THE POETRY OF EZRA POUND, 1908–1920

The Poetry of Ezra Pound

Forms and Renewal, 1908-1920

Hugh Witemeyer

University of California Press
Berkeley and Los Angeles 1969

University of California Press
Berkeley and Los Angeles, California
University of California Press Ltd.
London, England
Copyright © 1969 by
The Regents of the University of California
L. C. 69–13136
Printed in the United States of America

For Dorothy and Benton Witemeyer

Preface

This is a critical study of Ezra Pound's poetry from *A Lume Spento* (1908) to *Hugh Selwyn Mauberley* (1920). It covers the work of his London years and traces his poetic development to the point where he began to devote himself almost exclusively to *The Cantos*. It is an account of Pound's poetic apprenticeship and early mastership.

My choice of topic probably needs no defense. The body of poetry Pound wrote in this period continues to attract and puzzle its share of readers, and whole books have been devoted to single poems in *Personae*. What may need some explanation is my emphasis, in the first part of this study, on Pound's very early poetry—much of which is not included in *Personae*. It is not, perhaps, generally known that Pound suppressed over one hundred early poems from the so-called "Edition to date of all Ezra Pound's poems except the unfinished 'Cantos.'" Though some have recently been reprinted in *A Lume Spento and Other Early Poems* (1965), there are still nearly seventy poems from the period 1905–1916 not available in modern editions. On the whole, Pound's editing was excellent. The poems omitted *are* inferior to those included, are in some sense juvenilia of which he should understandably wish to disembarrass himself. Yet I have given two chapters to some of this work (and am by no means the first to write about it). The reader may justifiably wonder why.

The first reason is my own conviction that these early efforts have intrinsic value. They include some graceful lyrics, humorous ripostes, and interesting personae which I happen to admire. Not all the confections in *A Lume Spento and Other Early Poems* merit Pound's harsh description of them as "a collection of stale creampuffs." But then I may have an inordinate taste for creampuffs. There are other reasons why someone interested in Pound might find the early poems significant.

Our picture of Pound's poetic development is oddly incomplete. We tend to focus on the high points—Imagism and the mature poems from *Homage to Sextus Propertius* (1917) onwards—without understanding very well how Pound got from one stage to another. This picture is altered when we take the early poems into account. We then see that the bewildering variety and rapid metamorphoses of his published work are part of a more natural pattern of growth. We do not need a theory of special creation, with T. E. Hulme or Ernest Fenollosa in the role of Divine Providence, to explain radical discontinuities in Pound's evolution.

No one can study Pound's early poetry and prose for long without sensing how much of his mature achievement they anticipate. Pound's mind was set at a very early stage, and the work of his later years is often an elaboration of the concerns and dispositions of his youth. Properly understood, his writings show remarkable consistency and continuity over a long career. My two opening chapters, which are of a general and theoretical nature, attempt to show how soon he formulated (1) his habitual methods of dealing with literary tradition and (2) his basic conception or theory of poetry. The remaining chapters discuss the poems from *A Lume Spento* to *Hugh Selwyn Mauberley* in roughly chronological order, emphasizing the patterns which link them together and making interpretive connections with *The Cantos* where possible.

Some readers may find this plan flawed by the absence of a chapter (or even a few pithy pages) on *Homage to Sextus Propertius*. To this I can only reply that J. P. Sullivan, in *Ezra Pound and Sextus Propertius* (1964), has already done for that poem precisely what I would have tried (and failed) to do with the approach I have chosen. He elucidates the *Homage* as a work of "criticism in new composition" far more thoroughly than a classicist of my abilities could hope to do. I find myself in complete agreement with his treatment of Pound's "creative translation," and cannot add much that would make *Propertius* more relevant to the argument of this study.

I can now combine a declaration of some further critical al-

legiances with a statement about my own methods. It seems to me
that the best critics of Pound have tried to interpret his poetry in
Pound's own terms. They have enlisted the aid of his prose essays,
letters, and reviews to illuminate his verse. And they have gone to
his literary sources to see what Pound's handling of them will
reveal. Hugh Kenner made the first extensive use of Pound's prose
in *The Poetry of Ezra Pound* (1951), in my opinion still the best
single book on Pound's total achievement. Four years later, in
Ezra Pound's Mauberley, John J. Espey showed "how effective
the traditional academic method of attack, with its full panoply
of textual collation, identification of sources, and historical method"
can be in studying a poem like *Hugh Selwyn Mauberley*. (Espey's
scholarship supplements some impressive critical insights about
the essential structure of the poem.) Sullivan in his reading of
Propertius and N. Christoph de Nagy in *The Poetry of Ezra Pound:
The Pre-Imagist Stage* (1960) have further confirmed the value
of this method.

These are my guides, but my own particular aim is more exposi-
tory than judicial. It seems to me that the most valuable service a
critic of Pound can perform at this point is to help his readers
understand the poems in fairly specific ways. For we are still
uncertain about Pound. In many of his simplest early poems (not
to mention *The Cantos*), we still find it difficult to say what he is
doing, or even trying to do. So long as we are in doubt about such
basic matters of interpretation, we cannot (or should not) attempt
to pass final critical judgments on Pound's art. We shall not be
able to "place" his achievement in the total context of literature
for many years to come. In the meantime, our job is simply to try
our best to understand what is happening in his poems.

A few more words about this book's indebtedness. In addition
to the scholars mentioned already, I owe a great deal to Professor
A. Walton Litz for initially suggesting the topic to me as the subject of my doctoral dissertation at Princeton University, and for
supervising and criticizing my early drafts. Without Donald Gal-
lup's *A Bibliography of Ezra Pound* (London, 1963), I literally
could not have finished the book. For permission to quote from the
works of Ezra Pound, I am indebted to Mrs. Dorothy Pound and
to Mr. James Laughlin of New Directions Publishing Corporation.

I quote from *The Letters of Ezra Pound, 1907–1941* by permission of its publisher, Harcourt, Brace & World, Inc. "Oread" is quoted from *H. D. Selected Poems*, copyright © 1957 by Norman Holmes Pearson, published by Grove Press, Inc. Richard Aldington's "Penultimate Poetry" is reprinted by the kind permission of Mr. Alister Kershaw. Some of the material in the second part of Chapter 4 appeared first in an article co-authored by George J. Bornstein and myself, "From *Villain* to Visionary: Pound and Yeats on Villon," *Comparative Literature*, XIX (Fall 1967); it is used here with the permission of that journal. For all of this assistance, I am deeply grateful.

H. W.

Contents

Abbreviations

Full Title and Date of First Publication	Abbreviation	Edition Cited
A Lume Spento (1908)	ALS	1965
A Quinzaine for This Yule (1908)	QFTY	1965
Exultations (1909)	E	1909
The Spirit of Romance (1910)	SR	1953
Canzoni (1911)	C	1911
Personae: The Collected Shorter Poems of Ezra Pound (1926)	P	1949
ABC of Reading (1934)	ABC	1960
The Letters of Ezra Pound, 1907–1941 (1950)	LETT	1950
Literary Essays of Ezra Pound (1954)	LE	1968

In the text and notes of this book, citations of Pound's poems and essays are often accompanied by the year of first publication (in parentheses) to locate them chronologically; but actual page references are to the most accessible modern editions. Pound almost never revised his work after its first publication, so that except for minor changes in punctuation and spelling the modern editions accurately duplicate the earlier ones.

All but three of the "Editions Cited" are published by New Directions. The 1965 New Directions edition of *A Lume Spento and Other Early Poems* contains both *A Lume Spento* and *A Quinzaine for This Yule*, and also some previously unpublished verses from a notebook kept by Pound in 1908. The 1953 New Directions edition of *The Spirit of Romance* incorporates as its fifth chapter the important essay, "Psychology and Troubadours," originally published in 1912.

Because many of the poems in *Exultations* and *Canzoni* are still out of print, I have cited the first editions (London: Elkin Mathews). Nearly seventy unreprinted poems by Pound from the period 1905–1916 are reproduced in an appendix to my doctoral dissertation (Princeton University Library).

The Letters of Ezra Pound, 1907–1941 is edited by D. D. Paige and published by Harcourt, Brace & World.

THE POETRY OF EZRA POUND

FORMS AND RENEWAL

1908–1920

> *the deathless,*
> *Forms, forms and renewal, gods held in the air,*
> *Forms seen, and then clearness*
>
> (CANTO 25)

CHAPTER 1

Tradition and Its Uses

To have gathered from the air a live tradition
or from a fine old eye the unconquered flame
This is not vanity.   (CANTO 81)

In his essay "Date Line" (1934), Pound outlined five categories of criticism:

1. Criticism by discussion, extending from mere yatter, logic-chopping, and description of tendencies up to the clearly defined record of procedures and an attempt to formulate more or less general principles. . .
2. Criticism by translation.
3. Criticism by exercise in the style of a given period. . . .
4. Criticism via music, meaning definitely the setting of a poet's words: e.g. in *Le Testament*, Villon's words, and in *Cavalcanti*, I have set Guido's and Sordello's. . . .
This is the most intense form of criticism save:
5. Criticism in new composition. . . . (LE, 74–75)

In this ascending hierarchy, every literary composition may become a critical act, an explicit or implicit commentary upon some part of the existing literary tradition. Nearly all of Pound's own work can be grouped under one or another of these headings, and we must understand what he meant by "tradition" and its relation to the new work of art at the outset of any attempt to deal critically with his own poetry. Because his approach to literary tradition is essentially the same no matter what form of "criticism" he is writing, we may begin by describing the method of his prose criticism. For that method, once understood, casts light on the techniques of his poetry ("criticism in new composition").

Pound's idea of tradition is identical, as he himself has said, to

T. S. Eliot's familiar formulation in "Tradition and the Individual Talent" (1919). The modern poet, Eliot argued, must have the "historical sense":

> ... the historical sense involves a perception, not only of the past-ness of the past, but of its presence; the historical sense compels a man to write not only with his own generation in his bones, but with a feeling that the whole of the literature of Europe from Homer and within it the whole of the literature of his own country has a simultaneous existence and composes a simultaneous order. . . . The existing monuments form an ideal order among them-selves, which is modified by the introduction of the new (the really new) work of art among them.[1]

In 1933, Pound assented to this view: "Mr. Eliot and I are in agreement, or 'belong to the same school of critics,' in so far as we both believe that existing works form a complete order which is changed by the introduction of the 'really new' work."[2]

Pound's statement is not surprising, for he had been crying very similar ideas in the London wilderness at least nine years before Eliot's essay appeared. In the preface to his first book of criticism, *The Spirit of Romance* (1910), Pound argued that tradition is eternally living and relevant because it exists in a timeless order:

> The history of an art is the history of masterwork, not of failures, or mediocrity. The omniscient historian would display the master-pieces, their causes and their inter-relation. . . . All ages are con-temporaneous. It is B.C., let us say, in Morocco. The Middle Ages are in Russia. The future stirs already in the minds of the few. This is especially true of literature, where the real time is inde-pendent of the apparent, and where many dead men are our grandchildren's contemporaries, while many of our contemporaries have been already gathered into Abraham's bosom, or some more fitting receptacle.
> What we need is a literary scholarship, which will weigh Theoc-ritus and Yeats with one balance. . . .
>
> (SR, 7–8)

Eliot's "existing monuments" corresponds to Pound's "master-pieces," his "ideal order" to Pound's "inter-relation," and his "simul-taneous existence" to Pound's "real time." (The "receptacle" is a uniquely Poundian embellishment.)

Pound habitually views criticism as a clarification of this time-less order. His entire career as a critic represents an endeavor to become that omniscient historian who displays the interrelations of masterpieces, and weighs past and present achievement in a delicate balance. His purpose has been to develop, in himself and others, what he called in "Date Line" the capability of "Excernment. The general ordering and weeding out of what has actually been performed. The elimination of repetitions. The work analogous to that which a good hanging committee or a curator would perform in a National Gallery or in a biological museum" (LE, 75). Throughout his life, in a continuous series of anthologies, translations, critical essays, reviews, and essays-cum-anthologies, Pound has arrayed his *musée imaginaire*. Perhaps his most familiar efforts are "How To Read" (1929) and the *ABC of Reading* (1934). But it is important to recognize that his basic critical method was established early in his career, and that his creative method has always marched hand in hand with it.

Pound used "excernment" in his two earliest important critical works, *The Spirit of Romance* (which originated in two series of adult-education lectures at the Regent Street Polytechnic in 1908–1910) and "I Gather the Limbs of Osiris" (a series of twelve articles in *The New Age* in 1911–1912).[3] His topic was the medieval literature of southern Europe from Apuleius to the Renaissance, but his method, as defined in the "Osiris" series, was one which he has since used for a wide variety of subjects. He seems to consider it useful for dealing with any complex body of material. He first called it "the method of Luminous Detail," and illustrated it with an example from history:

Any fact is, in a sense, "significant." Any fact may be "symptomatic," but certain facts give one a sudden insight into circumjacent conditions, into their causes, their effects, into sequence, and law. . . . when in Burckhardt we come upon a passage: "In this year the Venetians refused to make war upon the Milanese because they held that any war between buyer and seller must prove profitable to neither," we come upon a portent, the old order changes, one conception of war and of the State begins to decline. The Middle Ages imperceptibly give ground to the Renaissance. A ruler owning a State and wishing to enlarge his possessions could, under one régime, in a manner opposed to sound economy, make war; but commercial sense is sapping this régime. In the history of the development of civilisation or of literature, we come upon such interpreting detail. A few dozen facts of this nature gave us intelligence of a period—a kind of intelligence not to be gathered from a great array of facts of the other sort. These facts are hard to find. They are swift and easy of transmission. They govern knowledge as the switchboard governs an electric circuit.[4]

This approach to history clearly anticipates *The Cantos*, which present their "intelligence" of various eras through clusters of "interpreting detail" (for example, of the Italian Renaissance through certain events in the career of Malatesta, or of Revolutionary America through selections from the correspondence of Adams and Jefferson).* And it is significant that as early as 1911 Pound was interpreting history primarily in terms of economics.† But he also employed his "method" in other areas.

In his literary criticism, excernment by means of luminous detail usually involves pinpointing the moment in literary history when one of two things happened: either a radical and fruitful innovation in technique and expression of feeling first appeared, or it was perfected by a master. In "How To Read" Pound calls the two highest kinds of poet *inventors* and *masters*, and he contrasts them to diluters, to "the men who do more or less good work in the more or less good style of a period," to belle-lettrists, and to starters

---

* "Osiris, Part XI" describes very clearly the technique of Pound's American-history Cantos: "As for the scholastic bearing, which matters much less than the artistic, if one wished an intimate acquaintance with the politics of England or Germany at certain periods, would one be wiser to read a book of generalities and then read at random through the archives, or to read through, let us say, first the state papers of Bismarck or Gladstone? Having become really conversant with the activities of either of these men, would not almost any document of this period fall, if we read it, into some sort of orderly arrangement? Would we not grasp its relation to the main stream of events?" (*New Age*, X [15 February 1912], 370.) Here is an early rationale for Pound's use of the Adams–Jefferson papers in *The Cantos*.

† The anecdote of Baldy Bacon and the Cuban currency which appears as an instance of usury in Canto 12 made its debut in the "Osiris" series under more benign circumstances. Bacon's monetary manipulations are there cited as an admirable instance of professionalism: "every man who does his own job really well has a latent respect for every other man who does *his* own job really well; this is our lasting bond; whether it be a matter of buying up all the little brass farthings in Cuba and selling them at a quarter per cent. advance, or of delivering steam-engines to King Menelek across three rivers and one hundred and four ravines. . . ." ("Osiris, Part IX," *New Age*, X [25 January 1912], 298.)

of crazes (LE, 23–24). He anticipated this classification in the "Osiris" series by distinguishing between "symptomatic" and "donative" authors. The first group makes no new contribution to the art, but the "donative author seems to draw down into the art something which was not in the art of his predecessors."[5] Excernment involves the identification of donative authors and the description of their donations. Pound's early poem, "Famam Librosque Cano" (1908), can be read as a portrait of the donative and the symptomatic poets, the sheep and goats of the craft.*

Donative authors may be either inventors or masters. Criticism in Pound's hands is not only the "history of masterwork," but also the resurrection of neglected "inventors" who have made valuable contributions later perfected by great masters. Like Browning, Pound seems almost to prefer focusing on the *pictor* or *scriptor ignotus*. The very title of the articles in which his first translations of the *Seafarer*, of Arnaut Daniel, and of Cavalcanti appeared—"I Gather the Limbs of Osiris"—reflects this interest. Isis gathered the dismembered limbs of Osiris, whose consequent rebirth was the legendary basis of an Egyptian fertility ritual. By identifying himself with Isis, Pound implied a hope that his translations of lesser-known inventors would assist a rebirth of English poetry.

The contribution of the donative author, according to Pound, is inseparable from his own personal *virtù*; he has discovered that unique quality in himself which differentiates him from all other men. In Part VI of the "Osiris" series, entitled "On Virtue," Pound first discussed a concept which has been central to his subsequent thought:

The soul of each man is compounded of all the elements of the cosmos of souls, but in each soul there is some one element which

---

* In this poem, the donative poet is addressed by the symptomatic. The former's songs have achieved "fame," the first item in the mock-Vergilian argument of the title (*arma virumque cano*). The symptomatic poet, however, has succeeded only in writing a few unread, remanded "books." His songs are known, not to the women and children of the land, but only to a learned bohemian wanderer, somewhat reminiscent of Browning's poet in "How It Strikes a Contemporary." This scholar obviously has great experience in diagnosing literary symptoms, and he "analyzes form and thought to see / How I 'scaped immortality" (ALS, 35–36). The speaker is a mask for Pound himself, giving humorous expression to fears about his own literary destiny; Pound called the poem "self-criticism" (see LETT, 6).

predominates, which is in some peculiar and intense way the quality or *virtù* of the individual; in no two souls is this the same. It is by reason of this *virtù* that a given work of art persists. It is by reason of this *virtù* that we have one Catullus, one Villon; by reason of it that no amount of technical cleverness can produce a work having the same charm as the original. . . . So far as mortal immortality is concerned, the poet need only discover his *virtù* and survive the discovery long enough to write some few scant dozen verses—providing, that is, that he have acquired some reasonable technique, this latter being the matter of a lifetime—or not, according to the individual facility.[6]

The donative author has both technique and self-knowledge.*

Individual works and even specific bodies of literature may also have *virtù*. Provençal poetry is important, in Pound's view, because it established the basic formal techniques of subsequent European poetry—"the Troubadours were melting the common tongue [Latin] and fashioning it into new harmonies depending not upon the alternation of quantities but upon rhyme and accent" (SR, 22). The medieval Tuscan poets are valued for their emphasis upon "the harmonies of the mind," their "objective imagination," and their "quality of vision"—all cardinal virtues, as we shall see, in Pound's own poetic (SR, 116). Each chapter in *The Spirit of Romance* seeks to ascertain the unique *virtù* of the individual writer or body of literature which it treats.

In the "Osiris" series, too, Pound attempted to describe the donative *virtù* of the works he was translating. His statements help to explain his lifelong interest in the *Seafarer* and the poems of Daniel and Cavalcanti. In the *Seafarer* he found "a certain element which has transmuted the various qualities of poetry which have drifted up from the South, which has sometimes enriched and made them English, sometimes rejected them, and refused combination."[7] He praised the work of Arnaut Daniel for three qualities:

---

* There is some indication that Pound thought the single line to be the best gauge of a poet's *virtù*. In *The Spirit of Romance*, he said: "The single line is, it is true, an insufficient test of a man's art, but it is a perfect test of his natural vigor, and of his poetic nature" (SR, 110). If so, this would explain Pound's critical technique (sometimes so irresponsible in appearance) of referring to the essential achievement of an author by quoting a favorite line or lines. Such lines are Pound's version of Matthew Arnold's "touchstones."

rhyme, organic unity, and poetic music. He argued that Daniel "bears to the technique of *accented* verse of Europe very much the same relation that Euclid does to our mathematics."[8] Cavalcanti's work interested Pound, "apart from its beauty, for his exact psychology, for an attempt to render emotions precisely."[9]

In its emphasis on *virtù*, Pound's critical method descends from that of Walter Pater. In his preface to *The Renaissance*, Pater declared:

The aesthetic critic, then, regards all the objects with which he has to do, all works of art, and the fairer forms of nature and human life, as powers or forces producing pleasurable sensations, each of a more or less peculiar and unique kind. . . . And the function of the aesthetic critic is to distinguish, analyze and separate from its adjuncts, the virtue by which a picture, a landscape, a fair personality in life or in a book, produces this special impression of beauty or pleasure, to indicate what the source of that impression is, and under what conditions it is experienced. His end is reached when he has disengaged that virtue, and noted it, as a chemist some natural element, for himself and others. . . .[10]

It was not Pater's impressionism that appealed to Pound, for Pound considered aesthetic values to be more than a matter of "pleasurable sensations." (In fact, Hugh Selwyn Mauberley falls victim to a Paterian aesthetic based too exclusively on a "special impression of beauty or pleasure.") But Pound was attracted by Pater's idea of a critical method which analyzes the virtue of a work "as a chemist" analyzes "some natural element." In the *ABC of Reading*, he advised a similar procedure based on the science of biology: "The proper METHOD for studying poetry and good letters is the method of contemporary biologists, that is careful first-hand examination of the matter, and continual COMPARISON of one 'slide' or specimen with another" (ABC, 17). The passages anthologized in the *ABC of Reading* are the "specimens" in which Pound's reader will hopefully perceive different poetic "virtues" (as Agassiz' wretched postgraduate student finally perceived the virtue of the "Ichthus Heliodiplokus"). Pound acknowledged his debt to the method outlined in Pater's preface by referring to it during a discussion of *virtù* in the introduction to his earliest translations of Cavalcanti.[11]

In Pound's view, then, criticism operates in a realm of masterwork and significant invention, where "real time is independent of the apparent" (sr, 8). It identifies and describes (or "excerns") the peculiar virtues of the works with which it is concerned. These virtues are assumed to have an objective existence and at least a potential order within the literature itself; they are not independent of the personal *virtù* of authors, but they can be perfectly expressed only when the author has achieved an impersonal mastery of technique. Comprehension of these pivotal developments gives standards of judgment to the critic, and an arsenal of techniques to the poet. The poet must grasp the tradition if he is not to duplicate past achievements, if he is to create "the really new work of art" and present an "adjunct to the Muses' diadem."

Given such a view of poetic tradition, it is not surprising that Pound's own poetry has displayed, from the very beginning of his career, such a vivid awareness of other literature. His poems often find their point of departure and self-definition in other poems, other prose, other words. In so doing, they become commentaries on the works whence they originate; they become, in short, what Pound called "criticism in new composition."

Pound's idea that criticism is not limited to prose "discussion" was scarcely original. Oscar Wilde had expressed it in 1891, for example, in his famous dialogue, "The Critic as Artist." Wilde has his protagonist, Gilbert, say: "And you see now, Ernest, that the critic has at his disposal as many objective forms of expression as the artist has. Ruskin put his criticism into imaginative prose, and is superb in his changes and contradictions; and Browning put his into blank verse and made painter and poet yield us their secret; and M. Renan uses dialogue, and Mr. Pater fiction, and Rossetti translated into sonnet-music the colour of Giorgione and the design of Ingres, and his own design and colour also. . . ."[12] Pound's conception of "criticism in new composition" is part of the tradition sketched here by the excellent Gilbert.

In practice, Pound's "criticism in new composition" has much in common with his "criticism by discussion." Both utilize the "method of Luminous Detail"; in verse criticism such details take the form of allusions, personae, and imitations. When Pound uses a line from Gautier or speaks through the mask of Villon, he creates a double perspective by which their work in some way comments on his, or vice versa. This technique can be used to resurrect the dead, to invoke an ideal standard, or to make an ironic observation. The past is always present in Pound's poetry, demanding recognition for its imperishable values.

This demand, however, raises questions which call the validity of Pound's method into doubt, and which must be confronted at this point. For in practice, Pound often seems to assume not only (1) that a "few dozen facts" of the right kind are enough "to give us intelligence of a period" in the history or literature of a civilization; but also (2) that his reader knows which facts these are; and (3) that his reader shares his own particular interpretation of these facts. In other words, he uses a system of cultural shorthand in which the *mere presentation* of a fact, a name, or an allusion is meant to convey a highly complex evaluation but often fails to do so because the reader is not privy to Pound's personal ratiocinations. He once wrote, without further explanation: "Criticism may be written by a string of names. Confucius, Ovid and Homer. Villon, Corbière, Gautier."[13] Little can be made of such a statement by a reader who is not familiar with Pound's more discursive critical writings. Similarly, the allusions and literary backgrounds in Pound's poems often require not only that the reader be able to identify them, but that he also know precisely what significance Pound attached to them. When Pound says "Turned from the 'eau-forte / Par Jaquemart,'" not only do we need to know that he is referring to the frontispiece of the 1884 edition of Gautier's *Emaux et camées*; we also need to know what he thought of Gautier's achievement in that book, if we are to evaluate Hugh Selwyn Mauberley's allegiances. The dangers of this method are obvious. The principal objection to Pound's *Cantos* will always be that he has pushed his theory of communication past the point of diminishing returns, and assigned more private and personal values to his "ideograms" than they convey by themselves to a reader.

Yet the missing information in Pound's poetry is often close to hand. If we undertake a thorough reading of Pound's work, we see that he seldom makes a judgment or discrimination that he has not *somewhere* argued fairly and openly. He seldom makes extensive use of a body of foreign literature that he has not translated or at least discussed at some length in his critical writings. Pound thought of his work in poetry and prose as complementary parts of *a single unified literary program*. As a result, his references in one context usually imply values which he has previously "excerned" in another. The careful reader of Pound's essays, translations, and letters will find himself in possession of innumerable hints, glosses, sources, and evaluations that illuminate the poetry. These clues are often more helpful than a knowledge of the sources themselves, for they give us Pound's personal interpretation of his materials (which does not, it must be admitted, always coincide with what Dr. Johnson called "the common sense of readers uncorrupted with literary prejudices, after all the refinements of subtilty and the dogmatism of learning"). In short, Pound is more responsible to his reader than he seems.

Perhaps his requirements *are* ultimately unsatisfactory. Recent writers such as Donald Davie, Graham Hough, and Frank Kermode have leveled some very intelligent and devastating criticism at the most basic assumptions of Pound's aesthetic.[14] But before we can pass final judgments, we must do Pound the justice of trying to read his poems on their own terms. Before we can reject his often difficult and frustrating work, we must be fair enough to accept his method at least provisionally, and to see how far into his poetry it can carry us. I hope to persuade my reader that it will carry us a great way.

II

Pound's leaning toward "criticism in new composition" and his experimentation with appropriate poetic techniques are apparent in his earliest poetry. At least three such techniques may be seen in his first volume, *A Lume Spento* (1908). None of the poems in question exhibits the finished mastery or emotional intensity of *Homage to Sextus Propertius* or *Hugh Selwyn Mauberley*, two later examples of Pound's most mature "criticism in new composition." But they are significant for showing how early his mind was set toward such poetry.

The first and simplest technique is that of allusion, which may be illustrated by the fourth poem in *A Lume Spento*, entitled "In Epitaphium Eius."

> Servant and singer, Troubadour
> That for his loving, loved each fair face more
> Than craven sluggard can his life's one love,
>
> Dowered with love, "whereby the sun doth move
> And all the stars."
> They called him fickle that the lambent flame
> Caught "Bicé" dreaming in each new-blown name,
>
> And loved all fairness though its hidden guise
> Lurked various in half an hundred eyes;
>
> That loved the essence though each casement bore
> A different semblance than the one before.
>
> (ALS, 20)

These humorous couplets, commemorating an anonymous but experienced troubadour, sport with the respectable platonic idea that essential beauty has its earthly incarnation in a variety of individual (in this case, female) forms. No, *our* singer was not fickle in his twenty-five amours, but a devoted servant of ideal "fairness"!

Pound uses allusion to set against this cavalier character the austere figure of Dante, model of spiritual monogamy. Both quotations in the poem are from Dante. The first translates the last line of *Il Paradiso*, "L'amor che move il sole e l'altre stelle." In *The Spirit of Romance*, Pound associates God's love as described in this line with Dante's love for Beatrice as described in *La Vita Nuova*.* To associate either with the troubadour's vagrant passion is very funny (but partly serious, as we shall see). The second quotation, "Bicé," is the Italian nickname for Beatrice, and is used by Dante in the fourteenth sonnet of *La Vita Nuova*. Here the

---

* After quoting the opening of *La Vita Nuova*, Pound goes on: "In this fashion he begins the tale of Love the revealer, of Love the door and the way into the intelligence, of Love infinite 'That moves the sun and all the other stars' " (SR, 120).

name is associated with that of Amor himself. Love appears to
Dante and draws his attention to two approaching women. The
second is Beatrice, and Amor renames her after himself:

> Io vidi monna Vanna e monna Bice
>
> .   .   .   .
>
> Amor mi disse: Quell' e Primavera,
> E quell' ha nome Amor, si mi somiglia.[15]

Pound's troubadour, however, finds his "Bicé" or Love "dreaming
in each new-blown name"; every one of the twenty-five was a true
Beatrice for him!

Yet this contrast between the two poets is more than a source of
humor in the epitaph. The allusion to Dante provides an historical
dimension of "criticism in new composition." For in Pound's view
of tradition, the love poetry of the vagabond troubadours ultimately provided Dante with many of the techniques and modes
of feeling for *La Vita Nuova* and the *Divine Comedy*: "I am constantly contending that it took two centuries of Provence and one
of Tuscany to develop the media of Dante's masterwork" (LE, 9).
Seen in this perspective, the anonymous troubadour was a "donative" inventor, and the allusion to Dante in his epitaph appropriately reminds us of his contribution to the development of
poetry.

One further allusion serves to equate the troubadour with
Dante, and also to recall the man who did most to revive Dante
and his contemporaries for Pound's generation through his translations of *The Early Italian Poets* (1861)—Dante Gabriel Rossetti.
The opening words of "In Epitaphium Eius" echo the second line
of Rossetti's poem, "Dante at Verona":

> Of Florence and of Beatrice
>   Servant and singer from of old,
>   O'er Dante's heart in youth had toll'd
> The knell that gave his lady peace.[16]

By applying to his troubadour the words that Rossetti applied to
Dante, Pound again suggests that the two *can* in some sense be
equated. The minstrel *was*, however fitfully, dowered with the
same love "whereby the sun doth move / And all the stars." The

allusion to Rossetti also closes an historical circuit between the troubadour and his commemorator, Pound. In "How To Read," Pound maintained that "exotic injections" such as Rossetti's translations "kept alive" British literature all through the nineteenth century (LE, 33–34).

Allusion is thus a technique of what Eliot called "the historical sense." The three luminous details in this poem suggest critical and historical connections between certain of the existing monuments. It is a far cry from this artist's epitaph to *Hugh Selwyn Mauberley*, but some of their aims and techniques are the same.

A second example of "criticism in new composition" in *A Lume Spento*—"Scriptor Ignotus"—combines allusion with the persona. Pound of course learned the dramatic monologue from Browning; he once called the monologues in Browning's *Men and Women* (1855) "the most vital form" of poetry in the Victorian period (LE, 419). "Scriptor Ignotus" takes its title from a poem in that volume, "Pictor Ignotus," and its speech rhythms and diction are strongly Browningesque.

Like "Pictor Ignotus," Pound's monologue portrays a failed artist. The "unknown writer" is identified in a note: "Bertold Lomax, English Dante scholar and mystic, died in Ferrara in 1723, with his 'great epic' still a mere shadow. . . ." Lomax (unlike Browning's *pictor*) is presented at the height of his confidence, in 1715. He comforts his lady friend

> From out the heights I dwell in, when
> That great sense of power is upon me
> And I see my greater soul-self bending
> Sibylwise with that great forty-year epic
> That you know of, yet unwrit
> But as some child's toy 'tween my fingers . . .
>
> (ALS, 38)

We know as we read his words that the project was abortive, that the eighteenth century produced no great epic in English, and that Lomax would probably have remained unknown were it not for Pound.

Pound's primary aim in the poem seems to be the presentation of Lomax's relationship to the lady, and of Lomax's sense of literary tradition. Pound does not attempt a Browningesque analysis of the psychological reasons for his character's failure, though several lines suggest a conflict between Lomax's religion and his epic ambitions.* The speaker would like his epic to immortalize the lady organist as his muse, and he alludes in this connection to two famous literary precedents.

The first is Ronsard's well known sonnet from *Les Sonnets pour Hélène* (Book II, XLIII):

> Quand vous serez bien vieille, au soir à la chandelle,
> Assise aupres du feu, devidant et filant,
> Direz chantant mes vers, en vous esmerveillant:
> Ronsard me celebroit du temps que j'estois belle.

This poem, which Pound also used in "Na Audiart" (1908), "Laudantes Decem Pulchritudinis Johannae Templi" (1909), and "Sonnet in Tenzone" (1910), and which inspired Yeats's early sonnet "When you are old and grey and full of sleep" (1893),† occurs to Lomax as he addresses his lady:

> A gift I give thee even as Ronsard gave it.
> Seeing, before time, one sweet face grown old,
> And seeing the old eyes grow bright
> From out the border of her fire-lit wrinkles,
> As she should make boast unto her maids,
> "Ronsard hath sung the beauty, *my* beauty,
>   Of the days that I was fair."
>
>   (ALS, 39)

The second precedent that occurs to the Dante scholar is the great Italian epic. Lomax recalls the passage near the end of *La Vita Nuova*, in which Dante expresses a hope to write of Beatrice, if God be willing that he live several years longer, that which has never been written of anyone. The passage refers, of course, to the

---

* "Surely if in the end the epic / And the small kind deed are one; / If, to God, the child's toy and the epic are the same." Such a view of the epic diminishes its importance considerably.

† In Canto 80, Pound refers to Yeats's poem: "and there was also Uncle William / labouring a sonnet of Ronsard / . . . before the world was given over to wars / Quand vous serez bien vieille."

then unwritten *Divine Comedy* and is perfectly appropriate for Lomax's situation: "Sicchè, se piacere sarà di Colui, a cui tutte le cose vivono, che la mia vita dura per alquanti anni, io spero di dire di lei quello che mai non fu detto d'alcuna."[17] Pound's version is a paraphrase of the original (and also echoes an earlier paraphrase by Rossetti*):

> "And if," for so the Florentine hath writ
> When having put all his heart
> Into his "Youth's Dear Book"
> He yet strove to do more honor
> To that lady dwelling in his inmost soul,
> He would wax yet greater
> To make her earthly glory more.
> Though sight of hell and heaven were price thereof,
> If so it be His will, with whom
> Are all things and through whom
> Are all things good,
> Will I make for thee and for the beauty of thy music
> A new thing
> As hath not heretofore been writ.
>   Take then my promise!
>
>   (ALS, 39–40)

Allusion and the persona in "Scriptor Ignotus," then, open multiple perspectives upon tradition. An unknown poet of the eighteenth century, whose heroes are Dante and Ronsard, "speaks" to

---

* Rossetti summarized the same passage in his "Dante at Verona" as follows:

> Such was the hope that love did blend
> With grief's slow fires, to make an end
>
> Of the "New Life," his youth's dear book:
> Adding thereunto: "In such trust
> I labour, and believe I must
> Accomplish this which my soul took
> In charge, if God, my Lord and hers,
> Leave my life with me a few years."

Pound's phrase, "Youth's Dear Book," no doubt echoes Rossetti's.

a modern audience. At the same time the title, form, and style of
the poem derive from Browning, and one passage recalls Rossetti.
These literary dimensions are inseparable from the poem's meaning; they set up a network of standards by which Lomax's ambition and failure may be judged. The persona, though it has many
other functions in Pound's poetry, is a primary technique of "criticism in new composition."*

A third and still more complex technique in *A Lume Spento*
combines allusion and the persona with what may be called "thematic transformation." By thematic transformation, I mean that
Pound makes an original use of themes and modes of feeling which
he has distilled from the work of another author after careful critical pondering. He writes "in the spirit" of that author without
actually translating him; Robert Lowell's *Imitations* (1960) represent a further development of this technique. A good example is
Pound's "Villonaud for This Yule," which he wrote as "what I
conceive after a good deal of study to be an expression akin to,
if not of, the spirit breathed in Villon's own poeting" (LETT, 3).

The poem is unusual among Pound's personae, in that it borrows parts of its actual form directly from the work of the persona himself. It is a slightly modified version of the traditional
French *ballade* used by Villon throughout *Le Testament*, most
notably in "Ballade des dames du temps jadis."† Pound's refrain
("Wineing the ghosts of yesteryear") echoes Rossetti's famous
translation of Villon's refrain, and his envoi is a variation on that
of Villon's *ballade*. In addition, the opening of the "Villonaud"
echoes the opening of Villon's *Lais*:

> En ce temps que i'ay dit deuant,
> Sur le Noel, morte saison,

---

* See Chapter 4 on its further functions. In "Scriptor Ignotus," the persona is also a mask for Pound himself. "I began the Cantos about 1904, I
suppose. I had various schemes, starting in 1904 or 1905," Pound declared
in a recent interview ("Ezra Pound: An Interview," *The Paris Review*, 28
[Summer–Fall, 1962], 23). If so, Lomax's epic aspirations may be taken to
equal Pound's. The "K.R.H." to whom the poem is dedicated is not Lomax's
lady-organist friend, but Katherine Ruth Heymann, an American pianist
whom Pound met in Venice in 1908.

† In Villon, the rhyme scheme in each stanza is a-b-a-b-b-c-b-c, whereas in
Pound it is a-b-a-b-a-b-a-b.

> Que les loups se viuent de vent,
> Et qu'on se tient en sa maison,
> Pour le frimas, pres du tison:

By recalling the setting in which Villon sat down to make his first legacy, Pound no doubt meant to set his poem in 1456, the year that Villon was forced to flee Paris to escape arrest for theft and began the *Lais*. These formal parallels and allusions in "Villonaud for This Yule" have been pointed out before.[18] But as "criticism in new composition" they are less important than what I have called "thematic transformation," Pound's attempt to capture the broader spirit of Villon's poetry.

To understand why Pound called the poem "an expression akin to, if not of, the spirit breathed in Villon's own poeting," we must consult his account of that spirit in "Montcorbier, *alias* Villon," the eighth chapter of *The Spirit of Romance*. There Pound treats Villon as the first "modern" poet, the first to base his poetry entirely on himself and his own experience.* In fact, he considered Villon's *virtù* as a poet to be the absolute accuracy and honesty with which he recorded this experience:

Villon's art exists because of Villon. . . . Villon has the stubborn persistency of one whose gaze cannot be deflected from the actual fact before him: what he sees, he writes. . . . Villon never forgets his fascinating, revolting self. . . . Human misery is more stable than human dignity; there is more intensity in the passion of cold, remorse, hunger, and the fetid damp of the medieval dungeon than [as compared to Whitman] in eating water melons. Villon is a voice of suffering, of mockery, of irrevocable fact. . . .

(SR, 168)

This voice "of suffering, of mockery, of irrevocable fact" is the voice which sings an elegiac drinking song over the Christmas wine in Pound's dramatic monologue.

---

* In 1908, he had written a little quatrain to the same effect:

> Some comfort 'tis to catch Will Shaxpeer stealing.
> All bards are thieves save Villon, master thief,
> Who pilfered naught but wine and then, wide reeling,
> Lilted his heart out,
>   Ballad-Lord in chief.

(ALS, 120)

The irrevocable fact is death, and the "Villonaud" is both a lament and a meditation on death. As in "Ballade des dames," the speaker especially mourns the death of beautiful women, and the dominant theme is the medieval *ubi sunt*:

> Where are the lips mine lay upon,
> Aye! where are the glances feat and clear
> That bade my heart his valor don?
>
> (ALS, 24)

Pound found this theme central and compelling in Villon's work, if we may judge from the passages he quotes in "Montcorbier, *alias* Villon": "Je cognois mort qui nous consomme, / Je cognois tout fors que moi meme"; "Where are the gracious gallants / That I beheld in times gone by"; "I mourn the time of my youth, / When I made merry more than another, / Until the coming of old age"; "Death, 'gainst thy harshness I appeal"; "A pitiful poor woman, shrunk and old, / I am . . ."; and (from Swinburne's translation of "Les Regrets de la belle Heaumière"):

> And he died thirty years agone.
> I am old now, no sweet thing to see;
> By God, though when I think thereon,
> And of that good glad time, woe's me,
> And stare upon my changèd body
> Stark naked, that has been so sweet,
> Lean, wizen, like a small dry tree,
> I am nigh mad with the pain of it.

The central theme of Pound's "Villonaud" is clearly, for him, the central theme of Villon's own poetry.

Pound's speaker certainly finds no consolation from religion in the course of his meditation on death. Pound saw a strong streak of religious skepticism in Montcorbier, alias Villon, and included it as an element of his own "Villonaud." Although at one point in his discussion Pound says that Villon accepted "unquestioningly . . . the dogma and opinion of his time," he suggests elsewhere (and more vigorously) that Villon was not a believer:

Villon holds his unique place in literature because he is the only poet without illusions. There are *désillusionnés*, but they are different; Villon set forth without the fragile cargo. Villon never lies to himself; he does not know much, but what he knows he knows: man is an animal, certain things he can feel; there is much misery, man has a soul about which he knows little or nothing. Helen, Heloise, and Joan are dead, and you will gather last year's snows before you find them. . . . Villon makes excuses neither for God nor for himself. . . . If Villon speculates, the end of his speculation is Omar's age-old ending: "Came out by the same door wherein I went." (SR, 169–176)

Pound also suggests that "Ballade pour prier Notre Dame" is one of the few poems in his work which Villon "does not actually feel." This is the element of "mockery" which Pound detected in Villon's voice.

In Pound's Christmas poem, the speaker finds no consolation in the promise of resurrection which the season brings. This is clear from the parentheses which punctuate the first three stanzas; their function in the poem is to convey Villon's "mockery," and they may be spoken almost bitterly:

> (Christ make the shepherd's homage dear!)
> (What of the magians' scented gear?)
> (Saturn and Mars to Zeus drawn near!)

The last of these, according to Pound's ironic note, is supposed to be a "Signum Nativitatis"! The mockery becomes most damaging in the last parenthetical line of the poem, if it may be considered as referring not only to Villon's lost love, but also to the newly born Jesus: "(Who knows whose was that paragon?)" Pound's envoi simply intensifies this note of religious skepticism:

> Prince: ask me not what I have done
> Nor what God hath that can me cheer
> But ye ask first where the winds are gone
> Wineing the ghosts of yester-year.

The "Villonaud," then, represents "criticism in new composition" in that it relies upon a careful transformation of selected themes in the work of its subject, themes which "after a good deal of study" seemed to Pound most characteristic and donative. Of the three techniques discussed here, this is obviously the most complex; but it also carries the greatest rewards for success. "Villonaud for This Yule" is Pound's earliest experiment with the technique which has since given us *Homage to Sextus Propertius*.

The relationship between these poetic techniques and the critical methods of Pound's prose should now be clearer. The choice of allusion and the transformation of carefully selected themes in poetry parallel the "method of Luminous Detail" in prose. Pound's mind seems always to work in terms of arrangements of significant particulars, patterns of luminous and irreducible facts—whether he be writing poetry, criticism, history, or economics. "Great poets seldom make bricks without straw," he said in 1910; "they pile up all the excellences they can beg, borrow, or steal from their predecessors and contemporaries, and then set their own inimitable light atop of the mountain" (SR, 162). Tradition provides straw for new bricks; originality lies less in the components of the structure than in the total design, less in the bricks than in the "inimitable light atop of the mountain."

Clearly tradition is a means rather than an end for Pound. A poem is not good *because* it represents "criticism in new composition," nor are the analyses in this chapter intended to show, for instance, that "Villonaud for This Yule" is really a great poem whose virtues have been undeservedly neglected. (For one thing, its "archaic" diction is simply too perverse.) Tradition is chiefly a *resource* to the poet, and "criticism in new composition" is the highest kind of criticism precisely because it singles out from the past what is still vital enough to nourish the life of art in the present. Ultimately Pound rejects the attempts of Arnold and Wilde to raise criticism from a subordinate and instrumental art to a primary art equal to poetry itself. If, he wrote, "Arnold considered poetry as a part of literature, then his definition of literature as 'criticism of life' is the one notable blasphemy that was born of his mind's frigidity. The spirit of the arts is dynamic. The arts are not passive, nor static, nor, in a sense, are they reflective, though reflection may assist at their birth. Poetry is about as much a 'criticism of life' as red-hot iron is a criticism of fire" (SR, 222).

CHAPTER 2

Delightful Psychic Experience

> So that the vines burst from my fingers
> And the bees weighted with pollen
> Move heavily in the vine-shoots:
>   chirr-chirr-chir-rikk—a purring sound,
> And the birds sleepily in the branches.
> ZAGREUS! IO ZAGREUS!
>   (CANTO 17)

Complementing Pound's view of an objective tradition is a psychological theory of poetry as the expression of certain kinds of subjective experience. The scholarship which "criticism in new composition" demands of both poet and reader is undertaken in the service of a visionary art. In his early writings, Pound outlined some of his fundamental aesthetic principles—principles which remain constant (though they are supplemented) in such later avatars as Imagism, Vorticism, and the Ideogram.

One approach to Pound's theory of poetry is through his theory of myth, as revealed by two statements made in 1912 and 1915:

I believe that Greek myth arose when someone having passed through delightful psychic experience tried to communicate it to others and found it necessary to screen himself from persecution. Speaking aesthetically, the myths are explications of mood: you may stop there, or you may probe deeper. (SR, 92)

The first myths arose when a man walked sheer into "nonsense," that is to say, when some very vivid and undeniable adventure befell him, and he told someone else who called him a liar. Thereupon, after bitter experience, perceiving that no one could understand what he meant when he said he "turned into a tree" he made a myth—a work of art that is—an impersonal or objective story woven out of his own emotion, as the nearest equation that he was capable of putting into words. (LE, 431)

Since Pound had earlier called poetry "equations for the human emotions," these remarks on myth-making are obviously relevant to other arts as well. Their importance is underlined by the fact that the second passage constitutes a perfect gloss on "The Tree," an early poem which Pound has placed at the head of all editions of *Personae* since 1926 as a sort of program poem.*

Pound's psychological theory of myth may be summarized as follows:

(1) The psychic experience is extraordinary, brief, and yet subjectively true. It is beyond the generally shared realm of common experience, but it is "vivid and *undeniable.*" Pound often calls it an "adventure."

(2) It is no more than *experience.* It does not reveal an objective, transcendental order. Myths are primarily "explications of mood," and Pound almost never chooses to "probe deeper."

(3) The myth or work of art is made out of this rare emotion.

(4) It is an objective verbal *equation* for a basically incommunicable experience. Language cannot convey the primary intensity of the experience itself; it can only reconstruct something else as the "nearest equation" that the myth-maker is "capable of putting into words."

(5) The myth-maker (poet) cannot relate his experience by speaking out directly in the first person. He must "screen himself" and speak indirectly through "an impersonal or objective story." Hence the need for masks and personae.

All of these ideas are central to Pound's theory of poetry as a record of delightful psychic experience. For him poetry is, like

---

* In this poem, the speaker is suddenly enabled to understand the myths of Daphne and of Baucis and Philemon from Ovid's *Metamorphoses* (I and VIII) when he inexplicably passes through a psychological experience similar to that which gave rise to them. He too "turns into a tree" and is able then to bring the gods "within / Unto the hearth of their heart's home" (P, 3). Pound wrote of such men: "Certain it is that these myths are only intelligible in a vivid and glittering sense to those people to whom they occur. I know, I mean, one man who understands Persephone and Demeter, and one who understands the Laurel . . ." (SR, 92). "The Tree" opens *Personae* because it is a paradigm of the kind of metamorphic experience (displacement from the poet's self into another mode of existence) out of which many poems in the volume grow. The persona is a means for bringing not only the gods but also the men of the past "within / Unto the hearth of their heart's home."

myth, a verbal approximation of such experience: "Poetry is a sort of inspired mathematics, which gives us equations, not for abstract figures, triangles, spheres, and the like, but equations for the human emotions" (sr, 14).

Whenever these emotions involve a sense of sudden transformation or revelation, as they often do in Pound's work, he locates the vision within the realm of ordinary experience. He speaks of "the indisputable and very scientific fact that there are in the 'normal course of things' certain times, a certain sort of moment more than another, when a man feels his immortality upon him" (sr, 94). Again, "there is, in what I have called the 'natural course of events,' the exalted moment, the vision unsought, or at least the vision gained without machination" (sr, 97). Such visionary episodes recur throughout *The Cantos*; in a letter to his father, Pound called them "the 'magic moment' or moment of metamorphosis, bust thru from quotidien into 'divine or permanent world' " (lett, 210). Yet he always hesitates to draw metaphysical conclusions from the rare experience. "Men think and feel certain things and see certain things not with the bodily vision," he wrote to Williams in 1908, but the psychological fact was all that he could be certain of (lett, 5). Rather than assert the existence of transcendental beings, he preferred to define a god as "an eternal state of mind," manifested when "states of mind take form."[1] It is in this sense that the gods still exist in Pound's world; the human psyche is their home. But psychology is not ontology, and the visionary strain in Pound's thought is resolutely empirical.

This curious secular mysticism is elaborated in a very important and almost unknown series of "Axiomata" which Pound published on the eve of his departure from England in 1921. The "Axiomata" state some of the unchanging philosophical assumptions behind all of Pound's work. (I quote at some length because the piece is both neglected and unavailable.)

I

(1) The intimate essence of the universe is *not* of the same nature as our own consciousness.

(2) Our own consciousness is incapable of having produced the universe.

(3) God, therefore, exists. That is to say, there is no reason for not applying the term God, *Theos*, to the intimate essence.

(4) The universe exists. By exists we mean normally: is perceptible to our consciousness or deducible by human reason from data perceptible to our consciousness.

(5) Concerning the intimate essence of the universe we are utterly ignorant. We have no proof that this God, Theos, is one, or is many, or is divisible or indivisible, or is an ordered hierarchy culminating, or not culminating, in a unity. . . .

III

(1) This is not to deny that the consciousness may be affected by the theos (remembering that we ascribe to this *theos* neither singular nor plural number).

(2) The theos may affect and may have affected the consciousness of individuals, but the consciousness is incapable of knowing why this occurs, or even in what manner it occurs, or whether it be the *theos*; though the consciousness may experience pleasant and possibly unpleasant sensations, or sensations partaking neither of pleasure nor its opposite. Hence mysticism. If the consciousness receives or has received such effects from the theos, or from something not the theos yet which consciousness has been incapable of understanding or classifying either as theos or a-theos, it is incapable of reducing these sensations to coherent sequence of cause and effect. The effects remain, so far as the consciousness is concerned, in the domain of experience, not differing intellectually from the taste of a lemon or the fragrance of violets or the aroma of dunghills, or the feel of a stone or of tree-bark, or any other direct perception. . . .

(3) This is not to deny any of the visions or auditions or sensations of the mystics, Dante's rose or Theresa's walnut; but it is to reaffirm the propositions in Section I.[2]

What emerges most clearly from Pound's "Axiomata" is the high value he places upon states of consciousness themselves as the ultimate knowable truths. We have no way of knowing whether our epiphanies are purely subjective or whether they proceed from an objective *theos*. "Le Paradis n'est pas artificiel," but "States of mind are inexplicable to us" (Canto 76). It is impossible to find a valid philosophical distinction between a vision of paradise and a sense perception of unusual intensity (Dante's rose and the taste

of a lemon). As Pound says in Canto 74, in lines which combine
Baudelaire and Leopold Bloom:

> Le Paradis n'est pas artificiel
> but spezzatto apparently
> it exists only in fragments unexpected excellent sausage,
> the smell of mint, for example,

What is the rare power of DTC sausage, or of mint, or for that
matter of Proust's *petits madeleines*? Pound hesitates to answer,
for he is aware of what Robert Langbaum calls, in *The Poetry of
Experience*, the "disequilibrium between the moment of insight,
which is certain, and the problematical idea we abstract from
it."[3] For Pound only the states of mind themselves are "vivid and
undeniable," and the gods are metaphors or "explications of mood."
He takes a firm stand "in the domain of experience."

Pound's early poem, "Erat Hora," illustrates these attitudes.

> "Thank you, whatever comes." And then she turned
> And, as the ray of sun on hanging flowers
> Fades when the wind hath lifted them aside,
> Went swiftly from me. Nay, whatever comes
> One hour was sunlit and the most high gods
> May not make boast of any better thing
> Than to have watched that hour as it passed.
>
> (P, 40)

The magical moment is in the past; we know only that "the hour
was." It was perfect and complete within the "domain of experience," for the gods themselves could not have known a finer. What
took place is not described, for delightful psychic experience is
ineffable. The poem is a verbal equation which seeks to adumbrate
the epiphany in images of sunlight and flowers, and expressions
of gratitude and triumph.

II

This view of poetry first emerged in Pound's medieval studies.
His entire aesthetic is present, explicitly or implicitly, in *The Spirit*

of Romance and "I Gather the Limbs of Osiris." It was later reinforced by the Bergsonian aesthetic of T. E. Hulme and by Fenollosa's *Essay on the Chinese Written Character*, but it was not
created by anyone but Pound himself. Imagism, Vorticism, and the
Ideogram, as I hope to show, were primarily the natural out-
growths of an earlier and more basic conception of poetry.

In 1912, Pound said of his favorite medieval mystic: "Richard
St. Victor has left us one very beautiful passage on the splendors
of paradise. They are ineffable and innumerable and no man having beheld them can fittingly narrate them or even remember
them exactly. Nevertheless by naming over all the most beautiful
things we know we may draw back upon the mind some vestige
of the heavenly splendor." He suggested that the Lady of Provençal love poetry is primarily a "catalogue" of such beauties, a
composite metaphor serving to recall the "heavenly splendor"
(SR, 96). Clearly this statement parallels his remarks on myth.
To behold the splendors of paradise is to know delightful psychic
experience, and to name over "all the most beautiful things we
know" is to seek the verbal equation for it.

Pound loved medieval literature generally (and the poetry of
Provence and Tuscany particularly) because he saw in it a supreme ability to deal precisely with ineffable and sometimes visionary states of consciousness: "The Tuscan poetry is, however, of
a time when the seeing of visions was considered respectable, and
the poet takes delight in definite portrayal of his vision" (SR, 105).
In Richard of St. Victor's treatises on the contemplation of God,
Pound found a "keenly intellectual mysticism" which he applied to
poetry (SR, 22). He declared that "poetry in its acme is expression
from contemplation,"* and he spoke much of "ecstasy," which is

---

* *Personae* (London, 1909), p. 58. In a note, Pound summarizes Richard's
distinction between cogitation, meditation, and contemplation (*Benjamin
Major*, I, 3 and 4). The poem to which this note refers—"Guillaume de Lorris
Belated: A Vision of Italy"—is a conscious attempt by Pound to imitate Wordsworth's contemplative style. Despite the allegorical dream-vision structure,
the style is more indebted to the English William than to the author of the
Romaunt de la Rose. Pound respected this vein in Wordsworth's poetry; he
quoted Arthur Symons' remark: "to translate Dante is an impossible thing,
for to do it would demand, as the *first* requirement, a *concise* and *luminous*
style equal to Wordsworth at his *best*" (SR, 144).

the highest state of contemplation (*mentis excessum*) on Richard's scale.†

But "definite portrayal" is the chief problem of the medieval poet, as of the myth-maker. For he must communicate the exact nature of an experience which is by nature incommunicable; he must "distinguish between the shades and the degrees of the ineffable"; he must discriminate "between one kind of indefinability and another."⁴ The paradox is dissolved by the faculty Pound called "objective imagination" (sr, 116). It mediates between the vision of the poet and the minds of others by finding in the sensible world the most precise possible analogue to the vision.*

Dante is, for Pound, the great master of "objective imagination." In the allegory of the *Divine Comedy*, he is able "to shed himself in completely self-conscious characters; to make a mood; slough it off as a snake does his skin, and then endow it with an individual life of its own" (sr, 85). Here we are reminded of Pound's definition of myths as "explications of mood." Dante is the epitome of "man conscious of the world within him,"⁵ and the *Divine Comedy* externalizes this world. Given Pound's theory of poetry, it is not surprising that he regarded the poem as lyrical: "It is in a sense lyric, the tremendous lyric of the subjective Dante" (sr, 153).

† Pound was not using Richard's terminology accurately. Poetry cannot be "expression from contemplation" by Richard's definitions, because speech is a function of reason and reason must "die" before contemplation may begin. Allegorically, Rachel (the type of reason) dies when Benjamin (the type of contemplation) is born. See *Benjamin Minor*, LXXIII and LXXIV. Nevertheless, it is interesting to note that Yeats, at about the same time (1909), was redefining the word "ecstasy" in terms of contemplation for his theory of tragedy: "A poet creates tragedy from his own soul, that soul which is alike in all men. It has not joy, as we understand that word, but ecstasy, which is from the contemplation of things vaster than the individual and imperfectly seen, perhaps, by all those that still live." See "Estrangement: Extracts from a Diary Kept in 1909," *Autobiographies* (London, 1955), p. 471. Richard Ellmann's description of "ecstasy" in Yeats could be applied with little alteration to Pound: "By ecstasy Yeats means no romantic agony; it is the liberation which comes from the perception of a pattern in intense human experiences. It frees the reader, like the writer, from isolating external circumstances. He escapes from confusion to radiant knowledge." *The Identity of Yeats* (New York, 1954), p. 106.

* Mario Praz has argued that T. S. Eliot's idea of the "objective correlative" came from *The Spirit of Romance*. See "T. S. Eliot and Dante," *Southern Review*, II (Winter, 1937), 525–548.

Dante's universe is psychological; Hell, Purgatory, and Paradise are conceived "as states, and not places." We are to regard them as Dante's "descriptions of men's mental states in life, in which they are, after death, compelled to continue: that is to say, men's inner selves stand visibly before the eyes of Dante's intellect" (SR, 128). Such an interpretation reveals the lyric bias of a post-Symbolist conception of poetry such as Pound's: the poem gives visible body to moods and "mental states." This may not be an accurate view of Dante's allegory, but it is a perfect description of Pound's own Hell Cantos, which portray "the state of English mind in 1919 and 1920" (LETT, 239).

The poet must exercise the utmost care in choosing his equations. In the 1910 introduction to his Cavalcanti translations, Pound declared his belief in absolute rhythm and absolute metaphor: "The perception of the intellect is given in the word, that of the emotions in the cadence. It is only, then, in perfect rhythm joined to the perfect word that the two-fold vision can be recorded."[6] The poet, in other words, must remain absolutely faithful to the particular "contour" of a given vision; a sort of psychic mimesis takes place "as the sculptor sees the form in the air" (Canto 25). For there is, in the mind, a "place where the ecstasy is not a whirl or a madness of the senses, but a glow arising from the exact nature of the perception" (SR, 91). And to communicate the exact nature of the perception, the poet needs "a sort of hyper-scientific precision," which is "the touchstone and assay of the artist's power, of his honor, his authenticity" (SR, 87). The Imagist emphasis on precise technique was but reiteration of a principle Pound had long held.

The function of "absolute metaphor" is made clear in Pound's pre-Imagist theory of figurative language. In his chapter on Dante, he distinguishes three kinds of epithet and three kinds of comparison (SR, 158–159). There are epithets of "primary apparition," of "secondary apparition," and of "emotional apparition." Epithets of primary apparition "describe what is actually presented to the sense or vision," and are the highest kind because they "give vividness to description and stimulate conviction in the actual vision of the poet." Pound cites Dante's "selva oscura" as an example, and points out that there can also be "clauses and phrases of

'primary apparition.' Thus, in Canto X of the Inferno, where Caval-
cante di Cavalcanti's head appears above the edge of the tomb,
'I believe he had risen on his knees,' has no beauty in itself,
but adds greatly to the verisimilitude." Concrete description, then,
gives verisimilitude to the poet's visionary adventure.*

Of the three kinds of comparison, simile is "leisurely," metaphor
is presumably a norm, and the "language beyond metaphor" is
"swift" and "compressed" in its expression of metaphorical perception (anticipating the Image). But to all three sensuous presentation is essential, because it "stimulates conviction" in the
authenticity of the vision. Pound notes that "Dante's vividness
depends much upon his comparison by simile to particular phenomena," and he praises Arnaut Daniel's "comparison of the heart
to the Rhone overflowing with the spring freshets" for its "vivid
and accurate description of the emotion" (SR, 28).

The similes in Pound's own early poetry follow these prescrip-
tions. One of them, in "Piere Vidal Old," even steals the Rhone
image for which he praised Daniel:

> Swift came the Loba, as a branch that's caught,
> Torn, green and silent in the swollen Rhone,
> Green was her mantle, close, and wrought
> Of some thin silk stuff that's scarce stuff at all,
> But like a mist wherethrough her white form fought.
>
> (P, 31)

The moment is ecstatic, but the similes are concrete. Loba moves
with the effortless, worn integrity of a branch on the Rhone flood,
and her white body seems to participate in the forward movement
as it looms with increasing clarity through the "mist" of its green
veil. An almost random selection of other similes from Pound's
early poems shows that their function is often to give sensuous
verisimilitude to an intangible tenor:

---

* Pound was later reminded of "primary apparition" by a passage in
Fenollosa's Essay on the Chinese Written Character. He appended a note, "Cf.
principle of Primary apparition. 'Spirit of Romance,'" to the following passage: "Poetry differs from prose in the concrete colors of its diction. It is not
enough for it to furnish a meaning to philosophers. It must appeal to emotions
with the charm of direct impression, flashing through regions where the intellect can only grope."

And we that are grown formless, rise above—
Fluids intangible that have been men,
We seem as statues round whose high-risen base
Some overflowing river is run mad,
In us alone the element of calm.

(P, 32)

Be in me as the eternal moods
    of the bleak wind, and not
As transient things are—
    gaiety of flowers.

(P, 67)

Slight are her arms, yet they have bound me straitly
And left me cloaked as with a gauze of aether;
As with sweet leaves; as with subtle clearness.

(P, 71)

See, they return, one, and by one,
With fear, as half-awakened;
As if the snow should hesitate
And murmur in the wind,
       and half turn back;

(P, 74)

Thy gracious ways,
       O Lady of my heart, have
O'er all my thought their golden glamour cast;
As amber torch-flames, where strange men-at-arms
Tread softly 'neath the damask shield of night.

(C, 6)

In each case, the simile gives concrete representation to an ineffable "mood." The world of the senses, shared by poet and reader, is the bridge across which the poet sends messages from his inner kingdom.

III

This visionary empiricism—with all of its unstated assumptions about epistemology and about the triangular relationship of words, things, and mental experience—is the foundation of Pound's Imagism. Stanley Coffman has said of Pound that the Imagist "can be seen all through the studies of the romance poets."[7] Let us reverse the focus, restore the chronology, and try to ascertain how much of the romanticist can be seen all through Imagism.

An "Image" is that which presents an intellectual and emotional complex in an instant of time. I use the term "complex" rather in the technical sense employed by the newer psychologists, such as Hart, though we might not agree absolutely in our application. It is the presentation of such a "complex" instantaneously which gives that sudden sense of liberation; that sense of freedom from time limits and space limits; that sense of sudden growth, which we experience in the presence of the greatest works of art. (LE, 4)

Thus Pound announced the latest word in *Poetry* for March 1913. The scientific tenor of his language makes it easy to overlook the counterthrusting mysticism of his ideas. Bernard Hart and Freudian psychology notwithstanding, Pound is talking about "delightful psychic experience" and visionary ecstasy.* The "intellectual and emotional complex" is but another way of naming the "twofold vision" of the earlier Cavalcanti introduction. The "sense of freedom from time limits and space limits" is explicitly mystical, a function of "the exalted moment, the vision unsought, or at least

---

* Bernard Hart, a distinguished Cambridge psychologist, used the term "complex" in an orthodox Freudian sense, as "a system of connected ideas, with a strong emotional tone, and a tendency to produce actions of a definite character." He went on in his popular primer, *The Psychology of Insanity* (1912), to explain that complexes become active "in the presence of a 'stimulus,' occurring whenever one or more of the ideas belonging to a complex is roused to activity, either by some external event, or by a process of association occurring within the mind itself" (4th ed. [New York, 1931], pp. 77–79). Pound's use of the term has only a tenuous connection with Hart's. Both are systems of ideas with "emotional tone," but Pound's complex does not lurk in the unconscious waiting to be triggered by the stimulus of a poetic image. It is presented *to* the mind by the Image. Nor would Pound and Hart "agree absolutely" in their application of the term, since Hart's chief concern is with the obsessive and insane actions that may be caused by the complex. Pound's "Image" does not lead to irrational behavior (except perhaps among his critics); it augments our sense of reality, not our obsessions with unreality. It is a tribute to Pound's eclecticism that he should seek to define an experience of mystical clarity with the help of a manual on the psychology of insanity, but his reference to Hart is little more than a pseudoscientific smokescreen.

the vision gained without machination" (SR, 97). And the "sense of sudden growth, which we experience in the presence of the greatest works of art" is simply a toned-down version of a statement made in 1910: "great art is made to call forth, or create, an ecstasy" (SR, 82).

In practice, the presentation of the Image involves the search for an equation that will approximate a beautiful but ineffable psychic adventure. This much Pound made clear when he described the process of composing "In a Station of the Metro":

For well over a year I have been trying to make a poem of a very beautiful thing that befell me in the Paris Underground. I got out of a train at, I think, La Concorde and in the jostle I saw a beautiful face, and then, turning suddenly, another and another, and then a beautiful child's face, and then another beautiful face. All that day I tried to find words for what this made me feel. That night as I went home along the rue Raynouard I was still trying. . . . I tried to write the poem weeks afterwards in Italy, but found it useless. Then only the other night, wondering how I should tell the adventure, it struck me that in Japan . . . one might make a very little poem which would be translated about as follows:

"The apparition of these faces in the crowd:
Petals on a wet, black bough."[8]

The moment of delightful psychic experience and the subsequent search for the precise equation could not be more clearly described. In some ways, the poem can be interpreted by means of the definitions in "A Few Don'ts by an Imagiste": the complex is presented "instantaneously," the transition from the Metro station to the wet bough somewhere outside liberates us from "space limits," and the transition from the present faces to the remembered petals breaks down "time limits." But the "Don'ts" don't account for one peculiarly powerful word in the poem—"apparition." This word veils the faces in mystery, for it suggests that they are not a mere visual impression but a vision of beauty appearing to the poet from another realm. "Apparition" links "Metro" with the aesthetic of *The Spirit of Romance*.

The second line of the haiku "super-poses" a concrete image which gives a sensory equation for the rare perception.[9] The heart of the poem lies neither in the apparition nor in the petals, but in the mental process which leaps from one to the other. "In a poem of this sort," as Pound explained, "one is trying to record the precise instant when a thing outward and objective transforms itself, or darts into a thing inward and subjective."[10] This darting takes place *between* the first and second lines. In the simplest possible verbal equation ($a=b$), the adventure lies in the unstated relation *between* the elements. The factors exist for the sake of the equivalence, the images for the sake of the Image. As Stanley Coffman puts it, "the images are so arranged that the pattern becomes an Image, an organic structure giving a force and pleasure that are greater than and different from the images alone."[11]

This can be seen in other important Imagist poems. In H. D.'s "Oread," for example, the experience is also external in origin and "darts" into the subjective realm through the pine metaphor:

> Whirl up, sea—
> Whirl your pointed pines,
> Splash your great pines
> On our rocks,
> Hurl your green over us,
> Cover us with your pools of fir.

The opening lines present first the sea, then the visual metaphor that only partially arrests the flux. But as the imperatives are repeated, a new energy enters the poem to harmonize with the sea's: namely, the poet's own strong desire for pleasant obliteration. From a poem like "Oread," one learns how Pound could call for "objectivity and again objectivity, and expression" without contradicting himself (LETT, 49).

The Imagist poem, then, was never meant to be a simple record of visual impressions, and R. P. Blackmur was probably wrong to call Imagism "a mere lively heresy of the visual in the verbal." The Imagist poem attempts to present, economically and metaphorically, a state of mind, a mood or feeling, or a reaction to an external observation. Pound constantly distinguished between "the *conception* of poetry" and "the *reception* of an impression." He argued that "no impression, however carefully articulated, can, recorded, convey that feeling of sudden light which the works of art should and must convey."[12] The Image is an equation for aspects of experience which can be known but not fully verbalized. In Suzanne Langer's terms, it is a "presentational" as opposed to a "discursive" symbol.[13] Frank Kermode is undoubtedly right in calling it "non-discursive," and relating it to a major post-Romantic tradition: "What it comes to in the end is that Pound, like Hulme, like Mallarmé and many others, wanted a theory of poetry based on the non-discursive *concetto*."* Pound himself admitted, in his essay on "Vorticism," that "the image is the word beyond formulated language." The Imagist poem is the perfectly tailored garb of the invisible spirit of romance.

IV

"Vorticism" was a movement toward formalism and abstractionism in several modern arts—chiefly painting, sculpture, and poetry. Pound continued to call the poetic branch of the movement "Imagisme," and he told John Gould Fletcher that Vorticism was "only an extension of the old principle of imagism to embrace all the arts."[14] This was an accurate description, for the concept which Pound developed to explain the unity of the arts was simply a new version of his older notion of art as an equation for emotions: "EVERY CONCEPT, EVERY EMOTION PRESENTS ITSELF TO THE VIVID CONSCIOUSNESS IN SOME PRIMARY FORM. IT BELONGS TO THE ART OF THIS FORM. IF SOUND, TO MUSIC. IF FORMED WORDS, TO LITERATURE; THE IMAGE, TO POETRY; FORM, TO DESIGN; COLOUR IN POSITION, TO PAINTING; FORM OR DESIGN IN THREE PLANES, TO SCULPTURE; MOVEMENT TO THE DANCE OR TO THE RHYTHM OF MUSIC OR VERSES."[15] In Vorticism, the media themselves become equations, each one appropriate for some kinds of experience but not others.

To illustrate "primary form," Pound gave a second account of

---

* *Romantic Image*, p. 136. The recent revaluation of Hulme's Imagism by such writers as Kermode and A. R. Jones has emphasized its Romantic, intuitional, Bergsonian character. The main point is that the Image for Hulme was a means of intuiting Bergson's "Intensive Manifold," which cannot be grasped by the "Intellect." See "T. E. Hulme," Chapter VII of *Romantic Image*, and "The Poetic Theory," Chapter III in Jones' *The Life and Opinions of Thomas Ernest Hulme* (Boston, 1960).

the composition of "In a Station of the Metro." He argues that he should have painted those faces, because color was really the proper equation for the experience:

And that evening, as I went home along the Rue Raynouard, I was still trying and I found, suddenly, the expression. I do not mean that I found words, but there came an equation . . . not in speech, but in little splotches of colour. . . . That evening, in the Rue Raynouard, I realized quite vividly that if I were a painter, or if I had, often, *that kind* of emotion, or even if I had the energy to get paints and brushes and keep at it, I might found a new school of painting, of "non-representative" painting, a painting that would speak only by arrangements of colour. . . .
Perhaps this is enough to explain the words in my "Vortex":—
"Every concept, every emotion, presents itself to the vivid consciousness in some primary form. It belongs to the art of this form."
That is to say, my experience in Paris should have gone into paint. If instead of colour I had perceived sound or planes in relation, I should have expressed it in music or in sculpture. Colour was, in this instance, the "primary pigment"; I mean that it was the first adequate equation that came into consciousness.[16]

Nothing could better illustrate the essential continuity of Pound's thought from *The Spirit of Romance* to *BLAST* than his use of the word "equation" in this passage.

The "Vortex" itself is the delightful psychic experience or the intellectual and emotional complex for which the work of art is an equation. It is the unique pattern of emotion which the artist must objectify: "Intense emotion causes pattern to arise in the mind. . . . Not only does emotion create the 'pattern unit' and the 'arrangement of forms,' it creates also the Image."[17] The objective arrangement of colors, images, musical tones, or sculptural planes in a work of art transmits a subjective vortex: "An organization of forms expresses confluence of forces. These forces may be the 'love of God,' the 'life-force,' emotions, passions, what you will."[18] The Vortex is identical to the "complex" presented by the Image; it is simply renamed to suggest its vital power ("complex" was too static a word for Pound): "The image is not an idea. It is a radiant node or cluster; it is what I can, and must perforce, call a VORTEX, from which, and through which, and into which, ideas are constantly rushing."[19]

If "Metro" is the program poem for Imagism, "The Game of Chess" is its Vorticist equivalent. It reveals much about the curious aesthetic which Pound saw as uniting the modern arts. Published in the second issue of *BLAST*, its subtitle clearly indicates its Vorticist orientation: "Dogmatic Statement Concerning the Game of Chess: Theme for a Series of Pictures." Here the poet generates a Vortex, and invites the painter to perfect it:

> Red knights, brown bishops, bright queens,
> Striking the board, falling in strong "L's" of colour.
> Reaching and striking in angles,
>   holding lines in one colour.
> This board is alive with light;
>   these pieces are living in form,
> Their moves break and reform the pattern:
>   luminous green from the rooks,
> Clashing with "X's" of queens,
>   looped with the knight-leaps.
>
> "Y" pawns, cleaving, embanking!
> Whirl! Centripetal! Mate! King down in the vortex,
> Clash, leaping of bands, straight strips of hard colour,
> Blocked lights working in. Escapes. Renewal of contest.
>   (P, 120)

The Vortex of color and energy is in the consciousness of the beholder; it is he who endows the chessboard with living light and form. The poem stands, in a sense, halfway between the actual chessboard and the finished painting; it has partially dissolved the game into its fundamental elements of form and color, and the painting would complete the elimination of representational elements. The kind of "series" for which this poem states a "theme" would be a set of abstract and energetic designs similar to Wyndham Lewis's *Timon* portfolio. The images and rhythms are the poet's equation for what the painter would express through form and color.

Pound's espousal of modern abstract art in his Vorticist period was a natural result of his earlier aesthetic. For if the best art presents equations for nondiscursive types of experience, then it is by nature nonrepresentational. The abstractionist simply follows the logic of his medium to its final conclusions.

V

Pound's "ideogrammic method" follows from his earlier aesthetic programs and "isms." The essence of the method is that general concepts are most meaningful (perhaps only meaningful) when expressed through a cluster of particular cases. Thus to define "red," the Chinese ideogram combines the characters for rose, cherry, iron rust, and flamingo (ABC, 22). Thus Aristotle says "philosophy is not for young men" because "their generalities cannot be born from a sufficient phalanx / of particulars" (Canto 74). The particulars, in other words, become a complex set of equations pointing to a single reality; but this reality cannot be expressed in any way other than through the particulars.

But the consistency of the ideogrammic method with its predecessors is not, for our purposes, the most important feature of Pound's later critical writings. What reveals even more is the fact that his aesthetic, born in his early medieval studies, comes back to its true home in the long essay called "Cavalcanti: Medievalism." First published in 1928 and then included as the preface to Pound's 1931 edition of Cavalcanti, this essay is Pound's last and most eloquent definition of the "spirit of romance" and the qualities that attracted him to medieval literature. Hugh Kenner has argued that it is essential to an understanding of Pound's methods in *The Cantos*.[20]

Following his usual procedure, Pound tries to isolate the *virtù* of medieval art, especially of Tuscan painting, sculpture, and writing. This consists in its ability to give concrete embodiment to invisible psychic forces and energies.

The Greek aesthetic would seem to consist wholly in plastic, or in plastic moving toward coitus. . . . Plastic plus immediate satisfaction. . . . The Tuscan demands harmony in something more than the plastic. . . . There is the residue of perception, perception of something which requires a human being to produce it. . . . This really complicates the aesthetic. You deal with an interactive force:

the *virtu* in short. . . . It is more than the simple athleticism of the *mens sana in corporo sano*. The conception of the body as perfect instrument of the increasing intelligence pervades. . . . Out of these fine perceptions, or subsequent to them, people say that the Quattrocento, or the sculpture of the Quattrocento, discovered "personality." All of which is perhaps rather vague. We might say: The best Egyptian sculpture is magnificent plastic; but its force comes from a non-plastic idea, i.e. the god is inside the statue. . . . The force is arrested, but there is never any question about its latency, about the force being the essential, and the rest "accidental" in the philosophic technical sense. The shape occurs. (LE, 150–152)

Pound goes on in the essay to describe the Renaissance breakdown of this Tuscan ideal, and to contrast the medieval outlook with the modern:

Certainly [in painting] the metamorphosis into carnal tissue becomes frequent and general somewhere about 1527. The people are corpus, corpuscular, but not in the strict sense "animate"; it is no longer the body of air clothed in the body of fire; it no longer radiates, light no longer moves from the eye, there is a great deal of meat. . . .

We appear to have lost the radiant world where one thought cuts through another with clean edge, a world of moving energies *"mezzo oscuro rade,"* *"risplende in sè perpetuale effecto,"* magnetisms that take form, that are seen, or that border the visible, the matter of Dante's *paradiso*, the glass under water, the form that seems a form seen in a mirror. . . . Not the pagan worship of strength, nor the Greek perception of visual non-animate plastic, or plastic in which the being animate was not the main and principal quality, but this "harmony in the sentience" or harmony *of* the sentient, where the thought has its demarcation, the substance its *virtu*, where stupid men have not reduced all "energy" to unbounded undistinguished abstraction.

For the modern scientist energy has no borders, it is a shapeless "mass" of force; even his capacity to differentiate it to a degree never dreamed by the ancients has not led him to think of its shape or even its loci. The rose that his magnet makes in the iron filings, does not lead him to think of the force in botanic terms, or wish to visualize that force as floral and extant (*ex stare*). (LE, 153–154)

Pound sees Tuscan art as the initial term in a series of dichotomies: essence *v.* accident, nonplastic idea *v.* plastic satisfaction, *anima v.* meat. In every case he distinguishes between the intangible energies of the spirit and the tangible body in which they are clothed. All of this bears out his earlier aesthetic. In the imagery of these passages, the poem is the stone and the delightful psychic experience is the god inside; the poem is the rose pattern in the iron filings of language, and the subjective perception of the poet is the floral magnetic force that arranges them.

VI

"What," the reader might be wondering by now, "does this so-called aesthetic have to do with all the talk about tradition in the first chapter?" To put the answer too simply, the elements of literary tradition may be among the equations for delightful psychic experience. Myth and earlier literature can supply a modern poet of the "historical sense" with luminous details which he can array to adumbrate certain moods and perceptions of his own.

The point can only be made by an example. Here is the early poem called "Speech for Psyche from the Golden Book of Apuleius" (1911). It is a dramatic monologue spoken by Psyche on the morning after Cupid's first visit:

> All night, and as the wind lieth among
> The cypress trees, he lay,
> Nor held me save as air that brusheth by one
> Close, and as the petals of flowers in falling
> Waver and seem not drawn to earth, so he
> Seemed over me to hover light as leaves
> And closer me than air,
> And music flowing through me seemed to open
> Mine eyes upon new colours.
> O winds, what wind can match the weight of him!
>
> (P, 39)

Quite obviously, the poem is about the delightful "psychic" experience of consummation with a god. The similes and metaphors—wind, air, petals of flowers, leaves, music—are Psyche's equations for the incorporeal presence of her husband. The delicate modulation of the rhythms of the first seven lines suggest the wavering and hovering of the god, while the firmer iambic beat of the last three lines builds toward the hyperbolic and synesthetic ecstasy of the climax. These are the absolute metaphors and absolute rhythms which serve the "two-fold vision."

But at the same time the poem could scarcely exist apart from its literary source. The framework for the magic moment is taken over from the Cupid–Psyche legend as told in Apuleius' *Golden Ass*, a work which Pound considered the earliest manifestation of "the spirit of romance" (sr, 12). Keats had employed the same source in his "Ode to Psyche," but Pound views Apuleius through Walter Pater's translation in "The Golden Book," chapter five of *Marius the Epicurean* (1885). The title of his poem speaks of "The Golden Book" rather than the *Golden Ass*.[21]

Not only did Pound take the dramatic situation from Apuleius, but the main images of his poem recapitulate the imagery of his source. In the tale which so deeply affected Pater's Marius, Psyche is placed upon a mountain as a sacrifice to an unknown and terrible power which has plagued the city of the king, her father. She is rescued and wafted to a valley of flowers by Zephyrus, the wind. There she enters a magical house, where invisible spirits play and sing for her:

And the feast being ended, one entered the chamber and sang to her unseen, while another struck the chords of a harp, invisible with him who played on it. Afterwards the sound of company singing together came to her, but still so that none was present to sight; yet it appeared that a great multitude of singers was there.

And the hour of evening inviting her, she climbed into the bed; and as the night was far advanced, behold a sound of a certain clemency approaches her. Then, fearing for her maidenhood in so great solitude, she trembled, and more than any evil she knew she dreaded that she knew not. And now the husband, that unknown husband, drew near, and ascended the couch, and made her his wife; and lo! before the rise of dawn he had departed hastily. And the attendant voices ministered to the needs of the newly married. And so it happened with her for a long season.[22]

Pound's summary of the legend in *The Spirit of Romance* singles out the images which he used in "Speech for Psyche": "Then come voices in the air; voices 'unclothed of bodily vesture'; the harping of invisible harpers, singing; the musicians invisible, subject to her will; the invisible Eros, and the wind Zephyrus, who does her bidding" (SR, 17). Wind, flowers, and music are the central images in Psyche's monologue; in effect, she recapitulates her own tale in describing its climax.* By transforming the imagery of his source into equations for delightful psychic experience, Pound has performed a careful act of "criticism in new composition."

In such ways, tradition complements the ecstasy of poetry. A poet's metaphors may come from personal experience ("Petals on a wet, black bough"), but they may also come from a traditional or literary context, replete with relevant associations (Sappho's "Pierian roses" in *Hugh Selwyn Mauberley*). This is to say that Pound's poetry must be viewed as a continuous dialectic between tradition and the individual talent, between criticism and lyricism. In the chapters that follow, we shall focus on both aspects of his art.

* There is dramatic irony in Psyche's simile, "as the wind lieth among / The cypress trees, he lay." After her disobedience in Apuleius, Cupid flies up and alights in a cypress to upbraid her. Pound's Psyche here foreshadows the end of her bliss.

CHAPTER 3

The Phantastikon of 1908

> And shall I claim;
> Confuse my own phantastikon,
> Or say the filmy shell that circumscribes me
> Contains the actual sun;
> confuse the thing I see
> With actual gods behind me?
> Are they gods behind me?
> How many worlds we have!
> (CANTO 1–1917 VERSION)

The two traditions which most concerned Pound in the poems he wrote before 1912 were the medieval literature of southern Europe discussed in *The Spirit of Romance* and British literature from 1840 to 1910 (especially Browning and the "aesthetes"—Swinburne, Rossetti, Pater, Morris, the writers of the nineties, and the early Yeats). The first of these possessed values which might bring new vigor to modern poetry, and the second was the strongest vein in recent poetry written in English. The two traditions are typically combined on the title page of Pound's first volume of poetry, *A Lume Spento* (1908). The volume is in memory of William Brooke Smith, a young painter and a friend of Pound's at the University of Pennsylvania.[1] The title itself comes from Dante's *Purgatorio* (III, 132), where the phrase "with tapers quenched" describes the funeral procession of Manfredi, a Ghibelline leader who died under papal excommunication. At the same time, Pound calls Smith "Painter, Dreamer of dreams," an allusion to Arthur O'Shaughnessy's "Ode" (1874):

> We are the music-makers
> And we are the dreamers of dreams,
> Wandering by the long sea-breakers,
> And sitting by desolate streams . . .[2]

The same combination of traditions occurs, as we have seen, in "In Epitaphium Eius," "Scriptor Ignotus," and "Speech for Psyche"; it pervades Pound's early work.

The extent of Pound's debt to late nineteenth-century England is gradually being recognized.[3] Accustomed to regarding him as a founder of "modern" poetry, we have too easily forgotten that Pound originally considered himself an heir of Swinburne and the tradition of "art for art's sake." In "Prolegomena" (1912), he made his allegiances clear:

As for there being a "movement" or my being of it, the conception of poetry as a "pure art" in the sense in which I use the term, revived with Swinburne. From the puritanical revolt to Swinburne, poetry had been merely the vehicle . . . the ox-cart and post-chaise for transmitting thoughts poetic or otherwise. And perhaps the "great Victorians," though it is doubtful, and assuredly the "nineties" continued the development of the art, confining their improvements, however, chiefly to sound and to refinements of manner. Mr. Yeats has once and for all stripped English poetry of its perdamnable rhetoric. He has boiled away all that is not poetic—and a good deal that is. . . . He has made our poetic idiom a thing pliable, a speech without inversions. (LE, 11–12)

Pound did not leap full-grown from the brow of Browning; his earliest poems (many of them now in print again for the first time since 1912) are the result of a far more natural parturition from the body of late nineteenth-century English traditions.*

These traditions were not remote. Swinburne was still living when Pound reached London in 1908, and though they did not meet Pound had already recorded his reverence and discipleship in a poem written two years earlier—"Salve O Pontifex: To Swinburne: an hemichaunt":†

> O High Priest of Iacchus,
> Wreathed with the glory of years of creating

---

* See *A Lume Spento and Other Early Poems* (New Directions, 1965). Pound reiterated his belief in "art for art's sake" in May 1913: "As touching 'art for art's sake': the oak does not grow for the purpose or with the intention of being built into ships and tables, yet a wise nation will take care to preserve its forests. It is the oak's business to grow good oak." See "America: Chances and Remedies," *New Age*, XIII (1 May 1913), 10.

† Swinburne died in 1909, and years later in Canto 82 Pound regretted that he had not met him: "Swinburne my only miss / And I didn't know he'd

Entangled music that men may not
Over-readily understand:
                              Breathe!
Now that evening cometh upon thee,
Breathe upon us that low-bowed and exultant
Drink, wine of Iacchus,
          That since the conquering†
Hath been chiefly contained in the numbers
Of them that even as thou have woven
Wicker baskets for grape clusters
Wherein is concealèd the source of the vintage,
          O High Priest of Iacchus,
Breathe thou upon us
          Thy magic in parting!
                    †Vicisti, Nazarenus! [Pound's note]
                              (ALS, 64–65)

Swinburne, according to this view, upheld the trobar clus tradition
of pure and difficult craftsmanship against Victorian Puritanism.
The "hemichaunt" is a prayer for inspiration which places its self-
conscious author squarely in the pagan apostolic succession.*

The High Priest was not without his followers in the religion of
art. Rossetti, too, had great influence on Pound's early poetry.
There are direct echoes of his poems in "Aegupton" (ALS, 58),
"Nicotine" (ALS, 78), and "The House of Splendour" (P, 49), as
well as "In Epitaphium Eius" and "Scriptor Ignotus." Pound's
"Donzella Beata" (ALS, 41) should be read as an affectionate and

---

been to see Landor." When the "hemichaunt" was reprinted in *Ripostes*
(1912), Pound added this note (p. 41): "This apostrophe was written three
years before Swinburne's death." See De Nagy's remarks on the "hemichaunt"
form and on the allusions to Swinburne's own work in the poem (*The Poetry
of Ezra Pound*, pp. 159–160).

* Pound spoke of his "Apostolic Succession" very explicitly in 1913: "Be-
sides knowing living artists I have come in touch with the tradition of the
dead. . . . I have relished this or that about 'old Browning,' or Shelley sliding
down his front banisters 'with almost incredible rapidity.' There is more,
however, in this sort of Apostolic Succession than a ludicrous anecdote, for
people whose minds have been enriched by contact with men of genius retain
the effects of it. I have enjoyed meeting Victorians and Pre-Raphaelites and
men of the nineties through their friends." See "How I Began," *T. P.'s Weekly*
(6 June 1913), p. 707.

witty riposte to Rossetti's "Blessed Damozel." Moreover, Rossetti's
Italian translations were constantly in the young Pound's view
when he undertook to translate Cavalcanti: "In the matter of these
translations and of my knowledge of Tuscan poetry, Rossetti is my
father and my mother. . . ."[4] The priesthood of Iacchus perpetuates
itself in strange ways.

This particular novice was raised on British poetry of the 1890s.
Born in a "half-savage country, out of date," he was gradually ex-
posed to the poets of the nineties by adventurous teachers and
publishers (such as the Maine pirate Thomas Mosher). Writing on Lionel Johnson in 1915, Pound described the American
literary climate in which many of his early poems were composed:
"In America ten or twelve years ago one read Fiona MacLeod, and
Dowson, and Symons. One was guided by Mr. Mosher of Bangor.
I think I first heard of Johnson in an odd sort of post-graduate
course conducted by Dr. Weygandt. One was drunk with 'Celt-
icism,' and with Dowson's 'Cynara,' and with one or two poems of
Symons' 'Wanderers' and 'I am the torch she saith'" (LE, 367).
These enthusiasms left their mark on Pound's early poetry. The
title page of *A Lume Spento* echoes Dowson's "Cynara" (*"somewhat after mine own fashion"*); and "In Tempore Senectutis; An
anti-stave for Dowson" (ALS, 80) is an optimistic answer to Dowson's poem of the same name, using Dowson's own meters and
rhymes. Arthur Symons's "Wanderer's Song" probably inspired
Pound's "Cino" (ALS, 17–19). Fiona MacLeod's "The Unknown
Wind" is the source for Pound's "Motif" (ALS, 73), and "her"
imagery of winds, dreams, and roses greatly resembles the dominant imagery of *A Lume Spento* and *A Quinzaine for This Yule*.[5]
Pound had clearly profited from reading the poets of the nineties
before he reached Venice with the manuscript of *A Lume Spento*
in 1908. (In fact, as the opening "Ode" of *Hugh Selwyn Mauberley*
later intimated, he found it difficult to liberate his style from their
influence.)

Yeats was the living apostle who linked Pound to all of these
figures. Pound had read Yeats at the University of Pennsylvania,
and he chose to settle in London partly because he had become
convinced that Yeats was the best poet writing in English at the
time.[6] His frequent mention of Yeats in *The Spirit of Romance* and

his statement of praise in "Prolegomena" ("He has become a classic in his own lifetime and *nel mezzo del cammin*") were based on the Irish poet's early work; and it was this work that influenced Pound most directly. At least eight of Pound's early poems are clearly indebted to specific poems by Yeats, and in every case to poems written by Yeats before 1900. (Five of the eight appeared in *The Wind Among the Reeds*.)* Yeats, through his own work and his personal contacts with the Pre-Raphaelites and Rhymers, symbolized for Pound the craft of "poetry as a 'pure art,'" and Pound apprenticed himself accordingly.

But in an account of the traditional influences on Pound's earliest poetry, specific writers are perhaps less important than the general *fin-de-siècle* conception of what poetry should be. *A Lume Spento* and *A Quinzaine for This Yule* are dominated by the spirit of Decadence. Put thus broadly, such a description may seem less than helpful, but Pound himself has pointed the way to a more specific account of that spirit. Writing to René Taupin in 1928, he said, "l'idée de l'image doit 'quelque chose' aux symbolistes français via T. E. Hulme, via Yeat [sic] < Symons < Mallarmé" (LETT, 218). He may have had in mind Symons's essay on Mallarmé in *The Symbolist Movement in Literature* (1899) and Yeats's essay on "The Autumn of the Body" in *Ideas of Good and Evil* (1903). Both discuss poetry in terms that readily apply to Pound's own early work.

Symons described the spirit of Decadence as a "revolt against exteriority, against rhetoric, against a materialistic tradition . . .

* Pound's "The Tree" (1908) is modeled on Yeats's "He Thinks of His Past Greatness When a Part of the Constellations of Heaven" in *The Wind Among the Reeds* (1899). The third section of "Und Drang" (*Canzoni*, 1911) alludes to "Song of the Wandering Aengus" in the same volume. The second, fourth, and ninth sections of "Laudantes Decem Pulchritudinis Johannae Templi" (*Exultations*, 1909) owe much to the titles and rose imagery of *The Wind Among the Reeds*. "La Fraisne" is modeled on "The Madness of King Goll" (*Crossways*, 1889), and "The Flame" (*Canzoni*, 1911) alludes to *The Wanderings of Oisin* (1889). In addition, three of Pound's early poems are humorous ripostes to poems by Yeats. "Au Jardin" (*Canzoni*, 1911) is a reply to "The Cap and Bells" (*The Wind Among the Reeds*), "Amities" (1914) is a sarcastic descant on "The Lover Pleads with His Friend for Old Friends" (*The Wind Among the Reeds*), and "The Lake Isle" (1916) rebuts "The Lake Isle of Innisfree" (*The Rose*, 1873).

[an] endeavour to disengage the ultimate essence, the soul, of whatever exists and can be realised by the consciousness . . . [a] dutiful waiting upon every symbol by which the soul of things can be made visible. . . ."[7] This already sounds something like Pound's idea of poetry as equations for ineffable experience, and when Symons writes of Mallarmé the resemblance grows even stronger:

"Poetry," said Mallarmé, "is the language of a state of crisis"; and all his poems are the evocation of a passing ecstasy, arrested in mid-flight. This ecstasy is never the mere instinctive cry of the heart, the simple human joy or sorrow. . . . It is a mental transposition of emotion or sensation, veiled with atmosphere, and becoming, as it becomes a poem, pure beauty. . . . [Quoting Mallarmé again:] "To be instituted, a relation between images, exact; and that therefrom should detach itself a third aspect, fusible and clear, offered to the divination. . . . The pure work," then, "implies the elocutionary disappearance of the poet, who yields place to the words, immobilised by the shock of their inequality; they take light from mutual reflection, like an actual train of fire over precious stones, replacing the old lyric afflatus or the enthusiastic personal direction of the phrase."[8]

Some of the central tenets of Pound's aesthetic are latent in these passages: ecstasy, the mental transposition of emotion, the exact relation of images, the elocutionary disappearance of the poet, and the craftsmanship which creates the effect of a train of fire over precious stones. Yeats quoted from these passages near the end of "The Autumn of the Body," and added his own comment: "Mr. Symons understands these and other sentences to mean that poetry will henceforth be a poetry of essences, separated one from another in little and intense poems. I think there will be much poetry of this kind, because of an ever more arduous search for a disembodied ecstasy. . . ."[9] Ideas of this sort are probably the "quelque chose" which the Image owes to the French symbolists "via Yeat <Symons<Mallarmé."

The first poem in A Lume Spento reveals Pound's commitment to this "spiritual romanticism."[10] Called "Grace Before Song," it is both a prayer for inspiration and a declaration of poetic principles:

> Lord God of heaven that with mercy dight
> Th' alternate prayer wheel of the night and light

Eternal hath to thee, and in whose sight
Our days as rain drops in the sea surge fall,

As bright white drops upon a leaden sea
Grant so my songs to this grey folk may be:

As drops that dream and gleam and falling catch the sun,
Evan'scent mirrors every opal one
Of such his splendor as their compass is,
So, bold My Songs, seek ye such death as this.

(ALS, 13)

Pound is clearly declaring his intention to write what Yeats called
"a poetry of essences, separated one from another in little and intense poems." Each lyric is to be a fleeting raindrop, momentarily
mirroring the celestial fire of Beauty (the sun). "Evan'scent mirrors every opal one" is parallel to Mallarmé's image of the train of
fire over precious stones, and the self-sufficient perfection of the
songs themselves implies the elocutionary disappearance of the
poet.

II

"The essential thing about a poet," Pound said in 1915, "is that
he build us his world."[11] In A Lume Spento and A Quinzaine for
This Yule, he creates a fairly coherent imaginative "world" by
means of recurring patterns of imagery. The poetic faculty involved in building a world he called the phantastikon, or image-
making faculty: "the consciousness of some seems to rest . . . in
what the Greek psychologists called the phantastikon. Their minds
are, that is, circumvolved about them like soap-bubbles reflecting
sundry patches of the macrocosmos" (SR, 92). The reflected patches of the macrocosmos provide the appropriate image equations for
the experience of the consciousness. Pound retained this notion of
the phantastikon in the first version of Canto 1 (1917) and emphasized its world-building power:

And shall I claim;
Confuse my own phantastikon,
Or say the filmy shell that circumscribes me

Contains the actual sun;
confuse the thing I see
With actual gods behind me?
Are they gods behind me?
How many worlds we have! If Botticelli
Brings her ashore on that great cockle-shell—
His Venus (Simonetta?),
And Spring and Aufidus fill all the air
With their clear-outlined blossoms?
World enough. Behold, I say, she comes
"Apparelled like the spring, Graces her subjects,"
(That's from *Pericles*).
Oh, we have worlds enough, and brave *décors*,
And from these like we guess a soul for man
And build him full of aery populations.
Mantegna a sterner line, and the new world about us:
Barred lights, great flares, new form, Picasso or Lewis.*

Botticelli, Shakespeare, Mantegna, and the cubists build their different worlds out of what they see, out of what is reflected by the "filmy shell" of their consciousness. Like the speaker in Pound's early poem, "Plotinus," each artist makes "New thoughts as crescent images of *me*" (ALS, 56). In his own early poems, Pound too sets forth a world built "full of aery populations."

This world is the nebulous and rarefied realm of "spiritual romanticism." Its main elements are (1) disembodied spirits seeking incarnation in an earthly form or union with the divine essence; (2) a magical wind conveying sometimes death but more often a transcendental inspiration; (3) dawn, and especially the false dawn, the strange illusory harbinger of day, real and unreal; and (4) dreams, symbolizing rare psychic states of contemplation and insight. In addition, fire is a ubiquitous symbol of inspired spirituality, and the literary tradition of the past is a vague but potent influence in the form of runes, legends, druidings, and old songs.[12]

---

* "Three Cantos—I," *Poetry*, X (June 1917), 120–121. Pound used the term humorously in answering a letter from William Bird in 1933: "As fer yr. final pp., that is about the kind of mess that has been trespassin on my phantastikon for several weeks" (LETT, 243).

The first of these elements—disembodied spirits—seems to have fascinated Pound as much as it intrigued his contemporaries. He was interested in the various mystical speculations so popular in London circles before the war, and though never as serious a student as Yeats, he did look into the literature.[13] The "Note Precedent to 'La Fraisne' " in *A Lume Spento* mentions several examples, including Yeats's own *The Celtic Twilight* (1893). Years later, Pound related the disembodied spirits which he encountered in Chinese poetry and Japanese drama to Celtic folk tales and to the traditions of European hermeticism.[14] Spiritist doctrines provided Pound, as they did Yeats, with equations or "metaphors for poetry." As Pound wrote later, perhaps with his own early work in mind, "Romantic poetry . . . almost requires the concept of reincarnation as part of its mechanism. *No apter metaphor having been found for certain emotional colours.*"[15]

The speaker in "Anima Sola," for instance, seems to be the world soul of the Greek philosophers, diffused throughout natural phenomena but especially present in nature's most indefinable processes—the appearance of dew, darkness, the light of meteors, the Shelleyan blowing of autumn winds (ALS, 31–32). He is also, however, the soul of the "God-man," the free spirit of the Decadence, superior to all conventions because of his wide experience and suffering. In "Prometheus," the disembodied souls of artists seek their eternal home, the divine fire which their songs have reflected. They are weary with a *fin-de-siècle* languor, but they keep the sacred flame alive in the surrounding darkness (ALS, 57). Their spiritual brothers are the chorus of unlocalized voices in "The Decadence" (ALS, 68). The voices of lovers are heard in two complementary sonnets, "That Pass Between the False Dawn and the True" and "In Morte De" (ALS, 44–45). Probably inspired by Dante's tale of Paolo and Francesca, these poems portray the souls of lovers afloat upon an undirected wind—not eternally together like Dante's pair, but separated after a momentary meeting and carried longingly apart. A similar moment is depicted in "Comraderie" [sic], where the lover can almost feel the brush of the cheek and Pre-Raphaelite long hair of his absent beloved (ALS, 47).[16] The speakers in "Threnos" (ALS, 46) and "Aegupton" (ALS, 58–59) are also spirits, and the eternal souls of artists are reincarnated in "Masks" (ALS, 52) and "Histrion" (QFTY, 108). In these early poems, Pound indeed emulates the decadent spirit as Symons had described it: "To fix the last shade, the quintessence of things; to fix it fleetingly; to be a disembodied voice, and yet the voice of a human soul: that is the ideal of Decadence."[17]

But Pound could not believe in the actual existence of his spirits. Plato had used the term *phantastikon* to mean the source of delusions, of the dangerous prevalence of imagination.[18] And Pound, always hesitant to make metaphysical assertions on the basis of "delightful psychic experience," retains this as a possible connotation:

> And shall I claim;
> Confuse my own phantastikon,
> Or say the filmy shell that circumscribes me
> Contains the actual sun;
>   confuse the thing I see
> With actual gods behind me?
>   Are they gods behind me?

Nearly all the disembodied voices of *A Lume Spento* and *A Quinzaine for This Yule* are dramatis personae, and therefore provisional and self-confessed fictions. It might be better to say that they are unborn personae, plaintively seeking the identity and incarnation which the speakers of the full-fledged dramatic monologues in these volumes have. In presenting these beings with their rarefied ecstasies, Pound seems to be working in an uncongenial convention. The poems convey the same longing for tangibility that Symons expressed when he wrote: "The whole visible world itself, we are told, is but a Symbol, made visible in order that we may apprehend ourselves, and not be blown hither and thither like a flame in the night."[19] Pound could not long be satisfied with personae possessing so little identity and *virtù*.

The spirits in this poetic "universe" are transported upon symbolic winds. Though sometimes associated with death, this wind is more often the "Correspondent Breeze" of English Romantic tradition, symbolizing transcendent inspiration.[20] The young Pound even had his own version of the Romantic Aeolian harp, which he gave in two of his least eloquent early poems:

For man is a skin full of wine
But his soul is a hole full of God
And the song of all time blows through him
As winds through a knot-holed board.

(ALS, 82)

As winds through a round smooth knot-hole
Make tune to the time of the storm,
The cry of the bard in the half-light
Is chaos bruised into form.

(ALS, 123)

The simile is used more subtly in "Marvoil" (*Personae*, 1909) when the troubadour addresses the niche in which he is about to conceal his last manuscript: "O hole in the wall here! be thou my jongleur / As ne'er had I other, and when the wind blows, / Sing thou the grace of the Lady of Beziers" (P, 23). In these cases, the wind is associated with poetic inspiration.

This magical wind ventilates the pages of *A Lume Spento* and *A Quinzaine for This Yule*. It is, for instance, the mysterious breeze in "Motif":

I have heard a wee wind searching
Through still forests for me,
I have seen a wee wind searching
    O'er still sea.

Through woodlands dim
    Have I taken my way,
And o'er silent waters, night and day
Have I sought the wee wind.

(ALS, 73)

The "Purveyors General" make "new songs from out the breeze" (QFTY, 93), while "winds and lutany" stir the poet's heart to song in "Vana" (later retitled "Praise of Ysolt"—ALS, 42, and P, 16). The spirit of spring sends out a warm "gust of breath" in "La Regina Avrillouse" (ALS, 74), and Childe Roland in "Oltre la Torre: Rolando" asks "who will lie in the bracken high / And laugh, and laugh for the winds with me?" (ALS, 81). The "Cry of the Eyes" of the scholar is to "feel the fingers of the wind" (ALS, 37).

In several of these early poems, Pound makes play with the etymological connection between breath and inspiration. This kind of wind is heard in the "wind-runeing" of "Cino" (ALS, 17), and it blows through Browning in "Mesmerism" when "you wheeze as a head-cold long-tonsilled Calliope" (ALS, 28). It is the inspiration Pound seeks in "Salve O Pontifex!" when he repeatedly invokes Swinburne to "Breathe!" and portrays Swinburne's disciples departing from him "toning thy melodies even as winds tone / The whisper of tree leaves, on sun-lit days" (ALS, 63–66). In *Personae* (1909), it is the "breath for beauty and the arts" possessed by Pound's soulmates "In Durance," whom he loves "as the wind the trees / That holds their blossoms and their leaves in cure / And calls the utmost singing from the boughs" (P, 20–21).

This wind imagery even permeates Pound's best-known dramatic monologues, where it preserves its special connotations. We have noted its function in "Marvoil"; it is also the "wind that flutters in the leaves" of the magical ash grove in "La Fraisne" (ALS, 15–16). It is heard by Bertran de Born in "Sestina: Altaforte" when "the winds shriek through the clouds, mad, opposing" (P, 28); and it bears the hot scent sniffed by Piere Vidal at the end of his monologue (P, 32). It is seen in the eyes of the "Goodly Fere," which are "like the sea that brooks no voyaging / With the winds unleashed and free" (P, 34).

The symbolic values of wind in Pound's early poetry receive their most explicit statement in "Aegupton" (later retitled "De Aegypto"). Here the spirit of beauty on the winds is the speaker of a dramatic monologue:

> I—even I—am he who knoweth the roads
> Through the sky, and the wind thereof is my body.
>
> (ALS, 58–59)

This spirit is wafted in an eternal search for earthly incarnation.*

---

* The speaker has beheld the "Lady of Life" with her green and gray raiment *because* she is an example of such incarnation. As T. W. West has noted, she is the picture of the soul painted by the fictional artist, Chiero

At present he seeks a poet or singer to inspire:

> Manus animam pinxit–
> My pen is in my hand

> To write the acceptable word,
> My mouth to chant the pure singing!

> Who hath the mouth to receive it,
> The song of the Lotus of Kumi?

The spirit of Egypt is thus a persona for the transcendent beauty which rides the winds of *A Lume Spento* and *A Quinzaine for This Yule*, bringing ecstasy to those it touches. Wind is one of the central equations for "delightful psychic experience" in Pound's early poems.

Ecstasy has a time, as well as an element, in this imaginative world. It is associated with the dawn, especially with the false dawn—the moment before sunrise when the light of day is reflected in the west rather than the east. Pound's first published poem was a translation of the *aube*, or dawn song, which contains the earliest Provençal poetry, and *A Quinzaine for This Yule* is dedicated "To the Aube of the West Dawn." In a critical essay on the Renaissance Latin poets, published early in 1908 by "Ezra Pound, Professor of Romance Languages in Wabash College," he attempted to describe the kind of beauty he associated with the dawn. It is "evanescent yet ever returning . . . warm without burning"; it is "no strong, vivifying power" but its "tones are as Whistler's when he paints the mist at moth hour. . . . It is not that other dream beauty, the Celtic beauty of sadness, that fills us with restless wave-longing

---

dell' Erma, in Rossetti's short story, "Hand and Soul." The words "Manus animam pinxit" and the "green and gray raiment" in Pound's poem come from Rossetti's story: "The picture I speak of is a small one, and represents merely the figure of a woman, clad to the hands and feet with a green and gray raiment, chaste and early in its fashion, but exceedingly simple. . . . You knew that figure, when painted, had been seen; yet it was not a thing to be seen of men. . . . On examining it closely, I perceived in one corner of the canvas the words *Manus Animam pinxit*, and the date 1239." See Rossetti, *Poems and Translations*, p. 170; and T. W. West, "D. G. Rossetti and Ezra Pound," *Review of English Studies*, IV (1953), 63–67. In Chiero's case, the "hand painted the soul," the kind of achievement which Pound declares to be the peculiar virtue of medieval art in his "Cavalcanti" essay.

and sets us a-following the wind of lost desire. . . . It is not the intense, surcharged beauty of blood and ivory that we find in Rossetti, but a beauty of the half-light of Hesper and Aurora, of twilight and the hours between the false dawn and the true."[21]

Many of Pound's early poems attempt to capture the kind of beauty he found in the Provençal *aube* and the poetry of Flamininus. One is actually titled "Between the False Dawn and the True" (ALS, 44), and in another ("In Tempore Senectutis") the undiminished psychic ecstasy of two aged lovers is associated with the "moth-hour" which "leadeth the dawn / As a maiden" (ALS, 33). In "Greek Epigram," praise of the dawn and the twilight differentiates the poet from other men (QFTY, 105); and years later in Canto 79 Pound recalled this poem:

> and when the morning sun lit up the shelves and battalions
> of the West, cloud over cloud
> > Old Ez folded his blankets
> Neither Eos nor Hesperus has suffered wrong at my
> hands.

In "The Decadence" (ALS, 68), the poet-martyrs have kept the flame burning until "new day glistens in the old day's room" (that is, until the new dawn is seen in the west). In "Famam Librosque Cano" the songs of the successful poet will be sung "when the night / Shrinketh the kiss of the dawn" (ALS, 35). In "Nel Biancheggiar," Katherine Ruth Heymann's playing reminds Pound of the soft unfolding of the west dawn: "Blue-grey, and white, and white-of-rose, / The flowers of the west's fore-dawn unclose" (QFTY, 109).[22] In "Aube of the West Dawn: Venetian June," Pound relates the west dawn to the ecstasy from which myth and poetry are created. The poem tells "How Malrin chose for his Lady the reflection of the Dawn and was thereafter true to her," and Pound explained in a note: "I think from such perceptions as this arose the ancient myths of the demi-gods; as from such as that in 'The Tree' (*A Lume Spento*), the myths of metamorphosis" (QFTY, 94). Dawn, then, is associated by Pound with "delightful psychic experience," and therefore with wind. In "Ballad Rosalind" (ALS, 48), the Lady Rosalind is "Fair as dawn and fleet as wind."[23]

The "Flamininus" essay reveals Pound's interest in varieties of "dream beauty," and in his own early work (as in that of Fiona MacLeod and Yeats) dreaming is a sign of spiritual insight, of an inward ecstatic contemplation. If the magical light of dawn is rejected, as it is in "To the Dawn: Defiance" (ALS, 67), it is only because it threatens the sacred state of dream. The last poem in *A Lume Spento* is entitled "Make strong old dreams lest this our world lose heart" (ALS, 82); and the value of dreams is asserted by the speaker in "Song":

> Love thou thy dream
> All base love scorning,
> Love thou the wind
> And here take warning
> That dreams alone can truly be,
> For 'tis in dream I come to thee.
>
>   (ALS, 72)

The identity of this speaker is left unrevealed, but "I" clearly represents inspiring vision. Perhaps "I" is one of the women who come to the "Scriptor Ignotus" in "his dreams / Of Iseult and of Beatrice" (ALS, 39). Or it may be the ineffable third vision of Malrin the jester: "And again Malrin, drunk as with the dew of old world druidings, was bowed in dream. And the third dream of Malrin was the dream of the seven, and no man knoweth it" (ALS, 51). In one of Pound's (unintentionally) funniest early poems, "Nicotine: A Hymn to the Dope," this admirable substance is praised chiefly because it induces dreams. Pound salutes it as "Goddess" and "Dream-Grace," because it weaves "Dreams that need no undeceiving." By alluding to Rossetti's "Love's Nocturn," he equates its spiritual power with that of love itself.[24] Dreams, then, symbolize states of rare and ecstatic contemplation; and when in *Hugh Selwyn Mauberley* Pound contrasts "the obscure reveries / Of the inward gaze" to what the age demanded, he is transferring to these "reveries" some of the values attached to dreams in his earlier poetry.

Pound seems to have given up this "world" after 1908. Perhaps he abandoned his magical winds, illusory west dawns, and unspecified dream visions for the same reason that he put aside his disembodied spirits—their insubstantiality. Not being in the natural world, they could not meet his Imagist rule "that the proper and perfect symbol is the natural object . . ." (LE, 9). Not being concrete or sensuous metaphors, they could not give convincing verisimilitude to the poet's vision. Perhaps Pound realized that his early symbols are vulnerable to the critique which he later used to distinguish Imagism from Symbolism: "The symbolists dealt in 'association,' that is, in a sort of allusion, almost of allegory. They degraded the symbol to the status of a word. . . . The symbolist's *symbols* have a fixed value, like numbers in arithmetic, like 1, 2, and 7. The imagiste's images have a variable significance, like the signs *a*, *b*, and *x* in algebra. . . . Almost anyone can realize that to use a symbol *with an ascribed or intended meaning* is, usually, to produce very bad art."[25] Certainly wind, dawn, dream, and fire *seem* to have a fixed and almost allegorical significance in *A Lume Spento* and *A Quinzaine for This Yule*. They are not embedded in any reality complex enough for them to have alternative meanings (like *a*, *b*, and *x* in algebra). They seem to suggest "belief in a permanent world" on the part of the poet, and to offer an associative shortcut to that world.[26] "Dream" is a word to conjure with, and nearly always carries the same visionary connotation; in the end it has become a symbol degraded to the status of a word. Pound uses many of the same favorite symbols in his dramatic monologues, but the richer context there allows them to have the multivalence of the true image. When the speaker in "La Fraisne" praises "Naught but the wind that flutters in the leaves," we may associate the wind with the divine inspiration of madness and poetry, or we may simply associate it with the physical setting of the monologue. The "wee wind" of "Motif" permits no alternative to the mystic interpretation. Pound turned increasingly to the richer world of the dramatic monologue, whither we now follow him.

CHAPTER 4

Personae: Historic Interest, Dramatic Ecstasy, and Personal Identity

Ghosts move about me
Patched with histories.
(CANTO 1—1917 version—
and CANTO 74)

In discussing "Scriptor Ignotus," we noted that the persona was both a device of "criticism in new composition" and a rather transparent mask for Pound himself, voicing Pound's own epic aspirations and fears. This double function is typical of the persona in all of Pound's early poetry. In this chapter, I shall argue that Pound's personae combine his concern for revitalizing history with his concern for portraying dramatic ecstasy; that they are exercises in historical imagination and also in creating a vivid personal identity; that, in other words, they stand somewhere between Browning's dramatic monologues and Yeats's masks.

I

For Browning the dramatic monologue involved a particular relationship between the poet and external reality. In his *Essay on Shelley* (1852), he distinguished between the "subjective poet" and the "objective poet," and related the dramatic poem to the second of these. The difference is largely one of attitudes toward the world outside the mind. The subjective poet is concerned primarily with presenting his own vision of things, and with the outside world only insofar as it relates to that vision. He is an idealist, a Platonist, a Shelley. The objective poet is concerned with presenting the outside world as it is, before it has been refracted through any particular vision:

> ... the objective, in the strictest sense, must still retain its original value. For it is with this world, as starting-point and basis alike, that we shall always have to concern ourselves: the world is not to be learned and thrown aside, but reverted to and relearned. The spiritual comprehension may be infinitely subtilized, but the raw material it operates on must remain. There may be no end of the poets who communicate to us what they see in an object with reference to their own individuality; what it was before they saw it, in reference to the aggregate human mind, will be as desirable to know as ever.[1]

The objective poet effaces himself in favor of his subject; his poetry is "substantive, projected from himself, and distinct." When he vanishes entirely, he leaves pure drama behind him: "The result ... in its pure form, when even description, as suggesting a describer, is dispensed with, is what we call dramatic poetry."[2] The monologue is, then, an empirical form presenting an unbiased account of the objective world.

Browning interpreted the word "objective" to include psychological and historical fact as well as physical; the objective poet should "reproduce things external (whether the phenomena of the scenic universe, or the manifested action of the human heart and brain)."[3] Browning is interested in the whole spectrum of psychological phenomena. Though he usually selects personae with extraordinary or even abnormal points of view, he appears to have no predisposition about the *kinds* of mental processes he will portray. There is room for everything from the elaborate rationalizations of Bishop Blougram and Sludge to the warped perception of Caliban and the monk in the Spanish cloister to the ineffable visions of Abt Vogler and Johannes Agricola. Likewise he is interested in many different historical periods and sets his monologues with circumstantial detail in a variety of past eras. As J. Hillis Miller has suggested, "he can approach an absolute vision only by attempting to relive, one by one, all the possible attitudes of the human spirit."[4]

Yeats's personae are less empirical and less historical in orientation. Yeats tended to choose a few traditional, preexisting types, whose associations might give his personal utterance weight. As he said in 1914, "I was about to learn that if a man is to write lyric poetry he must be shaped by nature and art to some one out of half a dozen traditional poses, and be lover or saint, sage or sensualist, or mere mocker of all life; and that none but that stroke of luckless luck can open before him the accumulated expression of the world."[5] These types are radically nonhistorical. Questions of historical period and verisimilitude of setting are irrelevant, for example, to the generic lover of *The Wind Among the Reeds*. Yeats's personae are temporal embodiments of types that exist out of time. He is chiefly interested in the handful of intensified moods and states of mind represented by the lover, beggar, fool, madman, poet, shepherd, fisherman, king, whore. In practice, the difference between Yeats and Browning is the difference between the Bishop of the Crazy Jane poems, and the Bishop who orders his tomb in St. Praxed's, Rome.

By a sort of useful oversimplification, we may think of Yeats and Browning as opposite ends of a spectrum along which Pound's dramatic monologues can be ranged. Pound's well-known definition of the dramatic lyric, in a letter to William Carlos Williams in 1908, emphasizes "the lyric element" in the form.[6]

To me the short so-called dramatic lyric—at any rate the sort of thing I do—is the poetic part of a drama the rest of which (to me the prose part) is left to the reader's imagination or implied or set in a short note. I catch the character I happen to be interested in at the moment he interests me, usually a moment of song, self-analysis, or sudden understanding or revelation. And the rest of the play would bore me and presumably the reader. I paint my man as I *conceive* him. Et voilà tout!   (LETT, 3–4)

The definition must be taken as Pound's attempt to distinguish his own practice from Browning's, which he later criticized for not being poetical enough: "Browning included a certain amount of ratiocination and of purely intellectual comment, and in just that proportion he lost intensity" (LE, 419–420). As this remark might lead us to expect, Pound's own monologues tend to concentrate on a narrower, more intense, and more specialized range of psychic states than Browning's. They contain in general less "ratiocination" and circumstantial detail of setting. Nevertheless, most of them still have an important Browningesque historical dimension. The "prose part" of the drama often plays a greater role than

Pound's definition suggests. It intensifies the lyric utterances of his personae by the narrative context it provides. If we seek a formulation that does justice to both aspects of Pound's art, we shall have to say something like this: Pound's personae are vital historic or pseudohistoric figures, caught in mid-career at some rare moment of intense passion, ecstasy, or contemplative lucidity.

This is but corroboration of our earlier discussion. Browning's conception of the persona appealed to Pound not just because it was the first he encountered, but because of Pound's native tendency toward empiricism and historicism—a tendency exemplified in his whole approach to literary tradition. At the same time, a "Yeatsian" conception also appealed to him because of his concern with poetry as a lyric record of purified and intense states of consciousness. Pound's constant endeavor is to accommodate history and poetry, to reconcile Truth and Calliope, the gentle maidens who are seen "slanging each other sous les lauriers" in Canto 8. By way of illustration, we may examine two poems from opposite ends of our hypothetical spectrum—"La Fraisne" and "Marvoil."

In "La Fraisne" a peculiar state of ecstasy is the principal subject, and all other elements are subordinate to it. The speaker is instrumental, and (so far as I know) purely fictitious. At first, however, Pound attempted to give him a legendary or pseudohistorical identity. In a "Note Precedent to 'La Fraisne,' " he cast the "prose part" of his drama in the form of an abbreviated Provençal *vida*: "Miraut de Garzelas after the pains he bore a-loving Riels of Calidorn and that to none avail, ran mad in the forest" (ALS, 14). To increase the verisimilitude, he cited the analogous legends of Piere Vidal and Garulf Bisclavret (a figure in one of the *Lais* of Marie de France), and he even gave the monologue a particular setting—"The Ash Wood of Malvern." But these "facts" add little to the poem, as Pound apparently realized when he omitted them from the collected edition of *Personae*. Far more important as background is the demonstrable fact that "La Fraisne" is modeled on Yeats's "The Madness of King Goll" (1889).* Both poems por-

---

* See N. Christoph de Nagy, *The Poetry of Ezra Pound*, p. 106. Pound's refrain, "Naught but the wind that flutters in the leaves," echoes Yeats's refrain, "They will not hush, the leaves a-flutter around me, the beech leaves old." See *The Collected Poems of W. B. Yeats* (London, 1961), pp. 17–20.

tray a powerful chieftain passing into isolation, madness, and a strange harmony with nature.

The delightful psychic experience of Miraut de Garzelas is a moment of metamorphic perception akin to that of the man who turned into "The Tree" in another of Pound's lyrics. In his "Note," Pound explained that the poem originated in such an experience:

When the soul is exhausted in fire, then doth the spirit return unto its primal nature and there is upon it a peace great and of the woodland. . . . Then becometh it kin to the faun and the dryad, a woodland-dweller amid the rocks and streams. . . . Also has Mr. Yeats in his *Celtic Twilight* treated of such, and I because in such a mood, feeling myself divided between myself corporal and a self aetherial, "a dweller by streams and in wood-land," eternal because simple in elements
"Aeternus quia simplex naturae."

We have learned to watch for the word "mood" in Pound's prose, and here he tells us frankly that the poem is an equation for a certain "mood" of his own. Its purpose is to evoke the primal peace of an "aetherial" soul from which all accidental qualities have been burnt away by the fires of passion. We are asked to participate in the psychic state of a man who can marry a dogwood tree by a pool in an ash grove, listen all day to the wind among the leaves, and find his lasting happiness in doing so. The integrity of the mood is threatened only by the memory of the consuming passion which created it, by "the love of women / That plague and burn and drive one away." The only dramatic development in the poem is the sudden menace and eventual defeat of memory. The threat of memory is reflected in a pattern of broken speech ("Once there was a woman . . . / . . . but I forget . . . she was . . . / . . . I hope she will not come again"). But it fails or is willed away, and the speaker's obsessive coherence is restored. The poem itself is *"simplex naturae,"* purposely avoiding a Browningesque dramatic complexity in order to present a Yeatsian ecstasy.

The other extreme is represented by "Marvoil," perhaps Pound's closest imitation of Browning before "Near Perigord." Here the speaker is an authentic historical figure—the troubadour, Arnaut of Marvoil. His monologue attempts to recreate the particular historical and psychological realities in which his art originated, in the manner of Browning's artist monologues such as "Fra Lippo Lippi" and "Andrea del Sarto." As De Nagy has pointed out, the first line of Pound's poem ("A poor clerk I, 'Arnaut the less' they call me") establishes its literary heritage by echoing the first line of "Fra Lippo Lippi" ("I am poor brother Lippo, by your leave").[7] Pound imagines the tangle of passion and circumstance behind the polite discretion and convention of Marvoil's surviving lyrics.[8] Pound's approach to Provence in this poem is the historical and empirical approach of his essay on "Troubadours—Their Sorts and Conditions" (1913), and not the mystical and visionary approach of his essay on "Psychology and Troubadours" (1912):* "No student of the period can doubt that the involved forms, and the veiled meanings in the 'trobar clus,' grew out of living conditions . . . the Middle Ages did not exist in the tapestry alone, nor in the fourteenth-century romances, but . . . there was a life like our own, no mere sequence of citherns and citoles, nor a continuous stalking about in sendal and diaspre" (LE, 94–101).

A knowledge of historical background is far more essential to a full appreciation of "Marvoil" than it is to "La Fraisne." It is important to realize that Pound is working from the *vida* of the troubadour, and that the major characters and relationships are (with one exception) taken directly from that source. The *vida*, for instance, opens with information about Arnaut's birthplace and his occupation before he became a troubadour: "Arnaut of Marvoil was of the diocese of Perigord, of a castle named Marvoil. And he was a clerk of low degree, who, because he could not earn his bread by letters, took to wandering through the world; and well knew to sing and rhyme." This information Pound integrates into his own opening:

> A poor clerk I, "Arnaut the less" they call me,
> And because I have small mind to sit

* Consider, in contrast, the following account of trobar clus in "Psychology and Troubadours." "Following the clue of a visionary interpretation," Pound speculates on the question: "Did this 'close ring,' this aristocracy of emotion, evolve, out of its half memories of Hellenistic mysteries, a cult—a cult stricter, or more subtle, than that of the celibate ascetics, a cult for the purgation of the soul by a refinement of, and lordship over, the senses?" (SR, 90). These two essays represent the antipodes, not only of Pound's thinking about Provence, but also of his thinking about poetry in general.

Day long, long day cooped on a stool
A-jumbling o' figures for Maître Jacques Polin,
I ha' taken to rambling the South here.

(p, 22)

(As De Nagy points out, Pound adds the anachronism of having
Marvoil designate himself by a title first applied to him posthu-
mously by Petrarch—" 'l men famoso Arnaldo.") All the rest of the
vida, all that is known about Marvoil's life, is related to the incident at the center of Pound's poem—Arnaut's love for the Countess
of Burlatz and Beziers, and his exile at the instigation of King Alphonso of Aragon. It comes down to this: Pound is attempting to
add an imaginary supplement to the *vida* which shall be consistent
with the facts of Marvoil's life as we know them, yet shall also illuminate his character and make him kin to us in a way that the
vida itself does not. And one major source of pleasure for the
reader can and should be a sense of how Pound has both followed
and transformed his source.*

In the *vida*, Arnaut goes to "Guillem of Montpellier, the which
was his trusty friend and lord," when he is exiled. But in Pound's
poem we see Arnaut in Avignon at an inn which seems to be his
first stopping place since his exile. The two-part structure shows
him first in a public room of the inn, speaking to us as if we were
other travelers, and telling us of himself and his misadventures. At
the end of the third strophe, the scene switches to the privacy of
Arnaut's own room, where he commits his only will and testament
—a parchment manuscript of "vers and canzone to the Countess of
Beziers"—to a hole in the wall. (Dreams of discovering such a

* The *vida* may be read in its entirety in *The Lives of the Troubadours*,
trans. Ida Farnell (London, 1896), p. 67. Pound mentions this translation in
The Spirit of Romance, p. 62, and his adherence to it is indicated by the cast
of characters he gives in a note to "Marvoil" in *Personae* (1909) on page 59:
"The Personae are:
Arnaut of Marvoil, a troubadour, date 1170–1200.
The Countess (in her own right) of Burlatz, and of Beziers, being the wife of
The Vicomte of Beziers.
Alfonso IV of Aragon.
Tibors of Mont-Ausier. For fuller mention of her see the 'razos' on Bertran of
Born. She is contemporary with the other persons, but I have no strict war-
rent for dragging her name into this particular affair."

cache must have haunted Pound when, as a young man just out of graduate school, he rambled through Provence on walking tours.)[9]

Pound is not primarily concerned to present an ecstatic state of consciousness in "Marvoil." Delightful psychic experience is implied only in the submerged myth of the fall from paradise which Pound acutely recognized in the *vida* and incorporated into his poem. This mythic pattern is suggested by the two summary tableaux which frame Arnaut's "fall":

> Beziers off at Mont-Ausier, I and his Lady
> Singing the stars in the turrets of Beziers,
> And one lean Aragonese cursing the seneschal
> To the end that you see, friends:
>
> Aragon cursing in Aragon, Beziers busy at Beziers—
> Bored to an inch of extinction,
> Tibors all tongue and temper at Mont-Ausier,
> Me! in this damn'd inn of Avignon,
> Stringing long verse for the Burlatz. . . .
>
> (P, 22)

Arnaut's paradise lasted while he and the Countess sat "singing the stars"; the serpent in his garden was Alphonso; and his resulting exile has brought him to the "damn'd inn" at Avignon. Beziers and its lady are Arnaut's lost paradise, as he implies when he prays for the eternal damnation of Alphonso and the salvation of himself:

> May her eyes and her cheek be fair
> To all men except the King of Aragon,
> And may I come speedily to Beziers
> Whither my desire and my dream have preceded me.
>
> (P, 22–23)

But in the poem this latent myth is a means of characterizing the troubadour sensibility, rather than an end in itself. Pound wishes primarily to portray the masculine vigor and passion of his speaker, and at the same time to show how this passion is combined with a sort of detached and sophisticated professional craftsmanship. (Arnaut can, for example, establish a graceful threefold comparison between himself and a hole in the wall by drawing his subject through the traditional *topoi* of rhetoric).* Arnaut is a skilled and forceful personality in a definite historical context, and the poem is beautiful propaganda designed to interest Pound's reader in that context.

"La Fraisne" and "Marvoil" differ, then, in their respective emphases upon an impersonal ecstasy and a concrete historical personality and situation. Neither emphasis is exclusive—"Miraut de Garzelas" has legendary associations just as Marvoil obliquely describes his moment of bliss—but they are relatively pure examples of the extremes to be found in Pound's early monologues. The other personae can be ranged between them.

We may begin with two lyrics in which the speakers' ecstasy has literally taken them out of themselves. Like the speaker in "La Fraisne," these personae have also been "exhausted in fire," and they share his mood of lucid peace. In "Paracelsus in Excelsis" (1910), Pound translates the hero of Browning's *Paracelsus* (1835). Browning had followed the vicissitudes of this questing soul through a repeating pattern of aspiration, temporary attainment and disappointment. In Part V, "Paracelsus Attains," the last words of the dying protagonist are: "I shall emerge one day." He emerges into Pound's poem. Here at last Paracelsus "attains"; in excelsis he is completed and purified. He exists in an eternal state of contemplative ecstasy:

> Being no longer human, why should I
> Pretend humanity or don the frail attire?
> Men have I known and men, but never one
> Was grown so free an essence, or become
> So simply element as what I am.
> The mist goes from the mirror and I see.
> Behold! the world of forms is swept beneath—
> Turmoil grown visible beneath our peace,
> And we that are grown formless, rise above—

---

* In addition to "dividing" his subject in the traditional manner, Arnaut uses more figures of rhetoric than do most of Pound's personae: "Day long, long day" (antimetabole); "Aragon cursing in Aragon, Beziers busy in Beziers" (diaphora, ploce, and prosonomasia); "O hole in the wall" (anaphora). The figures are, of course, highly appropriate in the mouth of a medieval poet.

Fluids intangible that have been men,
We seem as statues round whose high-risen base
Some overflowing river is run mad,
In us alone the element of calm.

(P, 32)

This spirit is nonhuman, stripped of all accidents, *"simplex na-turae"* if anything ever was. "Paracelsus in Excelsis" is Browning mysticized.

A different mood of peace is expressed by Tristram and Iseult, the unnamed speakers in "Threnos." They differ from most of the disembodied spirits in Pound's 1908 poems, in that they exhibit neither passion nor restlessness. They are simply the "fair dead" who will never again tryst at Tintagoel, King Mark's castle:

No more do I burn.
No more for us the fluttering of wings
That whirred in the air above us.

Lo the fair dead!

No more desire flayeth me,
No more for us the trembling
At the meeting of hands.

Lo the fair dead!

(ALS, 46)

Of the many post-Arnoldian versions of their tale, that which most closely approximates the mood of "Threnos" is "The Sailing of the Swan," the last book of Swinburne's *Tristram of Lyonesse* (1882):

So, crownless of the wreaths that life had wound,
They slept, with flower of tenderer comfort crowned;
From bondage and the fear of time set free,
And all the yoke of space on earth and sea
Cast as a curb for ever: nor might now
Fear and desire bid soar their souls or bow,
Lift up their hearts or break them: doubt nor grief
More now might move them, dread nor disbelief
Touch them with shadowy cold or fiery sting,
Nor sleepless languor with its weary wing,

Nor harsh estrangement, born of time's vain breath,
Nor change, a darkness deeper far than death.[10]

"Threnos" expresses not the Paracelsian ecstasy of contemplation, but the Swinburnian ecstasy of death.

But these postmortal states are not typical of Pound's best-known personae. Fullness of life rather than separation from it is the usual condition of his drama. His speakers are carried out of themselves *by* passion, not beyond passion. In "Piere Vidal Old" (1909), for example, the protagonist is far from having transcended what Miraut de Garzelas called "the love of women / That plague and burn and drive one away." Rather he is possessed by it so completely that he attains another kind of psychic purity. But though the emphasis is still upon the rare state of mind, "history" is more important in this tale. In comparison to "La Fraisne" (a comparison which Pound invites in his "Note Precedent to 'La Fraisne'"), "Piere Vidal" is a step closer to the other end of our spectrum.

Piere Vidal (1175–1215) had the advantage over most of his fellow troubadours of being chronicled in one of the longest and most detailed of the *vidas*. The Loba incident, referred to in the introductory note to "Piere Vidal Old," runs as follows in the *vida*:

Now the Loba [She-Wolf] was of Carcassone, and Piere Vidal made himself to be called Lop [Wolf] for love of her, bearing a wolf in his coat of arms. And in the mountains of Cabaret he made men hunt him forsooth with dogs, and with mastiffs, and with greyhounds, even as men hunt a wolf. And he donned the skin of a wolf to make the shepherds and dogs believe him one. Then the shepherds with their dogs hunted him and so evilly dealt with him, that he was brought as one dead to the dwelling of the She-Wolf of Penautier. And when she saw that it was even Piere Vidal, she made right merry over his folly, and laughed greatly, and also her husband; and she welcomed him joyfully, and her husband bade his servants take him and lay him in a privy chamber, and give him gentle usage, and bade a leech be sent for, and had him tended till he was healed of his wounds.[11]

It is clear that Pound has made significant changes in the original legend, chiefly to suggest that Vidal was actually mad. The original chronicler presents the hunt as one of several conscious stratagems on Vidal's part. Pound himself seems to recognize the man's cun-

ning when he calls Vidal a "mad poseur" in *The Spirit of Romance*
(178). But in his poem, Pound suggests that Vidal truly went mad,
thought himself a wolf, dominated the wolf pack, hunted and
pulled down deer, and attacked the hounds. His folly was touched
with a divine inspiration:

> Behold me, Vidal, that was fool of fools!
> Swift as the king wolf was I and as strong
> When tall stags fled me through the alder brakes,
> And every jongleur knew me in his song,
> And the hounds fled and the deer fled
> And none fled over long.
>
> Even the gray pack knew me, and felt fear.
> God! how the swiftest hind's blood spurted hot
> Over the sharpened teeth and purpling lips!
>
> (P, 30)

Though working from an "historical" or legendary source, then,
Pound has not hesitated to change the emphasis in order to bring
out what he conceives to be the true spirit of the tale.

His changes are in keeping with his practice of portraying highly
unusual states of human consciousness, bordering on or merging
with the nonhuman (as in "La Fraisne" or "The Tree"). What
caught his imagination in Vidal's life was the idea of metamorphosis. Later, in Canto 4, he related Vidal's transformation to the metamorphosis of Actaeon in Greek mythology. It is possible that in
handling Vidal's tale he had some help from Arthur O'Shaughnessy, who had previously portrayed in a dramatic monologue the
man-to-wolf metamorphosis of Garulf Bisclavret (the legendary
figure to whom Pound compared Vidal in the "Note Precedent to
'La Fraisne'"). O'Shaughnessy's "Bisclavret" (1870) might have
helped Pound to pick out the mythic pattern in Vidal's adventure.[12]
In any case, Pound's primary concern in "Piere Vidal Old" is a psychological recreation of the myth.

Vidal's spirit is youthful and untamed, though his body has de-
cayed. The memory of his moments of ecstasy gives him the su-
periority over his listeners. The "Age gone lax" which he upbraids
is clearly Pound's own and ours, capable of a life like his only vi-
cariously, through the masks of poetry. When Vidal speaks of

"stunted followers, / That mask at passions and desire desires,"
the created mask is mocking its own creator and all poets who do
not live their verse but use personae instead. Whereas memory is a
threat to Miraut de Garzelas in "La Fraisne," it is salvation to Vidal, when the rehearsing of the past induces its supreme madness
again in the present. Recalling the beauty of Loba and his final
possession of her, he reexperiences his metamorphosis and throws
off restraining hands (either remembered or the actual hands of
his present auditors):

> Ah! Cabaret! Ah Cabaret, thy hills again!
> ·
> Take your hands off me!   [*Sniffing the air.*]
>   Ha! this scent is hot!
>
>   (P, 32)

Clearly historical verisimilitude is still secondary to delightful psychic experience in "Piere Vidal Old."

In "Sestina: Altaforte" (1909), the passionate and masculine vitality of Vidal and Marvoil is seen in Pound's other major troubadour persona. Warrior, politician, friend, and lover, Bertran de
Born had many sides which fascinated Pound. He figures in five
poems written by Pound before 1916: translations of De Born's "Si
tuit li dol elh plor elh marrimen" ("Planh for the Young English
King"—1909) and "Dompna pois de me no'us cal" (1914); and
three original poems, "Na Audiart" (1908), "Sestina: Altaforte,"
and "Near Perigord" (1915). In the "Sestina," the warrior is central, as Pound attempts to catch the aspect of the man which Dante
saw when he placed De Born in Hell (*Inferno*, XXVIII) for stirring
up strife. War was De Born's greatest ecstasy, as he himself pro-
claimed in his sirventes, and Pound's monologue depicts the pure
ferocity and vigor of the man.

The chief impact of the poem is in the speaker's rage. But at the
same time, Pound has also tried to capture the spirit of De Born's
own poetry. "Altaforte" originated, in fact, in an effort to translate
De Born:

My other "vigorous" poem, the "Alta forte," was also written in the
British Museum reading-room. I had had De Born on my mind. I
had found him untranslatable. Then it occurred to me that I might

present him in this manner. I wanted the curious involution and recurrence of the Sestina. I knew more or less of the arrangement. I wrote the first strophe and then went to the Museum to make sure of the right order of permutations. . . . I did the rest of the poem at a sitting. Technically it is one of my best, though a poem on such a theme could never be very important.[13]

The dramatic monologue was in this case clearly a substitute for translation; the persona, a means of "criticism in new composition." In effect, Pound asked us to view it as such when he wrote: "Judge ye! Have I dug him up again?" (P, 28). It was the spirit of De Born's own war poems that Pound was trying to regain.

He admired these poems greatly: "the passages on the joy of war . . . enter the realm of the universal. . . . De Born is at his best in the war songs" (SR, 46–47). In *The Spirit of Romance*, he translated two which are especially relevant to the "Sestina." The first strophe of "Quan vey pels vergiers desplegar" is rendered by Pound as follows:

> When I see the standards spread through the gardens
> Yellow and indigo and blue,
> The cries of the horses are sweet to me,
> And the noise of jongleurs from tent to bivouac,
> The trumpets and horns and shrill clarions.
> Wherefore I would make me a sirvente,
> Such as the Count Richard shall hear it.
>
> (SR, 46)

These unfurling flags appear in "Altaforte" in a color scheme close to the original ("grocs, indis e blaus"): "But ah! when I see the standards gold, vair, purple, opposing." And the cries of horses which are so sweet to De Born ("M'adoussa la votz dels chavaus") become in Pound's poem "the shrill neighs of destriers in battle rejoicing."

Pound also translated another and more famous poem by De Born, usually called "In Praise of War." It opens with a comparison of spring blossoming to the emergence of armies in the field (perhaps after a winter lull):

> Well pleaseth me the sweet time of Easter
> That maketh the leaf and the flower come out.

And it pleaseth me when I hear the clamor
Of the birds, their song through the wood;
And it pleaseth me when I see through the meadows
The tents and pavilions set up, and great joy have I
When I see o'er the campagna knights armed and horses
    arrayed.

(SR, 47)

Now, in this passage, De Born's use of nature follows a Provençal
convention which Pound admired and imitated. The poet uses nature at the outset of his poem to comment upon the rest of the
poem. As Pound put it, "in most Provencal poetry one finds nature
in its proper place, i.e. as a background to the action, an interpretation of the mood; an equation, in other terms, or a 'metaphor by
sympathy' for the mood of the poem" (SR, 31). This account does
two things: it fits perfectly with Pound's idea of poetry as equations for "complete moods," and it describes his own use of nature
in "Sestina: Altaforte." In the second and fourth stanzas, the speaker praises summer and dawn because he sees in them the strife he
loves. Ruskin's "pathetic fallacy" is reborn as "metaphor by sympathy" in Pound's theory and practice. These parallels suggest that
Pound was imitating the imagery and conventions of De Born's
own poetry.

Pound's use of the sestina itself represents an act of "criticism by
new composition." Though De Born wrote no sestina (or at least
none by him has survived), the form was invented in Provence by
Arnaut Daniel. Traditionally associated with elegies and love poetry, it was used in English most notably by Sidney and Swinburne
before Pound. Pound called it "a form like a thin sheet of flame
folding and infolding upon itself."* The obsessive intensity of the
repeated monorhyme makes it an excellent vehicle for the presentation of De Born's warped vision. Pound adapted the sestina to

---

* SR, 27. Pound wrote two other sestinas—"Sestina for Ysolt" (1909) and
"The Golden Sestina: From the Italian of Pico della Mirandola" (1911). Formally, they are perfect sestinas; "Altaforte" is imperfect because the last three
lines contain four of the rhyme words instead of the three or six which convention demands, and because in the fourth stanza the rhyme words of the third
and fourth lines should be reversed. For a riposte to "Sestina: Altaforte," see
Donald Hall's "Sestina," in The Dark Houses (New York, 1958).

the exigencies of the dramatic monologue, as De Nagy has pointed out, by moving the conventional envoi of De Born's sirventes (nearly always an address to De Born's jongleur, Papiols) from the end of the poem to the beginning.[14] This creates an audience and a dramatic situation at the outset of the monologue. In all of these ways, then, "Sestina: Altaforte" maintains a verisimilitude to the historical realities of De Born's poetry while it presents the quintessence or *virtù* of the war songs.

But De Born is a man of many faces. In "Na Audiart" (1908), he speaks in his capacity as lover. And here he is represented as a far more complex personality. Though commonly read as a straightforward lyric effusion chiefly distinguished by its unusual rhythm, "Na Audiart" is actually the portrait of a detached, sophisticated, and ironic character. It is a descant upon six lines from De Born's "Dompna pois de me no'us cal," the poem which also occasioned "Near Perigord." The doubts about De Born's simplicity and sincerity which Pound expressed in that later poem are also reflected in "Na Audiart," though they do not enter "Sestina: Altaforte" at all. "Na Audiart" approaches the Browningesque end of our spectrum in being a portrait of some psychological complexity.

Ostensibly, De Born wrote "Dompna pois de me no'us cal" to regain the favor of his beloved Lady Maent of Montaignac. In the poem, he creates an ideal or "borrowed" lady by piecing together the best features of a number of other famous Provençal women. But in the end he decides that he prefers the Lady Maent herself to this imaginary paragon. One of the ladies from whom he borrows is Audiart of Malemort. When Pound translated De Born's poem in 1914, he rendered the passage that is relevant to "Na Audiart" as follows:

> Of Audiart at Malemort,
> Though she with a full heart
> Wish me ill [si be'm vol mal],
> I'd have her form that's laced
> So cunningly,
> Without blemish, for her love
> Breaks not nor turns aside.[15]

In "Na Audiart," we start from the assumption that Lady Audiart was displeased at being thus mentioned. Pound imagines Bertran addressing a new song to pacify her, just as he had written the original to mollify Lady Maent. But the difference is that De Born has changed his tactics; now his tone is a skillful blend of admiration, lewdness, irony, and genuine pity. By the end of the poem, he has so manipulated matters that *he* is forgiving *her* for being angry.

To begin with, the stylized adoration of the poem's opening section is leavened with a great deal of ironic wit:

> Though thou well dost wish me ill,
> > Audiart, Audiart,
> Where thy bodice laces start
> As ivy fingers clutching through
> Its crevices,
> > Audiart, Audiart,
> Stately, tall, and lovely tender
> Who shall render
> > Audiart, Audiart,
> Praises meet unto thy fashion?
> Here a word kiss!
> > Pass I on
> Unto Lady "Miels-de-ben,"
> Having praised thy girdle's scope,
> How the stays ply back from it;
> I breathe no hope
> That thou shouldst . . .
> > Nay no whit
> Bespeak thyself for anything.
> Just a word in thy praise, girl,
> Just for the swirl
> Thy satins make upon the stair,
> 'Cause never a flaw was there
> Where thy torse and limbs are met:
> > (ALS, 21–22)

Now, De Born does not have any real doubts about whether he is adequate to render the lady's praises; the rest of the poem testifies to that. And he does not pass on to Lady Miels-de-ben as he does in "Dompna pois"; it is a feint, designed to arouse Audiart's jealousy. Actually, his contemplation of Audiart is lewd. We notice that the seat of her displeasure is precisely the first focus of his fascination —that magnificent breast in its swelling bodice.[16] His attention moves systematically downward from her bodice to her girdle and finally to "Where thy torse and limbs are met." Picking up the word "entiera" from the Provençal ("without blemish" in the 1914 translation), De Born applies it genitally: "'Cause never a flaw was there." We are beginning to see why he has requisitioned this perfect body for his borrowed lady, and in what sense "her love / Breaks not nor turns aside." The respectful distance of the hopeless admirer quite disappears as he continues to address this "girl."

We are also beginning to understand why Lady Audiart dislikes De Born, but at this point he anticipates her and changes direction for the middle section of his song. She may hate his presumption, but she can do nothing for it. He has immortalized her, like it or not, and he is after all Bertran, no inconsiderable lord and singer:

> . . . never a flaw was there
> Where thy torse and limbs are met:
> Though thou hate me, read it set
> In rose and gold,
> Or when the minstrel, tale half told,
> Shall burst to lilting at the praise:
> > Audiart, Audiart.
> Bertrans, master of his lays,
> Bertrans of Aultaforte thy praise
> Sets forth, and though thou hate me well,
> Yea though thou wish me ill,
> > Audiart, Audiart,
> Thy loveliness is here writ till,
> > Audiart,
> Oh, till thou come again.

In this passage, the refrain is positively teasing.

The last section of the poem is governed by the spirit of Ronsard's sonnet, "Quand vous serez bien vieille," which, as we have seen, Pound used in "Scriptor Ignotus" and several other early poems.[17] Step by step, De Born reduces any pride Audiart might have in her own beauty, and reveals his true estimate of her by setting her in the long perspective of time. At this great distance, Audiart is seen as proud, vain, and scarcely worth attention were it not for her present physical beauty. By the end of the poem, the tables have turned completely. De Born is no longer a suppliant, but a disenchanted observer, forgiving and genuinely pitying an ignorant, pettish, but beautiful girl. The last line of the poem, far from representing a love-sick "dying fall," scornfully reduces Audiart's hatred to pathetic insignificance. "Na Audiart," then, presents the skillful rhetoric of a complex and ironic troubadour.

Another of Pound's early troubadour monologues also involves a more detailed dramatic situation and a greater psychological complexity than may at first appear. "Cino" (1908) resembles Miraut de Garzelas in that he is determined to reject the passions of love, but he does not succeed in doing so until he has enacted a more complex subjective drama and presented a more substantial historical environment.

The factual background of the poem is relatively slight. Pound gives no note to convey the "prose part" of his drama. De Nagy suggests that "Cino Polnesi" is modeled on the Italian poet, Cino da Pistoia, who was exiled from his city in 1307.[18] (Pound's setting is "Italian Campagna 1309.") But the parallel sheds little light on the poem. A more probable source is Arthur Symons's "Wanderer's Song" (1899). We should recall Pound's statement that "one or two poems of Symons's 'Wanderers'" were among the things "one was drunk with" during his youth in America (LE, 367). The opening mood of Symons's poem is very similar to that of Pound's:

> I have had enough of women, and enough of love,
> But the land waits, and the sea waits, and day and night is
>   enough;
> Give me a long white road, and the grey wide path of the
>   sea,
> And the wind's will and the bird's will, and the heart-ache
>   still in me.[19]

> Bah! I have sung women in three cities,
> But it is all the same;
> And I will sing of the sun.
>
> (ALS, 17)

Symons's generic wanderer probably inspired Pound more than the biography of any specific Italian troubadour. Pound told Williams: "'Cino' . . . he might be anyone" (LETT, 6).

Nevertheless, the poem has an important historical dimension. It turns on the relationships between patron and poet in a medieval aristocratic society. Among the ladies of the nobility, Cino's success has been great; but it has also been illusory. For his *social* inferiority has prevented them from taking him seriously as a lover. Any landed lord may easily oust him from their favor, even though, as Cino hints with Browningesque innuendo, such "lords" are often bastards no more legitimately qualified to hold their property than he himself ("And all I knew were out, My Lord, you / Were Lackland Cino, e'en as I am, / O Sinistro"). At the same time, the *spiritual* inferiority of the ladies prevents them from appreciating his art. They admire his amorous qualities—his passion, his gaiety, his laughter, daring, sauciness, and the deceptive strength in his apparently frail frame—but they do not understand his art except insofar as it is seductive. They are "forgetful in their towers of our tuneing / Once for Wind-runeing," and they do not know or care that he is an original composer: "Peste! 'tis his own songs? / Or some other's that he sings?"

The curious result of this double barrier is that neither party really exists in the eyes of the other. Cino does not exist for the ladies because of his social inferiority ("Oh they are all one these vagabonds"), and they do not exist for him because of their spiritual inferiority ("I have sung women in three cities / But it is all one"). In Cino's view, the ladies are only material for songs which they are too obtuse to understand. They have no existence beyond the bedchamber and the songs which result from it:

> Lips, words, and you snare them,
> Dreams, words, and they are as jewels,
> Strange spells of old deity,

Ravens, nights, allurement:
And they are not;
Having become the souls of song.

Eyes, dreams, lips, and the night goes.
Being upon the road once more,
They are not.

(ALS, 17)

Only the sun and sky over the campagna are real for Cino now, as
he bursts into praise of " 'Pollo Phoibee, old tin pan" in what De
Nagy aptly calls "a kind of facetious 'Cantico del Sole.' "[20]
    Yet Cino does not win peace of mind without a struggle. He still
has some of the heartache of Symons's wanderer, and like Miraut
de Garzelas he is troubled by memories of his former loves. As in
"La Fraisne," the threat of memory is reflected in a pattern of
broken speech:

I will sing of the sun.
. . . eh? . . . they mostly had grey eyes,
But it is all one, I will sing of the sun.

(ALS, 18)

His resolve is not yet strong enough, and the song itself is inter-
rupted by reminiscences:

Seeking e'er the new-laid rast-way
To the gardens of the sun . . .
. . . .
I have sung women in three cities
But it is all one.

Finally, however, the effort of will succeeds. Cino ends on a burst
of song, and the peaceful ecstasy of metaphorical perception
descends upon him:

I will sing of the white birds
In the blue waters of heaven,
The clouds that are spray to its sea.

Pound's monologue catches the character at the "moment of song,
self-analysis, or sudden understanding or revelation" (LETT, 4).

But this moment transpires in a definite historical or legendary context.

Historicity is even more important to "Ballad of the Goodly Fere," which presents another of Pound's vitalistic heroes. It is important because the poem wants us to accept a certain conception of its protagonist. In most of Pound's monologues, his view of the speaker does not compete with any preconceived view of the reader's; few of his readers *have* a definite picture of Marvoil or Bertran de Born. But in the "Ballad," the poet's conception of Christ must appear more valid than any differing conception the reader might previously have formed. The poem originated as an angry answer to a "cheap" conception of Jesus, as Pound explained:

In the case of the "Goodly Fere" I was not excited until some hours after I had written it. I had been the evening before in the "Turkish Coffee" café in Soho. I had been made very angry by a certain sort of cheap irreverence which was new to me. I had lain awake most of the night. I got up rather late in the morning and started for the Museum with the first four lines in my head. I wrote the rest of the poem at a sitting, on the left side of the reading-room, with scarcely any erasures.[21]

To make his own view seem the true one, Pound angrily used the dramatic monologue to create historical verisimilitude.

Beneath its pseudo-Burnsian surface, the "Ballad" is rooted in Browning. In several monologues ("Cleon," "An Epistle," "A Death in the Desert"), Browning's speaker considers the events and miracles of early Christianity from the viewpoint of an historical contemporary. But there is an important difference between Browning's Cleon and Karshish and Pound's Simon Zelotes. For Browning's speakers are never actual eyewitnesses of miracles. They all accept (or desire to accept) second-hand testimony. And their state of mind is Browning's primary interest, for he is concerned to portray the *Zeitgeist*, the mental climate which facilitated the rapid spread of the new religion. He assiduously avoids the question of whether or not the miracles truly occurred. Pound, however, blithely makes the leap which Browning refused. His speaker is one of the twelve apostles and has *seen* Christ healing the ill, raising the dead, calming the storm, suffering crucifixion, and eating honeycomb after His Resurrection. Simon Zelotes is

Pound's attempt to create the illusion of a reliable and historically irrefutable first-hand witness.*

Zelotes emphasizes the masculine vitality of his "fere" because, for the young Pound, Christianity was a religion of ecstasy, *virtù*, and the life force. In "Psychology and Troubadours" (1912), Pound distinguished between institutional and "ecstatic" religions:

> There are, as we see, only two kinds of religion. There is the Mosaic or Roman or British Empire type, where someone, having to keep a troublesome rabble in order, invents and scares them with a disagreeable bogie, which he calls god.
>
> Christianity and all other forms of ecstatic religion, on the other hand, are not in inception dogma or propaganda of something called the *one truth* or the *universal truth*; they *seem* little concerned with ethics; their general object appears to be to stimulate a sort of confidence in the life-force.[22]

This distinction is operative in "Fifine Answers" (1908), where Jesus is associated with gypsies and vagabonds who "drink all of life" (ALS, 29). "Ballad for Gloom" (ALS, 60) also foreshadows the muscular Christianity of the "Goodly Fere." This was the religion—more vitalistic than transcendental—which the "cheap irreverence" in a Soho café disturbed so deeply. Zelotes, accordingly, speaks of Christ's vigor and masculinity. Christ's blood was "hot and free"; he was a lover of "brawny men," "a man o' men," "a brave man," and "a master of men" (P, 33–34). The life force that was in him cannot be confined in an institutional "Mosaic" religion based on a written record:

> They'll no' get him a' in a book I think
> Though they write it cunningly;
> No mouse of the scrolls was the Goodly Fere
> But aye loved the open sea.

The "Goodly Fere" moves in the manly company of Pound's early personae, jostling shoulders with De Born, Vidal, Cino, and Marvoil.

* No meek character himself, Zelotes is thought, because the name "zealous" is given him in Luke (6:15), to have belonged to a fanatic nationalist group called the "Zealots." It was because of a "Zealot" rebellion that the Romans destroyed Jerusalem in A.D. 70. This background makes him an appropriate persona to present Pound's vigorous Christ. As an eyewitness, moreover, Zelotes is reminiscent of the narrator of The Gospel According to John.

"The study of literature is hero-worship," wrote Pound (SR, 7), and certainly his own poet-heroes grow out of that powerful nineteenth-century tradition which venerated the life force and the men who most embody it. Pound once said that the poet's task is to "departmentalise such part of the life-force as flows through him,"[23] and clearly De Born, Vidal, and Marvoil have done just that. Similarly, the Goodly Fere fulfills the aim of "ecstatic religion"—namely, "to stimulate a sort of confidence in the life-force" (SR, 95). The "factive heroes" of *The Cantos* are in the same line of descent. Pound is an heir of the vitalist philosophies of the nineteenth century who, via his medieval studies, relocates part of the sacred life force in the human psyche.

II

Beyond their significance to his reader, Pound's personae perform a special personal function for their creator. They are masks of virtue which enable him to establish provisional identities for himself as a poet.

At the outset of his career, Pound had trouble finding a "self" of which his poetry could be the expression. Together with many of his contemporaries, he was still under the influence of nineteenth-century "expressive" theories of poetry, but he was also skeptical about the relevance of any simple concept of personality to himself. When he looks into a mirror in an early poem called "On His Own Face in a Glass" (1908), Pound sees not one person but a "myriad" (ALS, 53). This is especially disconcerting to a poet who believes that "the soul of man is compounded of all the elements of the cosmos of souls, but in each there is some one element which predominates, which is in some peculiar and intense way the quality or *virtù* of the individual."[24] Where is his own *virtù*? Which face in the glass is the "true" Pound? The persona provides a viable way not of begging this question, but of beginning to construct an answer.

Browning had resorted to the technique out of a similar necessity. The incoherent *Pauline* had been a failure; stung into experimentation by John Stuart Mill's review, he finally evolved a poetry "often Lyric in expression, always Dramatic in principle, and so

many utterances of so many imaginary persons, not mine."[25] But
Browning did not use the persona as a means of working toward
an identity for himself. Rather, as J. Hillis Miller suggests, he used
it to try to relive all the possible attitudes of the human spirit. It
was Wilde, Yeats, and the men of the *fin-de-siècle* who perfected
the notion of the persona as a means of self-construction.[26] They
saw that, by giving its wearer a temporary identity, the mask allows him to mold a virtue, to create himself out of the inner chaos.

Yeats began consciously to formulate his theory of the mask in
1909, the year he met Pound. His initial terminology had a ring
that Pound would have liked, for Yeats argued that the mask en-
hances the artist's "active virtue": "If we cannot imagine ourselves
as different from what we are and assume that second self, we cannot impose a discipline upon ourselves, though we may accept
one from others. Active virtue as distinguished from passive acceptance of a current code is therefore theatrical, consciously dramatic, the wearing of a mask. It is the condition of arduous full
life."[27] According to Yeats, "virtue" is not something we *find* in
ourselves, but something we must *make* by strenuous dramatic
endeavor.

In both art and life, Pound attempted to use the mask in this
way. Even before he had reached London, he had written a poem
to describe his own experience of creating personae:

> 'Tis as in midmost us there glows a sphere
> Translucent, molten gold, that is the "I"
> And into this some form projects itself:
> Christus, or John, or eke the Florentine;
> And as the clear space is not if a form's
> Imposed thereon,
> So cease we from all being for the time,
> And these, the Masters of the Soul, live on.
>
> (QFTY, 108)

The poem is no more an expression of literal belief in reincarnation
than is Wordsworth's "Ode on the Intimations of Immortality." But
it is an apt equation for Pound's experience. The "I" is a shapeless
mass of gold, minted into momentary identity by the "form" of a
master soul. A poem is the resulting coin.

Pound wore an actual mask after he arrived in London. From all accounts, he adopted the pose of a sort of Pre-Raphaelite trouba- dour, a kinsman of the speakers of his own poems. He dressed in- formally and colorfully, sported a red beard and a great shock of red hair, spoke his mind outright, and made a formidable first im- pression.[28] This elaborate pose was a life mask in the Wilde tra- dition.

The same effort to establish an identity helped to produce *Personae* (1909), the second volume of poems that Pound pub- lished in London. A well-known passage in his later essay on "Vorticism" suggests the urgent personal motives behind these early monologues: "In the 'search for oneself,' in the search for 'sincere self-expression,' one gropes, one finds some seeming veri- ty. One says, 'I am' this, that, or the other, and with the words scarcely uttered one ceases to be that thing. I began this search for the real in a book called *Personae*, casting off, as it were, com- plete masks of the self in each poem."[29] They were not mere tech- nical exercises, but part of a search for the real, for himself, for "sincere self-expression."

At the heart of Pound's problem were an assumption and a desire. He believed that some poets are single-natured while others are many-natured. He was convinced that he himself was of the second kind, but he desired to be of the first. The dilemma is most clearly formulated in *The Spirit of Romance*, in the contrast be- tween Villon and Dante. We have seen that Pound admired Villon for his absolute honesty and integrity: "His depravity is not a pose cultivated for literary effect. . . . Many have attempted to follow Villon, mistaking a pose for his reality. These experi- menters, searchers for sensation, have, I think, proved that the 'taverns and the whores' are no more capable of producing po- etry than are philosophy, culture, art, noble character, conscien- tious effort, or any other panacea" (SR, 171–176). Villon, in short, *was* what the Decadents were trying self-consciously to become. Like Piere Vidal, he had no need to "mask at passions, and desire desires." He had found his own *virtù*, and achieved what Pound calls "his reality" by the discovery. "Villon is no theorist, he is an objective fact" (SR, 176).

Because of his reality, Villon neither had nor needed dramatic imagination. His life went directly into his poetry, and the man who suffers is the man who speaks there. There is no inner vision or division by which immediate experience is transformed: "Villon is destitute of imagination . . . thief, murderer, pander, bully to a whore, he is honored for a few score pages of unimaginative sincerity; he sings of things as they are. . . . The dramatic imagination is beyond him, yet having lived himself, he has no need to imagine what life is. . . . He scarcely ever takes the trouble to write anything he does not actually feel" (sr, 171–173). Pound argues that even when Villon adopted a persona, as in "Les Regrets de la belle Heaumière," the voice is still unmistakably his own (sr, 175). Pound underlines his point by a lengthy comparison of Villon to Dante, who is *par excellence* a poet of the dramatic imagination. Villon is more comparable to a dramatic character than to a dramatist:

Villon's poetry seems, when one comes directly from the *Paradiso*, more vital, more vivid; but if Dante restrains himself, putting the laments in the mouths of tortured spirits, they are not the less poignant. He stands behind his characters, of whom Villon might have made one. . . . Dante is many men, and suffers as many. Villon cries out as one. He is a lurid canto of the *Inferno*, written too late to be included in the original text. . . . Dante's vision is real, because he saw it. Villon's verse is real, because he lived it; as Bertran de Born, as Arnaut Marvoil, as that mad poseur Vidal, he lived it.   (sr, 177–178)

For Pound there is a strong contrast between the indirect dramatic utterance of Dante, and the simple *cri du coeur* of Villon.

Clearly the relationship between Dante and his characters in this description is analogous to the relationship between Pound and his personae. Like Dante, Pound is a complex poet of the dramatic imagination who "stands behind his characters," who "is many men, and suffers as many." We may recall Pound's claim that in the *Divine Comedy* Dante is "able to shed himself in completely self-conscious characters; to make a mood; slough it off as a snake does his own skin, and then endow it with an individual life of its own" (sr, 85). This is precisely what Pound does in "casting off, as it were, complete masks of the self." He gives us characters and moods, human states that he has seen and been and embodied in the people of the past. He is forced to be a poet of many selves precisely because he cannot be a Villon—a poet of "sincere self-expression." He must choose for his masks men like Villon who have succeeded in "living their verse," because he cannot "live" his own. Only by speaking through Villon, Bertran de Born, Arnaut Marvoil, and Vidal can he approximate the integrity of "objective fact."

CHAPTER 5

The Phantastikon of 1911

and the light became so bright and so blindin'
in this layer of paradise
that the mind of man was bewildered.

(CANTO 38)

In 1911, Pound began to publish "I Gather the Limbs of Osiris," the articles which contained his first translations of Cavalcanti and Arnaut Daniel. He also published a volume of poems entitled *Canzoni*. As its name suggests, this volume attempts to capture the spirit and revive the verse forms of Tuscan and Provençal poetry. In the second "Osiris" piece, Pound acknowledged that he had allowed his medieval studies "to impinge on my own poetry in 'Canzoni.' "[1] With his imagination dominated by the literature he had been translating and popularizing, Pound created another poetic world. "In the Trecento the Tuscans are busy with their *phantastikon*," he wrote. "In Provençe we may find preparation for this . . ." (SR, 93). And in *Canzoni*, he might well have added, we find continuation of it.

This world is, in a sense, Pound's first version of what he later called "the radiant world . . . of moving energies . . . magnetisms that take form, that are seen, or that border the visible, the matter of Dante's *paradiso*" (LE, 154). Its most important personage is the beloved lady, a nearly divine Beatrice figure. Its most important element is a radiant light, symbolizing the lady's prepotent *virtù*. Pound adopted both from his Tuscan masters. Here, for instance, is his translation of Cavalcanti's sonnet "Chi è questa," followed by his imitation of it in *Canzoni*:

> Who is she coming, drawing all men's gaze,
> Who makes the air one trembling clarity

Till none can speak but each sighs piteously
Where she leads Love adown her trodden ways?
Ah, God! The thing she's like when her glance strays,
Let Amor tell. 'Tis no fit speech for me.
Mistress she seems of such great modesty
That every other woman were called "Wrath."
No one could ever tell the charm she hath
For toward her all the noble Powers incline,
She being beauty's godhead manifest.
Our daring ne'er before held such high quest;
But ye! There is not in you so much grace
That we can understand her rightfully.[2]

Who is she coming, that the roses bend
Their shameless heads to do her passing honour?
Who is she coming with a light upon her
Not born of suns that with the day's end end?
Say is it Love who hath chosen the nobler part?
Say is it Love, that was divinity,
Who hath left his godhead that his home might be
The shameless rose of her unclouded heart?
If this be Love, where hath he won such grace?
If this be Love, how is the evil wrought,
That all men write against his darkened name?
If this be Love, if this . . .
                    O mind give place!
What holy mystery e'er was noosed in thought?
Own that thou scan'st her not, nor count it shame!

                              (c, 12–13)

In both cases, the lady radiates an ambience of light as she approaches, and the rational mind is powerless to comprehend her
glories. J. E. Shaw's commentary on "Donna Mi Prega" is also relevant to these poems: "The consideration of the ideal image in the
imagination and memory is the shining of the Intellectual Light
upon that image, Love in its first perfection, sensitive and intellectual, but not rational, for the logical faculty which forms syllo-
gisms and reaches conclusions is not concerned."[3]

This "ideal image" is Pound's version of the "Romantic Image,"

that mysterious female whose omnipresence in English and Conti-
nental poetry and painting of the late nineteenth century has been
demonstrated by Mario Praz and Frank Kermode.[4] She had appeared in Pound's poetry before *Canzoni*, but in a rather different
guise. Initially, she is Iseult (Yseult, Ysolt, Isolt) from the Tristan
legend, and Pound wrote poems with titles like "Praise of Ysolt" (p,
17), "To Ysolt, for Pardon" (ALS, 119), and "Sestina for Ysolt" (E,
23–24). In these poems she is the poet's muse or white goddess. She
is indeed "beauty's godhead manifest," and she descends from the
speaker in Arthur Symons's "Modern Beauty," who says: "I am
Yseult and Helen. . . ."*

Then in *Exultations* (1909) Pound's lady takes on a more Pre-
Raphaelite look. Like Matthew Arnold's Iseult, she becomes a
figure in a tapestry: "Out of you have I woven a dream / That
shall walk in the lonely vale" (E, 28). Richard Ellmann has pointed
out the importance of Pre-Raphaelite tapestry to the early Yeats
as "the primary model for his poetry of the late 'eighties and the
'nineties," and he has noted "an image-cluster of words like
'weave,' 'entwine,' and 'enwind' " in that poetry.[5] It would appear
that Pound was working with similar terms when he set out to
"weave this praise" (E, 24). Here, for instance, is "Portrait":

> Now would I weave her portrait out of all dim splendour.
> Of Provence and far halls of memory,
> Lo, there come echoes, faint diversity
> Of blended bells at even's end, or
> As the distant seas should send her
> The tribute of their trembling, ceaselessly
> Resonant. Out of all dreams that be,
> Say, shall I bid the deepest dreams attend her?
> Nay! For I have seen the purplest shadows stand
> Alway with reverent chere that looked on her,

---

* *Images of Good and Evil*, pp. 118–119. Pound quoted from "Modern
Beauty" in his Preface to the *Poetical Works of Lionel Johnson* (LE, 367) and
in his essay "Arthur Symons," *Athenaeum*, XCIV (21 May 1920), 663–664.
He also placed the poem first in his anthology, *Profile* (Milan, 1932), suggesting that for him it marked the beginning of "modern poetry." He quotes
from it in Canto 74 ("My fondest knight lie dead") and Canto 80 ("I am the
torch," wrote Arthur, "she saith").

Silence himself is grown her worshipper
And ever doth attend her in that land
Wherein she reigneth, wherefore let there stir
Naught but the softest voices, praising her.

(E, 25)

The poem is indeed woven; one by one the colored threads of the
tapestry are introduced into the sonnet loom: evening bells, distant
seas, deepest dreams, purplest shadows, softest voices. Pound's
aim is to adumbrate the ineffable beauty of the unknown woman
by associating her with as many delicate manifestations as possible. Even the rhymes are muted, exhibiting the "faint diversity /
of blended bells" appropriate to the subject.

But to turn from *Exultations* to *Canzoni* is to move away from a
Pre-Raphaelite medieval atmosphere to Pound's own medieval
world, suffused with its peculiar radiance. Here the lady's light is
a beacon toward which the lover journeys, as in "Canzon: The
Spear": " 'Tis the clear light of love I praise / That steadfast
gloweth o'er deep waters, / A clarity that gleams always" (c, 3).
But more often it is an ambience, trailing behind the lady and
clinging to the air through which she moves. Pound sometimes uses
the word "calyx" to describe this effect; the light is like the leaves
enclosing some precious flower: "A splendid calyx that about her
gloweth, / Smiting the sunlight on whose ray she goeth" (c, 9).
The calyx is "The cloak of graciousness, that round thee gloweth"
(c, 7), but it is curiously transferable and may come to bless the
lover: "Thy gracious ways, / O Lady of my heart, have / O'er all
my thought their golden glamour cast" (c, 6). The transferal may
involve synesthesia:

E'en this air so subtly gloweth,
Guerdoned by thy sun-gold traces,
That my heart is half afraid
For the fragrance on him laid;

(c, 5)

Or this "lustrous sheath" may appear to the lover as a halo, surrounding the head of his beloved (c, 9). He may notice "the
sheen / About her brows" or the "two bands of gold" that "make

more fair her delicate fair face" (c, 13 and 26). Indeed the volume as a whole is "full of faces / with gold glories behind them" (c, 24). But perhaps the handsomest instance of the calyx is "Balla-tetta," with its opening echo of the Gospel of St. John:*

> The light became her grace and dwelt among
> Blind eyes and shadows that are formed as men;
> Lo, how the light doth melt us into song:
>
> The broken sunlight for a healm she beareth
> Who hath my heart in jurisdiction.
> In wild-wood never fawn nor fallow fareth
> So silent light; no gossamer is spun
> So delicate as she is, when the sun
> Drives the clear emeralds from the bended grasses
> Lest they should parch too swiftly, where she passes.
>
> (P, 38)

In ascertaining the symbolic significance of this light, we should note how often it seems to emanate from precious stones and rare metals. In addition to the calyx, it also takes the form of jewel fire. Thus in "Canzon: The Spear," the "light within her eyes" is "like the gold where sunlight plays," and when the lady is angry "there comes a keener gleam instead, / Like flame that burns beneath thin jade" (c, 4–5). And in "Canzone: Of Angels," the "azure feldspar hight the microline" has the same "subtlety of shimmering" as the lady "round whom a graciousness is cast / Which clingeth in the air where she hath past." Her spirit is declared to be "akin unto the feldspar" (c, 9–10). This association of the lady with the crystal, especially when seen in connection with several passages of Pound's prose, points to the meaning of the light imagery in *Canzoni.*

Pound's favorite instance of the word *virtù* in all medieval liter-ature occurs in the last line of Cavalcanti's fifth *ballata,* "Vedrai la sua virtù nel ciel salita," which Pound translated as "Then shalt

---

* St. John 1:14: "And the Word was made flesh, and dwelt among us, (and we beheld his glory, the glory as of the only begotten of the Father,) full of grace and truth."

thou see her virtue risen in heaven."[6] Pound twice compared the poet's attitude toward the lady in this line to the alchemist's attitude toward his stone, suggesting a relationship between the spiritual power of the lady and the chemical power of the rare rock:

In this *ballata*, Guido speaks of seeing issue from his lady's lips a subtle body, from that a subtler body, from that a star, from that a voice, proclaiming the ascent of the virtu. For effect upon the air, upon the soul, etc., the "lady" in Tuscan poetry has assumed all the properties of the Alchemist's stone. (SR, 90)

Virtute, "virtue," "potency," requires a separate treatise. Pater has explained its meaning in the preface to his "The Renaissance," but in reading a line like
> "*Vedrai la sua virtù nel ciel salita*"
one must have in mind the connotations alchemical, astrological, metaphysical, which Swedenborg would have called the correspondences.

The equations of alchemy were apt to be written as women's names and the women so named endowed with the magical powers of the compounds. *La virtù* is the potency, the efficient property of a substance or person. Thus modern science shows us radium with a noble virtue of energy. Each thing or person was held to send forth magnetisms of certain effect; in Sonnet XXXV, the image of his lady has these powers. It is a spiritual chemistry, and modern science and modern mysticism are both set to confirm it.[7]

The radiant calyx of light surrounding the ladies of *Canzoni*, in its "effect upon the air, upon the soul" of the poet and its appearance in the depths of precious jewels, clearly represents the "magnetisms" and "potency" of the lady's spirit. In "Canzone: Of Angels," the poet has "looked upon such potencies / And glories" (C, 10). As Pound put it in Canto 74, "in the light of light is the *virtù*."

This "spiritual chemistry" is the theme of Pound's dramatic lyric, "The Alchemist," written in 1912.[8] This "Chant for the Transmutation of Metals" is uttered by a medieval alchemist as he heats and then cools his crucible. The alchemist invokes the virtues of a long list of famous ladies, both Provençal and Classical; in other words, his equations are "written as women's names and the women so named endowed with the magical powers of the compounds." The virtues of the ladies are associated with the virtues of sunlight and precious metals, as they are throughout *Canzoni*. Under a general Provençal rubric ("Midonz"), the alchemist summons their potencies to transform his base metal: *

> Midonz, with the gold of the sun, the leaf of the
>   poplar, by the light of the amber,
> Midonz, daughter of the sun, shaft of the tree,
>   silver of the leaf, light of the yellow of the amber,
> Midonz, gift of the God, gift of the light, gift of
>   the amber of the sun,
>   Give light to the metal.
>
> (P, 75)

"The Alchemist" is an explicit statement of the values governing the imagery of Pound's medieval imitations.

The phantastikon of 1911 is given its fullest rationale, however, in the essay called "Psychology and Troubadours," written in 1912.[9] This essay attempts to evaluate the significance of Provençal love poetry in the trobar clus tradition. Pound cautiously speculates whether the "love code" might not have been the manifestation of an underground religion, fundamentally pagan despite its Christian trappings. "Following," as he puts it, "the clue of a visionary interpretation," he proceeds to suggest the kind of secular and "unofficial" mysticism that might have been involved:

The question: Did this "close ring," this aristocracy of emotion, evolve, out of its half memories of Hellenistic mysteries, a cult— a cult stricter, or more subtle, than that of the celibate ascetics, a cult for the purgation of the soul by a refinement of, and lordship over, the senses? . . . If a certain number of people in Provence developed their own unofficial mysticism, basing it for the most part on their own experience, if the servants of Amor saw visions quite as well as the servants of the Roman ecclesiastical hierarchy, if they were, moreover, troubled with no "dark night of the soul,"

---

* "Midonz" (my lord) is a conventional address to the lady in Provençal poetry, despite its gender. Pound once called it "the inexplicable address to the lady in the masculine" (SR, 92). The "Midonz" passage marks the end of the heating stage; afterwards the crucible is cooling, and at the end of the poem the alchemist is about to open it.

and the kindred incommodities of ascetic yoga, this may well have
caused some scandal and jealousy to the orthodox. . . . The problem, in so far as it concerns Provence, is simply this: Did this
"chivalric love," this exotic, take on mediumistic properties? Stim-
ulated by the color or quality of emotion, did that "color" take on
forms interpretive of the divine order? Did it lead to an "exteriorization of the sensibility," and interpretation of the cosmos by
feeling? (SR, 90–94)

Whether or not this be an accurate view of Provençal poetry (and
Pound refused to conclude that it was), it is a very accurate description of the world of his own *Canzoni*. The love poems in
Canzoni are based on a kind of visionary and "unofficial" mysticism, in which love becomes a medium interpreting the divine
order and the world itself becomes an "exteriorization of the
sensibility." The *Canzoni* are not simply experiments in medieval
metric forms.* They are serious attempts to imitate the medieval
sensibility as Pound conceived it.

II

This sensibility Pound contrasted to the modern in a series of
twelve poems in *Canzoni* entitled "Und Drang." The series has
been broken up in later editions, and only the last six poems ("The
House of Splendour," "The Flame," "Horae Beatae Inscriptio,"
"The Altar," "Au Salon," and "Au Jardin") are currently reprinted
(P, 49–53). But these poems should be read in their original context, because the whole series represents an important dimension
of Pound's medievalism in *Canzoni*. Up to this point, Pound's
world has been hermetically sealed and apart—the "soap-bubble"
of the phantastikon (SR, 92). "Und Drang" now tests the relevance
of medieval values in the modern world. However awkwardly, it

---

* I have purposely neglected the technical aspects of *Canzoni* to call attention to its content and imagery. Anyone who wishes to know the sources
of Pound's verse forms will find most of them identified in a series of short
notes by Pound himself in *Provença* (Boston, 1910). The *Canzoni* which em-
ploy medieval forms seldom depend upon their sources for more than the
forms themselves; that is, little allusion, cross-reference, or "criticism in new
composition" plays back and forth between Pound's poems and the medieval
originals.

introduces the modern world *as a subject* into Pound's poetry, and places it in contrast to the past (a contrast which, once introduced, occupied more and more of the poet's attention after 1911).

The first five poems portray the confusion and malaise of modern life. They express moods of weariness and disorientation, sometimes rather quaintly: "I am worn faint," "The will to live goes from me," "Yea I have been dead right often." Occasionally they anticipate later treatments of the same theme, such as Eliot's "Hollow Men": "The deed blots out the thought / And many thoughts, the vision." The poet finds his Nietzschean burden too heavy: "There is no comfort being over-man." Even the pursuit of his "romantic image" has exhausted him:

> And I was Aengus for a thousand years,
> And she, the ever-living, moved with me
> And strove amid the waves, and
> > would not go.*

What most plagues him, however, is meaninglessness—the loss of an objective order of values:

> How our modernity,
> Nerve-wracked and broken, turns
> Against time's way and all the way of things,
> Crying with weak and egoistic cries!
> . . . .
> All things are given over,
> Only the restless will
> Surges amid the stars
> Seeking new moods of life,
> New permutations.
> . . . .
> See, and the very sense of what we know
> Dodges and hides as in a sombre curtain
> Bright threads leap forth, and hide, and leave no pattern.
> > (c, 43–46)

For all their languor and self-pity, these poems do at least bring

---

* In these lines Pound borrows the figure of the quester from Yeats's "Song of the Wandering Aengus" in *The Wind Among the Reeds*.

into Pound's work for the first time the kind of direct commentary on contemporary cultural conditions which was to become the principal motivation of his later poetry. What begins as the shrinking of a sensitive plant will soon become the "sterilized surgery" of the *Lustra* satires.[10]

The last six poems of "Und Drang" all reaffirm, in their different ways, an order of values based on Pound's medievalism. This order is qualified and clarified as the sequence moves on. First of all, "The House of Splendour" presents a radiant vision of the beloved lady which explicitly transcends time and space. The "bright threads" which "leave no pattern" in the poem last quoted are here restored into a meaningful tapestry:

> 'Tis Evanoe's,
> A house not made with hands,
> But out somewhere beyond the worldly ways
> Her gold is spread, above, around, inwoven;
> Strange ways and walls are fashioned out of it.
>
> (p, 49)

As in "Ballatetta" Pound strengthens his epiphany by alluding to the Bible, in this case to St. Paul's second letter to the Corinthians: "For we know, if our earthly house of this habitation be dissolved, that we have a building of God, a house not made with hands, eternal in heaven" (II Cor. 5:1). So high does Pound exalt Pater's House of Beauty and Rossetti's House of Life. Like the other women in *Canzoni*, Evanoe is surrounded by a radiant calyx of light ("Her hair was spread about, a sheaf of wings, / And red the sunlight was, behind it all"),[11] and the walls of her house emit the usual jewel fire ("through the claret stone, / Set to some weaving, comes the aureate light").* This radiance represents the lady's

---

* An interesting dispute over the jewel images in one line of the poem ("With six great sapphires hung along the wall") arose between Pound and William Carlos Williams in 1920. In the "Prologue" to *Kora in Hell: Improvisations* (Boston, 1920), Williams attacked the obscurantism of certain American poets (chiefly Pound and Eliot), citing a conversation some years before between his father, himself, and Pound: "My parent had been holding forth in downright sentences upon my own 'idle nonsense' when he turned and became equally vehement concerning something Ezra had written: what in heaven's name Ezra meant by 'jewels' in a verse that had come between

virtù, and the *virtù* is a positive energy inducing delightful psychic
experience:

> Here am I come perforce my love of her,
> Behold mine adoration
> Maketh me clear, and there are powers in this
> Which, played on by the virtues of her soul,
> Break down the four-square walls of standing time.
>
> (P, 49)

Mystical certainty and clarity are posed against modern *Sturm
und Drang* in "The House of Splendour."

In "The Flame" these values are asserted even more aggressive-
ly. Here Pound gives a "visionary interpretation" of Provençal
chivalric love which is far more dogmatic than his discussion in
"Psychology and Troubadours." Love in Provence was a means to
"immortal moments" of vision, and the heirs of Provence in the
modern world can escape the tyranny of time into the realm of
"clear light / Where time burns back about th' eternal embers." In
contrast, modern love is a mere sexual chess game of "mates and
mating" and a market for "barter, lands and houses" (P, 50). M.
L. Rosenthal rightly calls this a "program-poem"; seldom did
Pound assert the reality of visionary experience so emphatically.[12]

As always in Pound, the vision occurs in the "domain of experience." The jewel-like blue of an Italian lake contains the mystery of the jeweled walls of a heavenly city:

> We are not shut from all the thousand heavens:
> Lo, there are many gods whom we have seen,

---

them. These jewels—rubies, sapphires, amethysts and what not, Pound went
on to explain with great determination and care, were the backs of books as
they stood on a man's shelf. "But why in heaven's name don't you say so
then?' was my father's triumphant and crushing rejoinder" (p. 13). Pound responded in a letter of 11 September 1920: "Re the dialog. with your old
man, which I don't bloody remember . . . remember we did talk about 'Und
Drang' but there the sapphires certainly are NOT anything but sapphires,
perfectly definite visual imagination" (LETT, 159). Williams' memory of the
poem was obviously faulty, and so perhaps was his memory of Pound's remarks. One tends to accept Pound's account if only because the chief function of all the jewel imagery in *Canzoni* is to add richness to the light of
virtù.

Folk of unearthly fashion, places splendid,
Bulwarks of beryl and of chrysophrase.

Sapphire Benacus, in thy mists and thee
Nature herself's turned metaphysical,
Who can look on that blue and not believe?

Benacus is Lake Garda in northern Italy; the speaker in another
Canzoni poem ("'Blandula, Tenulla, Vagula'") founds his earthly
paradise on the permanent blue of the same lake, with its penin-
sula, Sirmio:*

If at Sirmio,
My soul, I meet thee, when this life's outrun,
Will we not find some headland consecrated
By aery apostles of terrene delight,
Will not our cult be founded on the waves,
Clear sapphire, cobalt, cyanine,
On triune azures, the impalpable
Mirrors unstill of the eternal change?
(P, 39)

In both poems, jewels and lake have a common quality—their exquisite blue—and it is on this blue, a quality within nature, that

---

* Garda is a favorite, almost magical, setting throughout Pound's poetry,
hallowed by its associations with Catullus and with the Renaissance Latin
poet whom Pound most admired, Marc Antony Flaminius. It is a recurrent
setting in *The Cantos*, especially in the Pisan sequence, and was the site of
Pound's first meeting with Joyce.

The title, "'Blandula, Tenulla, Vagula,'" echoes the address by the dying
Emperor Hadrian to his own soul:

Animula vagula blandula
hospes comesque corporis,
quae nunc abibis in loca
pallidula rigida nudula?
nec ut soles dabis iocos!

See the life of Hadrian by Aelius Spartianus, in *Scriptores Historiae Augustae*
(Loeb Classical Library), I, 78. Pater used the first four lines as the epigraph to Chapter VIII of *Marius the Epicurean*, and Pound used his version
of the first line as an epitaph for Remy de Gourmont (*Pavannes and Divisions*,
p. 128). Pound's poem proposes an alternative to the Christian heaven, to
the bleak abode of Hadrian's poem, and to Marius's lack of faith (at that
point) in immortality.

Pound will base his cult. As he says in Canto 5, "Topaz I manage, and three sorts of blue; / but on the barb of time." For Pound, it is always "Nature herself" who "turns metaphysical."*

"The Flame" also contrasts the medieval and the modern in literature. By means of several allusions, Pound ranges the heirs of Provence (himself) and the heirs of medieval Celtic legend (Yeats) against the modern impressionist poets (Arthur Symons). Referring to Yeats's "The Wanderings of Oisin" (1889), Pound asserts that he and Yeats show man to be independent of time and space:

> We have gone forth beyond your bonds and borders,
> Provençe knew;
> And all the tales of Oisin say but this:
> That man doth pass the net of days and hours.

Symons and the impressionists, on the other hand, write a love poetry in which man is bound to time and to his own body; it is a poetry

> . . . "of days and nights" and troubling years,
> Of cheeks grown sunken and glad hair gone gray.
>   (P, 50)

The quotation here is an allusion to Symons' first book of poems, *Days and Nights* (1889).[13] This piece of "criticism in new composition" marks the first shot in Pound's war against impressionism— a war which culminates, as we shall see, in the portrait of Hugh Selwyn Mauberley.

Pound's affirmation of medieval values in "Und Drang" takes a surprising new turn in the eleventh poem of the series, "Au Salon." After the passionate assertions of "The House of Splendour" and "The Flame," he undertakes to show the mode of life which the modern world necessarily imposes upon the artist who wishes to preserve such values. The principal requirement for such an artist

---

* This interpretation disagrees with N. Christoph de Nagy's argument that in "The Flame" Pound is relying upon "the hidden symbolic significance" of gems such as beryl and chrysophrase in "various occult traditions" (see *The Poetry of Ezra Pound*, p. 102). I think the whole point of the passage is that vision does *not* depend on occult aids.

is a salon, a small and very cultivated coterie of friends for whom he may write exclusively. "Au Salon" is concerned with social institutions and practical arrangements, and its style is correspondingly urbane and conversational:

> I suppose, when poetry comes down to facts,
> When our souls are returned to the gods
>   And the spheres they belong in
> Here in the every-day where our acts
> Rise up and judge us . . .
>
> (P, 52)

The gods of this poem are not the "folk of unearthly fashion" in "The Flame," but the dear domestic gods of social formalities and rituals—Lares and Penates.* Nevertheless, in the world of contemporary letters these gods are as important as the others; the speaker praises

> Some certain peculiar things,
>   cari laresque, penates,
> Some certain accustomed forms,
>   the absolute unimportant.

"Au Salon," then, is about the implementation of ancient ideals in the modern literary world.

In "Au Jardin," the final poem of "Und Drang," Pound demonstrates that his medievalism is compatible with a certain kind of tough-minded humor. In order to preserve his attitude toward "chivalric" love from possible misconceptions, he dissociates it from the attitude of the early Yeats. Though in "The Flame" he identified Provence and Oisin, here he attempts to show that his medievalism is made of sterner stuff. "Au Jardin" is a riposte to Yeats's "The Cap and Bells" in *The Wind Among the Reeds*.

Yeats's poem opens with the line quoted twice in Pound's "Au

---

* Pound might sympathize with some of the practices of today's "Flower Children." In "Religio, or the Child's Guide to Knowledge," he wrote: "To what gods is it fitting . . . to give incense? To Koré and Demeter, also to lares and oreiads and to certain elemental creatures. How is it fitting to please these lares and other creatures? It is fitting to please and to nourish them with flowers." (*Pavannes and Divisions*, p. 25.)

Jardin": "The jester walked in the garden." The jester woos his
"young queen" in vain (as do most of the lovers in *The Wind
Among the Reeds*), and decides to send her his most prized possessions (his cap and bells) as a last despairing gesture: "I will
send them to her and die." As soon as he expires, of course, the
lady begins to love him. Pound is having none of it:

> "The jester walked in the garden."
>   Did he so?
> Well, there's no use your loving me
> That way, Lady;
> For I've nothing but songs to give you.
>   (P, 53)

It is the Yeatsian view of the lady herself that Pound contests.
He is equally capable of endowing her with supreme virtues, but
he remains aware of the difference between the ideal image and
the real woman (a difference which, in some ways, Yeats was slow
to perceive). The actual nature of woman is not to be a stately
and mysterious queen, as in Yeats's poem, but something very
different:

>   And I loved a love once,
>   Over beyond the moon there,
>   I loved a love once,
>   And, may be, more times,
>   But she danced like a pink moth in the shrubbery.

The image of the pink moth is a happy one, suggesting slightness
and fickleness on the one hand, yet a residuum of strangeness and
visual fascination on the other. Only in certain moods of the poet
is the lady a radiant divinity, one of the "folk of unearthly fashion."
In other moods, he sees her simply as another woman, and can
assure frustrated lovers like Yeats's jester of imminent success:

> Oh, I know you women from the "other folk,"
> And it'll all come right
> O' Sundays.

Such are the means employed by Pound in "Und Drang" to
qualify the medievalism of the foregoing poems in *Canzoni*. By

writing directly about modern spiritual malaise, by demarcating his own literary values from those of impressionism and Yeatsian Romanticism, and by addressing himself to the preservation of those values in the salons of contemporary London, he seeks to make his medievalism relevant to modern conditions. In his next volume, *Ripostes*, he continued to invoke medieval values and images, but he expanded his attack against modernity by incorporating a greater range of satiric methods.

What is even more prophetic in "Und Drang" is the substance and structure of the series as a whole. Pound's subject is the contrast between past and present, between visionary clarity and eviscerated confusion, between civilization and chaos. His formal structure consists of an aggregation of separate units, locally unrelated but contributing in each case some new dimension to the total meaning of the sequence. It is a dialectic structure which juxtaposes conflicting values between poems and within poems, working toward clearer definitions without arriving at a definitive synthesis. Within the structure, we encounter a variety of moods and voices, ranging from the lyric and exalted to the ironic and casual. In all of these respects, "Und Drang" anticipates Pound's later and more famous sequence poems: *Propertius, Mauberley,* and *The Cantos*. It is Pound's characteristic long poem in embryonic form.

CHAPTER 6

Ripostes: Recapitulations and Innovations

Wilderness of renewals, confusion
Basis of renewals, subsistence,
(CANTO 20)

The most striking single difference between *Ripostes* and the preceding volumes was pointed out by T. S. Eliot a half-century ago. It is the greater overall assurance in style and expression. Eliot called it a gain in maturity:

In *Ripostes* there are traces of a different idiom. Superficially, the work may appear less important. The diction is more restrained, the flights shorter, the dexterity of technique is less arresting. By romantic readers the book would be considered less "passionate." But there is a much more solid substratum to this book; there is more thought; greater depth, if less agitation on the surface. The effect of London is apparent; the author has become a critic of men, surveying them from a consistent and developed point of view; he is more formidable and disconcerting; in short, much more mature.[1]

Nemi d'Agostino, one of Pound's most distinguished Italian critics, agrees with Eliot: "*Ripostes* sarà la sua prima produzione veramente originale e matura."[2] In fact most of those who have written about the matter "agree on one point: that the publication of 'Ripostes' (1912) is a sharp caesura in Pound's development. . . ."[3] My choice of epigraph for this chapter is designed to suggest that "caesura" is a misleading metaphor. Without denying the justice of Eliot's remarks, we should also see the "subsistence" in *Ripostes* of many features from Pound's earlier work. And we should see that Pound is laying the "basis of renewals" which will take place in his later poetry. *Ripostes* is transitional, a volume of recapitula-

tions and innovations, a conjunction rather than a caesura. There is
no radical break in the line of Pound's development.

The transition to the "different idiom" of which Eliot speaks is
reflected in the poem which opens *Ripostes*. "Silet" is a rewritten
version of a sonnet that had already appeared in *Canzoni*, and the
difference between the two poems epitomizes the greater excellence of *Ripostes* as a whole. The difference is partly one of diction
and syntax; the earlier poem, "Sonnet," employs the archaic diction
and clotted syntax characteristic of *Canzoni*. Indeed, it is a particularly charming example, with its initial conceit recalling Shakespeare's thirtieth sonnet:

> If on the tally-board of wasted days
> They daily write me for proud idleness,
> Let high Hell summons me, and I confess,
> No overt act the preferred charge allays.
>
> To-day I thought—what boots it what I thought?
> Poppies and gold! Why should I blurt it out?
> Or hawk the magic of her name about
> Deaf doors and dungeons where no truth is bought?
>
> Who calls me idle? I have thought of her.
> Who calls me idle? By God's truth I've seen
> The arrowy sunlight in her golden snares.
>
> Let him among you all stand summonser
> Who hath done better things! Let whoso hath been
> With worthier works concerned, display his wares!
>
> (c, 16)

The poem is a sufficiently jaunty record of delightful psychic experience, in the vein of "Erat Hora" ("the most high gods / May
not make boast of any better thing / Than to have watched that
hour as it passed"). But in "Silet" the gusto is freer and the feeling
has deeper range, because the poet has employed a more colloquial
diction and a smoother syntax.

> When I behold how black immortal ink
> Drips from my deathless pen,—ah, well-away!

Why should we stop at all for what I think?
There is enough in what I chance to say.

It is enough that we once came together;
What is the use of setting it to rime?
When it is autumn do we get spring weather,
Or gather may of harsh northwindish time?

It is enough that we once came together;
What if the wind have turned against the rain?
It is enough that we once came together;
Time has seen this, and will not turn again;

And who are we, who know that last intent,
To plague to-morrow with a testament!

(P, 59)

There can be little doubt which sonnet is the superior moment's
monument. Both are "literary," but the diction and rhythm of
"Silet" capture some of the true ease and nobility of the Eliza-
bethan convention.

But the "different idiom" did not mean that Pound had changed
his habitual techniques of "criticism in new composition." The
Shakespearean and Biblical echoes in "Sonnet" (St. John 8:7—"He
that is without sin among you, let him first cast a stone at her")
are replaced in "Silet" by three significant allusions. These allusions
all support the basic theme of the poem—its own futility. The most
obvious is to Villon's *Testament*. The poet sees no point in leaving
a record of his experience such as Villon's (though of course by
saying so he does leave one). The second allusion is to Arnaut
Daniel's canzon beginning "En breu brisaral temps braus," a line
which Pound translated in part as "harsh northwindish time" (SR,
37). Pound denies the power of poetry to portray such love as his,
or to "gather may [that is, May weather] of harsh northwindish
time" as it does in Daniel's canzon.* The third allusion is the title

* Pound's earliest complete translation of the relevant passage was in prose:
"Soon will the harsh time break upon us, the north wind hoot in the branches
which all swish together with their closed-over boughs of leaves; no bird
sings nor 'peeps' now, yet love teaches me to make a song that shall not be
second nor third, but first for freeing the embittered heart." ("Osiris—Part
XI," *New Age*, X [15 February 1912], 369.) For a later verse translation, see
The Translations of Ezra Pound, p. 169.

itself, which comes from a Renaissance Latin poem by Andrea
Navigeri. In this poem the speaker, gazing at a picture of Pytha-
goras, imagines the sage to be reincarnated in accordance with his
own doctrines, but silent with a portentous knowledge of un-
speakable mysteries. Pound translated it in *The Spirit of Romance*,
and called attention to the word "silet": †

> He who, Fame saith, hath lived so oft a soul re-born,
> Into a changèd body oft returning.
> Behold! once more from heaven
> He comes and through Asyla's skill hath life,
> And serves the ancient beauty with his lineament.
>
> Some worthy thing he broodeth certainly,
> So stern of brow, so mightily withdrawn within himself,
> He could the high perceptions of the soul show forth
>   were't not
> That held from the older cult, he doth not speak.
>
> (SR, 226)

The title thus implicitly relates the lover's "silence" in Pound's
sonnet to this massive Pythagorean meditation; the lover too
"broodeth" some worthy thing, some high perception of the soul.
Pound may be speaking in a "different idiom" in this volume, but
he is still using his old allusive sleight of hand. "Be influenced by
as many great artists as you can, but have the decency either to
acknowledge the debt outright, or to try to conceal it" (LE, 5).

   Ripostes links the themes and techniques of Pound's early work
to those of his later. "A Girl," for instance, is a typical Poundian
reinterpretation of myth in psychological terms. As in "The Tree,"
the myth is one of metamorphosis. The speaker is a modern Daphne, able to understand the myth because of her own "delightful
psychic experience," but unable to communicate her "folly to
the world." Pound here implies that the myth originated in a
sexual experience, for as Sister Bernetta Quinn has pointed out, the
tree is "employed metaphorically to symbolize her lover":[4]

> The tree has entered my hands,
> The sap has ascended my arms,

   † After giving his translation, Pound notes: "In the last line, 'silet' suggests
the 'silentes anni' of the Pythagorean disciples" (SR, 226).

The tree has grown in my breast—
Downward,
The branches grow out of me, like arms.

Tree you are,
Moss you are,
You are violets with wind above them.
A child—*so* high—you are,
And all this is folly to the world.

(P, 62)

Not only does "A Girl" recall "The Tree," but it also looks forward
to Pound's more ironic use of the Daphne myth in *Hugh Selwyn
Mauberley* ("'Daphne with her thighs in bark / Stretches toward
me her leafy hands,'— / Subjectively").

Another "linking" poem is "Pan Is Dead" (P, 72). It employs the
motif of fertility gods and pagan rites which Pound first used in
"La Regina Avrillouse" and "A Rouse" (ALS, 74–76). In those
poems, the April-like Queen is a goddess of spring and fertility;
her name derives from a Provençal song which according to
Pound "may have been used in connection with such fragments of
the worship of Flora and Venus as survived in the spring merrymakings" (SR, 39). In *Canzoni*, the opening poem—"Canzon: The
Yearly Slain"—is a psychological reinterpretation of the myth of
Koré (Persephone). The death of the fertility goddess symbolizes
the death of love in the poet's heart. "Pan Is Dead" is a straightforward and graceful song lamenting the god's death at the approach of winter. As we shall see, this Frazerian motif becomes a
dominant theme in Pound's next volume of poems, *Lustra* (1916).

Pound continued to use the persona in *Ripostes*. In "The Tomb
at Akr-çaar" (P, 60), the soul of Nikoptis reproaches his mummified
body in the tones of a neglected woman. As Robert Langbaum has
noted, part of the poem's effect is due to the historical perspectives
created by the dramatic-monologue form: "Integral to the meaning
is our modern awareness that the monologue takes place as the
tomb is about to be opened, and that this is the five-thousand-year-
old situation the archaeologists will break into."[5] But form is not
the only feature which links this poem to its predecessors. For the

persona itself—this speaking soul—is yet another version of the disembodied spirit, the *anima sola,* of *A Lume Spento.*

Other important "recapitulations" in *Ripostes* include four
poems which are variations of Pound's medievalism, as we have
seen it in *Canzoni.* In the sonnet, "A Virginal," the speaker has acquired part of the sheath of light which radiates from the lady and
symbolizes her *virtù.* Her touch has communicated the calyx of
grace, and the speaker does not want to lose it by touching another
(*noli me tangere*):

> No, no! Go from me. I have left her lately.
> I will not spoil my sheath with lesser brightness,
> For my surrounding air hath a new lightness;
> Slight are her arms, yet they have bound me straitly
> And left me cloaked as with a gauze of aether;
> As with sweet leaves; as with subtle clearness.
>
> (P, 71)

In "Sub Mare" the advent of the lady causes familiar alterations
in the speaker's environment; it is of course she who has brought
the "goldish colour" which transforms his world:

> It is, and is not, I am sane enough,
> Since you have come this place has hovered round me,
> This fabrication built of autumn roses,
> Then there's a goldish colour, different.
>
> (P, 69)

In "The Needle" (P, 69), the lovers are drawn on their voyage by
a mysterious tidal magnetism that can only be a manifestation of
that "world of moving energies . . . magnetisms that take form,
that are seen, or border the visible" which Pound associated with
the medieval imagination (LE, 154). The force attracting the
speaker combines external fate with internal *virtù* ("the needle
trembles in my soul").

The fourth medievalist poem, "Apparuit," contains perhaps the
most beautiful of Pound's ideal ladies. The vision is all the more
passionate and compelling because the verse rhythms are subtler
and freer than in the fixed stanza forms of *Canzoni.* The Sapphic

stanza (three 11-syllable lines and one 5-syllable line) allows
Pound to manipulate his stresses and ignore rhyme:

> Half the graven shoulder, the throat aflash with
> strands of light inwoven about it, loveli-
> est of all things, frail alabaster, ah me!
> > swift in departing.

> > > > (P, 68)

"Absolute rhythm" could not be better illustrated. This apparition
possesses the standard accoutrements of Pound's goddesses: the
light woven about the throat, a "shell of gold," an "oriel," a "goldish weft," "the tissue / golden about thee." Perhaps more important, though, is her vital relationship to her surroundings. She is
the organizing center of her environment, giving and taking life
forces; like the singer in Stevens' "Idea of Order at Key West," she
is "the single artificer of the world":

> Crimson, frosty with dew, the roses bend where
> thou afar, moving in the glamorous sun,
> drinkst in life of earth, of the air, the tissue
> > golden about thee.

And lest there be any doubt about her lineage, Pound's title con-
nects her directly to Dante's Beatrice.*

If this woman is the reincarnation of Beatrice, the women in
"The Picture" and "Of Jacopo del Sellaio" are reincarnations of
Venus. The first of these companion poems concerns the poet's
reaction to a painting of *Venus Reclining* by Del Sellaio, and introduces the linking line: "The eyes of this dead lady speak to me."
In the second poem, the poet sees the very same eyes in his
modern Venus:

> And now she's gone, who was his Cyprian,
> And you are here, who are "The Isles" to me.

> And here's the thing that lasts the whole thing out:
> The eyes of this dead lady speak to me.

> > > > (P, 73)

---

* "Apparuit" echoes the words of Dante's "spirito animale" when he first
sees Beatrice in *La Vita Nuova* (II); the spirit says "Apparuit iam beatitudo
vestra" ("your beatitude now appears").

These eyes reappear "dans un visage stupide" in Pound's French poem, "Dans Un Omnibus de Londres," published in 1916: "Les yeux d'une morte / M'ont salué" (P, 160). As Hugh Kenner has noted, when the goddess "turns up" in Pound's poetry we can often "identify her by her eyes."[6] We shall see the importance of "Yeux Glauques" and eye imagery in general to *Hugh Selwyn Mauberley*.

Kenner has noted that the women in Pound's poetry tend to merge into two basic archetypes: the goddess, radiant with a *virtú* which organizes the world about her; and the fragmented woman, lacking identity and organized by her environment.[7] We may say that Yseult, the medieval ladies of *Canzoni*, and the recurrent Aphrodite figure who helps to organize the flux of *The Cantos* are examples of the goddess; while the sterile females of the *Lustra* satires, Lady Maent in "Near Perigord," and Lady Valentine in *Hugh Selwyn Mauberley* are examples of the fragmented woman. In *Ripostes*, these opposites may be seen clearly in the contrast between the heroines of "Apparuit" and "Portrait d'une femme."

The subject of "Portrait" is a modern woman without identity or *virtú*. She is but "a sort of nodal point in the flux," defined by her environment.[8] Whereas the lady of "Apparuit" is organically inseparable from her setting ("Green the ways, the breath of the fields is thine there"), the London *femme* gains no identity from her oddments ("No! there is nothing . . . that's quite your own"). She is the cultural "Sargasso Sea" of London, and her "spars of knowledge" are lifeless and stationary in that backwater. The light in her world is not self-generated, but reflected from above, shifting and uncertain: "the slow float of differing light and deep" (P, 61). Yet despite her lack of unity, the lady is not nothing. The poem is a study of the second rate qualified by the poet's implied awareness of third, fourth, and fifth rates. If we say that this fragmented lady is the prototype of the figures satirized in *Lustra*, we must add that the perspective and balance of the "Portrait" are missing from most of Pound's later sketches. It was probably this poem that Eliot had most in mind when he spoke of "the effect of London" and said that Pound had become "more mature."

The balanced irony of "Portrait d'une femme" brings us to the "innovations" of *Ripostes*. Pound's experiments with irony, satire, and epigram in this volume represent significant new departures in the general direction of *Lustra*. Actually, these innovations begin in *Canzoni*, with the "Translations and Adaptations from Heine," with "Au Salon," and with "Redondillas" (a poem originally scheduled to appear in *Canzoni* but canceled in page proof at the last minute). The easy speech rhythms, natural diction, and satiric bent of these poems contrast strongly with the stilted language and lyric intensity of Pound's medieval imitations. Pound was already moving toward the modernity which Ford Madox Ford was shortly to urge upon him so dramatically. (Ford ridiculed the medieval poems in *Canzoni* by rolling on the floor in gales of laughter when he read them.)*

The Heine translations mark Pound's first real venture into *moeurs contemporaines* and the satirical mode of his later blasts and ripostes. Chosen principally from *Die Heimkehr*, these translations carried Pound into areas of style and sensibility as yet unexplored by him.[9] Heine's confident and urbane irony furnishes a wholly new note to Pound's poetry:

> This delightful young man
> Should not lack for honourers,
> He propitiates me with oysters,
> With Rhine wine and liqueurs.
>
> (P, 46)

Likewise, "Au Salon" is almost an exercise in the low style of the classical *sermones*, the traditional style of satire. In the context of "Und Drang," it offers a vivid contrast to the high style of poems like "The House of Splendour."

---

* Pound was traveling in Germany with Ford at about the time *Canzoni* was published (July 1911). Ford found the diction of Pound's poems absurdly archaic, and demonstrated his criticism graphically. Pound remembered the moment vividly almost thirty years later: "And he felt the errors of contemporary style to the point of rolling . . . on the floor of his temporary quarters in Giessen when my third volume displayed me trapped, flypapered, gummed and strapped down in a jejune provincial effort to learn, *mehercule*, the stilted language that then passed for 'good English' . . . And that roll saved me two years, perhaps more." See "Ford Madox (Hueffer) Ford; Obit," *The Nineteenth Century and After*, CXXVI (August 1939), 179.

This reward for our works,
        sic crescit gloria mundi:
Some circle of not more than three
        that we prefer to play up to,
Some few whom we'd rather please
        than hear the whole aegrum vulgus*
Splitting its beery jowl
        a-meaowling our praise.

                       (P, 52)

These two modes, lyric and ironic, were to govern the poems of
Lustra. But even more prophetic of the *Lustra* style is "Redondillas, or something of that sort." The following passage, for instance, anticipates the satirical concerns and Whitmanian stance
of the later poems:

I sing of natural forces
        I sing of refinements
I would write of the various moods
        of nuances, of subtleties.
I would sing of the hatred of dullness,
        of the search for sensation.

I would sing the American people,
        God send them some civilization;
I would sing of the nations of Europe,
        God grant them some method of cleansing
The fetid extent of their evils.†

"Redondillas" shows that the distance from *Canzoni* to "Contempo-
rania" was not so great as it may seem.

---

  * The phrase "aegrum vulgus" is borrowed from Aurelius Augurellus, a
Renaissance Latin poet. As Pound explained: "His 'aegrum vulgus,' 'diseased
rabble,' is one degree more contemptuous than the 'profanum vulgus' of
Horace" (SR, 239). Pound used the expression again in "The Serious Artist"
(LE, 47).
  † The poem was published for the first time through the good offices of
Noel Stock in *Poetry Australia*, XV (April 1967), 5–11. The title looks back
to a passage in *The Spirit of Romance* where Pound quotes and translates four
lines from Lope de Vega, and says: "These lines are at the beginning of some
careless redondillas, representing the thoughts he takes with him journeying"
(SR, 208).

In *Ripostes*, Pound expanded these experiments with satire by
writing four poems in the mode of the Latin epigram. "An Object"
satirizes a man incapable of friendship, and introduces the comparison of people to inanimate things which recurs in many of
Pound's later epigrams (P, 63). "Quies" (be silent) begins as
praise for a lady, but in the traditional manner of the Latin epigram saves its satiric sting for the last half-line (P, 63). "In Exitum
Cuiusdam" refuses to mourn the passing of friends (P, 59).

The fourth exercise, "Phasellus Ille," is more complex. Here
Pound's satire of a conservative Victorian magazine editor relies on
an implied contrast to a lyric by Catullus (IV). The Latin poem
praises a seaworthy pinnace (*phasellus*) which has seen its last
service; it opens:

> Phasellus ille quem videtis, hospites,
> ait fuisse navium celerrimus
> [That pinnace which you see, friends,
> Says it was the swiftest of ships . . .]

Pound's opening lines adapt those of Catullus humorously:

> This *papier-mâché*, which you see, my friends,
> Saith 'twas the worthiest of editors . . .
>
> (P, 63)

The unstated interplay continues throughout Pound's poem. Catullus' pinnace boasts that its course toward a limpid lake ("limpidum
lacum") was never deflected by winds calling it to right or left
("laeva sive dextra / vocaret aura"), nor by Jupiter himself. All of
these details have counterparts in Pound's boast that his editor
remains unmoved by all new ideas:

> Nor will the horrid threats of Bernard Shaw
> Shake up the stagnant pool of its convictions;
> Nay, should the deathless voice of all the world
> Speak once again for its sole stimulation,
> 'Twould not move it one jot from left to right.

In his subsequent satires, Pound often used allusion in this way—
to invoke a literary standard against which the object of his satire
may be judged.

Ripostes also exhibits significant innovations of a nonsatiric kind, innovations which point the way to Pound's Imagism. "The Cloak," for example, represents Pound's first adaptation from the *Greek Anthology*, a major source of material and inspiration for the Imagists. "The Cloak" (P, 67) is a free translation of a song by Julianus Aegyptus Aesclepiades, into which Pound interpolated the rose imagery from his own early poems.[10] Two other poems in *Ripostes*—"Δώρια" and "The Return"—were actually included in Pound's 1914 anthology, *Des Imagistes*, as examples of the new technique, even though both were first published prior to the beginning of the movement. To see why Pound considered "Δώρια" appropriate for his collection, we should notice how one of his later discussions of the Image might almost have been written with this poem in mind.

In his important essay on "Vorticism" (1914), Pound again advances his familiar notion that poetry is an equation for moods; he compares it to the equations of analytical geometry: "By the 'image' I mean such an equation; not an equation of mathematics, not something about *a, b,* and *c,* having something to do with form, but about *sea, cliffs, night,* having something to do with mood."* "Δώρια" is just such an equation for a mood, involving sea, cliffs, and night:

> Be in me as the eternal moods
> of the bleak wind, and not
> As transient things are—
> gaiety of flowers.
> Have me in the strong loneliness
> of sunless cliffs
> And of grey waters.

* "Vorticism," *Gaudier–Brzeska,* p. 100. The same essay contains Pound's well-known remark that "The Return" is comparable to abstractionist sculpture: "Secondly, I made poems like 'The Return,' which is an objective reality and has a complicated sort of significance, like Mr. Epstein's 'Sun God,' or Mr. Brzeska's 'Boy with a Coney' " (p. 98). The analogy is plausible—the poem is "non-representative" in that it is impossible to say just what the returning huntsmen represent. It refers to nothing outside itself, but presents an arrangement of images in rhythmic movement. This arrangement is the "objective reality" that conveys a certain emotional "Vortex."

> Let the gods speak softly of us
> In days hereafter,
> The shadowy flowers of Orcus
> Remember thee.

(P, 67)

The kind of mood in question is suggested by the title, "Doria"; it implies the martial sternness of Dorian music and architecture. The images present a contrast in types of passion: the "eternal" and "strong" suggested by "bleak wind," "sunless cliffs," "grey waters," and the "shadowy flowers of Orcus" (Dis or Pluto, the flowers of the kingdom of death); and the "transient" suggested by the "gaiety of flowers." The Dorian mood partakes of the eternal and will be remembered by the gods (indeed, Pound later defined a god *as* "an eternal state of mind").[11] In *Hugh Selwyn Mauberley* this integrity of mood is associated with Victor Plarr, whose *In the Dorian Mood* appeared in 1896. Plarr is of course "M. Verog," the only survivor of the nineties, a man who still preserves the obscure reveries of the inward gaze which constituted the strength of that generation:

> So spoke the author of "The Dorian Mood,"
>
> M. Verog, out of step with the decade,
> Detached from his contemporaries,
> Neglected by the young,
> Because of these reveries.

(P, 193)

Clearly, "Δώρια" foreshadows much that was to come in Pound's career.

II

Pound's translation of *The Seafarer* also partakes in the "transitional" character of *Ridpostes* as a whole. It should be seen as a successor to his early voyage poems, such as "Purveyors General" (QFTY, 92–93), "At the Heart o' Me" (*Personae* [1909], 34–35), and "Guido Invites You Thus" (P, 25), and seen also as a precursor of the major poems structured around the Odyssean quest, such as *Hugh Selwyn Mauberley* and *The Cantos*. In these other poems, the ocean voyage symbolizes a "sailing after knowledge," the hero's

quest for a civilized city or the artist's quest for beauty. Converse-
ly, those who decline or abandon the voyage are seen as philistines
and failures, the landlubbers of the soul. Pound's *Seafarer* incorporates some of the same values.

The earliest "voyage" poem is "Purveyors General." It sets up a
contrast between "the lonely ones" who sail the sea and "the
home-stayers" who consume the rare articles brought back by the
purveyors. The adventurers are thinly disguised artists; they seek
"new things / And quaint tales," "dreams," and "new mysteries /
New songs." While they suffer in their quest, the home-stayers
live in "ease" and "peace":

> We, that through chaos have hurled
> Our souls riven and burning,
> Torn, mad, even as windy seas
> Have we been, that your ease
> Should keep bright amongst you.

The "Purveyors General" traffic in goods of the soul, earning pain
while others enjoy the profit.

"At the Heart o' Me: A.D. 751" foreshadows the eventual merging
of this theme with the Anglo-Saxon *Wanderer* and *Seafarer*. The
speaker is an unnamed Anglo-Saxon sailor, who contrasts his life
to life on land as he sings a love lyric. The poem is Pound's
earliest experiment with Anglo-Saxon diction and meter:

> What should avail me
>   booty of whale-ways?
> What should avail me
>   gold rings or the chain-mail?
> What should avail me
>   the many-twined bracelets?

"Guido Invites You Thus" was the opening poem in *Exultations*
(1909), and presents the voyage motif by means of riposte. Here
the speaker is Cavalcanti, and he is answering a sonnet by Dante
in which a voyage is proposed. Pound's note to the poem suggests
that he wishes the reader to keep Dante's poem in mind:

> Dante's "Guido vorrei . . ."
> Guido, I wish that Lapo, thou, and I,
>   Could be by spells conveyed, as it were now,

Upon a barque, with all the winds that blow
Across all seas at our good will to hie.
So no mischance nor temper of the sky
    Should mar our course with spite or cruel slip;
    But we, observing old companionship,
To be companions still should long thereby.
And Lady Joan and Lady Beatrice,
    And her the thirtieth on my roll, with us
    Should our good wizard set, o'er seas to move
And not to talk of anything but love:
And they three ever to be well at ease,
    As we should be, I think, if this were thus.[12]

Pound's "Guido Invites You Thus"
"Lappo I leave behind and Dante too,
Lo, I would sail the seas with thee alone!
Talk me no love talk, no bought-cheap fiddl'ry,
Mine is the ship and thine the merchandise,
All the blind earth knows not th' emprise
Whereto thou calledst and whereto I call.
Lo, I have seen thee bound about with dreams,
Lo, I have known thy heart and its desire;
Life, all of it, my sea, and all men's streams
Are fused in it as flames of an altar fire!
Lo, thou hast voyaged not! The ship is mine."

Pound's intenser voyage is the quest of the artist, full of fiery
dreams, away from the "blind earth" of bourgeois society.

When Pound came to translate *The Seafarer*, his reading of the
poem was governed by the assumptions of these earlier voyage
poems. The changes he made in the original text subtly modify
its spirit and bring it into line with his own preoccupations. In a
recent interpretation, Donald Davie points out that Pound's alterations "romanticize" the poem by introducing a strong new motive
not in the original: *épater le bourgeois*.[13] The major change is
Pound's systematic elimination of all Christian elements from the
poem. He simply eliminates the last nine lines (containing moral
instruction and a hymn to God's power and mercy). And he purposely alters the passage in which men are advised to combat the

malice of devils so as to win eternal fame among the angels of
heaven. He accomplishes the latter by two manipulations: the
half-line "deofle togeanes" (against the devil) is dropped (hence
the hiatus in the translation after "Daring ado"); and the word
"engles" (angels) is read as "angles" (the English). The upshot is
that both devils and angels vanish from the poem, and Pound has
in effect made "malice the source of everlasting renown among the
English":[14]

> And for this, every earl whatever, for those speaking
>   after—
> Laud of the living, boasteth some last word,
> That he will work ere he pass onward,
> Frame on the fair earth 'gainst foes his malice,
> Daring ado, . . .
> So that all men shall honour him after
> And his laud beyond them remain 'mid the English. . . .
>
> (P, 66)

Pound's translation paganizes the poem. That he was fully conscious of this is proved by the note which he published with the
poem when it first appeared in *The New Age*:

Philological note: The text of this poem is rather confused. I have
rejected half of line 76, read "Angles" for angels in line 78, and
stopped translating before the passage about the soul and the
longer lines beginning, "Mickle is the fear of the Almighty," and
ending in a dignified but platitudinous address to the Deity:
"World's elder, eminent creator, in all ages, amen." There are many
conjectures about how the text came into its present from [sic]. It
seems most likely that a fragment of the original poem, clear
through about the first thirty lines, and thereafter increasingly il-
legible, fell into the hands of a monk with literary ambitions, who
filled in the gaps with his own guesses and "improvements." The
groundwork may have been a longer narrative poem, but the
"lyric," as I have accepted it, divides fairly well into "The Trials
of the Sea," its Lure, and the Lament for Age.[15]

Despite the scholarly rationale, the changes mesh too perfectly
with Pound's own poetic biases to be motivated by sheerly textual
considerations. His use of the term "lyric" suggests that he considered the poem a dramatic lyric; certainly he has made its

speaker reflect the same kind of *secular* vitality that his other personae exhibit (for example, the "Goodly Fere").

Moreover, Pound goes out of his way to introduce and satirize the bourgeois in a poem where they actually have no role. He has committed two other significant "mistakes" (unremarked by Davie and Sisam) which serve to transform the comfortable shore-dwellers in the poem into Old English Babbitts. He translates "in burgum" (in the dwellings of men) as " 'mid burghers" and "beorn" (man, warrior) as "Burgher." Thus the philistine middle class makes a sudden and surprising appearance in the society of Anglo-Saxon England:

> This he little believes, who aye in winsome life
> Abides 'mid burghers some heavy business,
> Wealthy and wine-flushed, how I weary oft
> Must bide above brine.
>
> (P, 64)

> Burgher knows not—
> He the prosperous man—what some perform
> Where wandering them widest draweth.
>
> (P, 65)

The anachronistic "burgher" is regarded with scorn here, whereas the landsman is regarded with some envy in the original. Clearly Pound has transformed the nonvoyagers into the despised "home-stayers" of "Purveyors General," and their habitation into the "blind earth" of "Guido Invites You Thus." The symbolic geography of his quest poems remains consistent.

Pound's Seafarer is the precursor of the Odysseus figure whose quest forms the structural skeleton of both *Hugh Selwyn Mauberley* and *The Cantos*. In "The Constant Preaching to the Mob" (1916), Pound associates the Anglo-Saxon poem with Book XI of the *Odyssey*, on which Canto 1 is based. And the association, in its context, illuminates the whole cluster of values embodied in Pound's symbolic voyages.

Pound writes this little essay because he has been made furious by a statement which he considers the "lie" of a "demagogue"— namely, that Old English poetry was "made by a rude war-faring people for the entertainment of men-at-arms, or for men at monk's tables." Not only is this statement false, but it also represents pernicious, simple-minded, self-satisfied, bourgeois assumptions about the nature of poetry in general. As such it must be blasted in no uncertain terms:

> Either such statements are made to curry favor with other people sitting at fat sterile tables, or they are made in an ignorance which is charlatanry when it goes out to vend itself as sacred and impeccable knowledge. "The beginnings—for entertainment"—has the writer of this sentence read *The Seafarer* in Anglo-Saxon? Will the author tell us for whose benefit these lines, which alone in the works of our forebears are fit to compare with Homer—for whose entertainment were they made? They were made for no man's entertainment, but because a man believing in silence found himself unable to withhold himself from speaking. . . . Such poems are not made for after-dinner speakers, nor was the eleventh book of the Odyssey. Still it flatters the mob to tell them that their importance is so great that the solace of lonely men, and the lordliest of the arts, was created for their amusement.   (LE, 64–65)

The well-fed middle class of this passage clearly corresponds to the home-stayers, burghers, Mr. Nixons—the Circe's swine of Pound's voyage poems generally. Against the aesthetic of the herd Pound poses two works involving individual suffering and solitary persistence. He not only associates the Greek and Anglo-Saxon poems, but he also identifies the poets with their heroes. The poets too are "lonely men" who obey only the laws of their own noble natures, and ignore the acclaim of "after-dinner speakers" at their "fat sterile tables." In other words, like the Seafarer and Odysseus they absent themselves from the tempting felicities of the banquet to pursue a solitary and inner-directed quest. Odysseus and the Seafarer are personae whose plight images that of their creators. And they become personae for Pound because the plight seems to him that of every serious artist. Just as "Δώρια" provides the transition from *Ripostes* to Imagism, so *The Seafarer* anticipates the figure of the artist-as-Odysseus in *Hugh Selwyn Mauberley* and *The Cantos*.

CHAPTER 7

Aspects of *Lustra*

> there in the glade
> To Flora's night, with hyacinthus,
> With the crocus (spring
> sharp in the grass)
> Fifty and forty together
> ERI MEN AI DE KUDONIAI
> Betuene Aprile and Merche
> with sap new in the bough
> (CANTO 39)

I. THE CULT OF BEAUTY AND THE CULT OF UGLINESS

If we turn from Pound's Imagist theory directly to *Lustra* (which collects most of the poems and translations he made between 1912 and 1916), we soon find that much of it cannot be described in terms of Imagist and Vorticist principles. The shorter poems fall into two general groups: lyrics and satires. Many of the satires are not "Imagist" in any obvious sense. Pound was aware of this dichotomy, and justified it in several critical statements. In "The Serious Artist" (1913), he defined the "cult of beauty" and the "cult of ugliness":

As there are in medicine the art of diagnosis and the art of cure, so in the arts, so in the particular arts of poetry and literature, there is the art of diagnosis and there is the art of cure. They call one the cult of ugliness and the other the cult of beauty.

The cult of beauty is the hygiene, it is sun, air and the sea and the rain and the lake bathing. The cult of ugliness, Villon, Baudelaire, Corbière, Beardsley are diagnosis. Flaubert is diagnosis. Satire, if we are to ride this metaphor to staggers, satire is surgery, insertions and amputations.

Beauty in art reminds one what is worth while. I am not now speaking of shams. I mean beauty, not slither, not sentimentalizing about beauty, not telling people that beauty is the proper and respectable thing. I mean beauty. You don't argue about an April wind, you feel bucked up when you meet it. You feel bucked up when you come on a swift moving thought in Plato or on a fine line in a statue.

Even this pother about the gods reminds one that something is worth while. Satire reminds one that certain things are not worth while. It draws one to consider time wasted.

The cult of beauty and the delineation of ugliness are not in mutual opposition.   (LE, 45)*

The lyrics in *Lustra* belong to the "cult of beauty" and the satires to the "cult of ugliness." Imagism–Vorticism itself has to do primarily with the "cult of beauty," as Pound explained in 1914:

. . . no artist can possibly get a vortex into every poem or picture he does. One would like to do so, but it is beyond one. Certain things seem to demand metrical expression, or expression in a rhythm more agitated than the rhythms acceptable to prose, and these subjects, though they do not contain a vortex, may have some interest, an interest as a "criticism of life" or of art. It is natural to express these things, and a vorticist or imagiste writer may be justified in presenting a certain amount of work which is not vorticism or imagisme. . . .[1]

The other "things," being criticism of life and art, find their expression in poetic satire and the "cult of ugliness." The nature of the two cults is our present concern.

The cult of beauty receives some clarification in Pound's initial description. It is associated with sun, air, sea, rain, lake bathing, gods, and an "April wind" that makes you feel "bucked up." This wind is obviously the same magical wind so often associated with beauty in the imagery of *A Lume Spento*, which suggests that the cult is one of ecstasy and life force. Its being an April wind implies spring and seasonal rebirth. And if we examine the poems of

* The same distinction is behind a remark made slightly over a year later: "There are only two passions in art; there are only love and hate—with endless modifications" ("Modern Georgics," *Poetry*, V [December 1914], 128). And it governs this statement in "Henry James" (1918): "Most good prose arises, perhaps, from an instinct of negation; is the detailed, convincing analysis of something detestable; of something which one wants to eliminate. Poetry is the assertion of a positive, i.e. of desire, and endures for a longer period. Poetic satire is only an assertion of this positive, inversely, i.e. as of an opposite hatred" (LE, 324).

Lustra, we find that they often do involve the coming of spring, fertility rites celebrating the new season, Greek gods and goddesses, and a stirring of human passion that mirrors the stirring of the earth. In *Lustra,* we see Pound moving closer to what he called the "germinal" consciousness:

And with certain others their consciousness is "germinal." Their thoughts are in them as the thought of the tree is in the seed, or in the grass, or the grain, or the blossom. And these minds are the more poetic, and they affect mind about them, and transmute it as the seed the earth. And this latter sort of mind is close on the vital universe; and the strength of the Greek beauty rests in this, that it is ever at the interpretation of this vital universe, by its signs of gods and godly attendants and oreads.   (SR, 92–93)

The beauty of the Imagist lyrics in *Lustra* is this "Greek beauty."[2]

We may begin with "Surgit Fama," because it illustrates not only the cult of beauty, but also the principles of Imagism itself.

> There is a truce among the gods,
> Korè is seen in the North
> Skirting the blue-gray sea
> In gilded and russet mantle.
> The corn has again its mother and she, Leuconoë,
> That failed never women,
> Fails not the earth now.
>
> The tricksome Hermes is here;
> He moves behind me
> Eager to catch my words,
> Eager to spread them with rumour;
> To set upon them his change
> Crafty and subtle;
> To alter them to his purpose;
> But do thou speak true, even to the letter:
>
> "Once more in Delos, once more is the altar a-quiver.
> Once more is the chant heard.
> Once more are the never abandoned gardens
> Full of gossip and old tales."
>
>   (P, 90)

Koré (the "Virgin" or Persephone) and Leuconoë are fertility goddesses reappearing after their annual deaths—Koré was last seen
in Pound's work making her autumnal exit in "Canzon: The Yearly
Slain."[3] They are harbingers of spring, like the April wind that
makes you feel "bucked up," and the movement of the poem is
toward the realization of the rumor (*fama*) they bring, toward the
arrival of the goddesses in Delos. Central island in the Cyclades,
Delos was the scene of yearly festivals in honor of Apollo, and
Pound portrays the festival as a hymn to the life force ("once
more is the altar a-quiver").

But the coming of spring also symbolizes the coming of poetic
inspiration, and "Surgit Fama" is a paradigm of Imagist composition. The threefold movement of the poem reflects the genesis of
an Imagist lyric—from its initial inspiration, through the arduous
search for the absolute equation, to the finished product. The first
strophe may be taken as the initial stirrings of the poet's imagination—once again he catches a visionary glimpse of the goddess. In
the second strophe, the poet is tempted by Hermes to make a careless or effusive statement. The mischievous god of rumor is ready
to spread abroad an inaccurate version of the poet's emotion
("Eager to catch my words / . . . To set upon them his change").
Hermes represents all the lapses of technique to which the Imagist
must never succumb. But the poet resists, and commands his words
to speak with Imagist precision, "even to the letter." (The image
of Koré's garment, a "gilded and russet mantle," typifies the desired precision, for it echoes one of Pound's favorite examples of
Imagist presentation—Shakespeare's "dawn in russet mantle
clad.")* The poet triumphs in the third strophe, which represents
the finished Imagist lyric and is appropriately set off in quotation
marks. The classical myths, of which he had only a glimpse at the
beginning, are fully reborn in a swelling chorus:

> "Once more in Delos, once more is the altar a-quiver,
> Once more is the chant heard.

---

* "When Shakespeare talks of the 'Dawn in russet mantle clad' he presents
something which the painter does not present. There is in this line of his nothing that one can call description; he presents" (LE, 6). Pound echoes the line
from *Hamlet* again in "The Garret": "Dawn enters with little feet / like a
gilded Pavlova" (P, 83).

Once more are the never abandoned gardens
Full of gossip and old tales."

In "Surgit Fama" we see not only the cult of beauty, but some of
its priestcraft.

Koré reappears in "The Spring" (P, 87) as "Cydonian Spring
with her attendant train, / Maelids and water-girls, / Stepping
beneath a boisterous wind from Thrace." Again she is associated
with wind and the renewal of crops. Her approach brings new and
painful desire to the poet because his beloved, who died with Koré,
cannot be reborn with her. The poem is based on a lyric by Ibycus,
the first line of which ("In springtime the Kydonian quinces . . .")
is Pound's epigraph. The same line recurs in Canto 39 in the
passage which celebrates "ver novum" and the god-engendering
sexual union of Odysseus and Circe. (See the epigraph to this
chapter.) "The Spring" is actually a free translation of the Greek
original, except for the last three lines, which Pound added to
introduce the note of sorrow in a haiku-like juxtaposition.[4] "Ibycus
and Liu Ch'e presented the Image," he declared, and his own
modification intensified what he found in the Greek original.[5]

A spring festival similar to the Delian rites of "Surgit Fama" is
presented in "Coitus" (P, 110). Here the growth of crocuses is
likened to the erection of innumerable potent "phaloi," the night
is "restless" with its new energy, and the "dead gods" of winter
are forgotten amid the "procession of festival." When the poem
was published in Lustra (1916), Elkin Mathews forced Pound to
change the title from "Coitus" to "Pervigilium," and the change
points to a source of inspiration—the Greek Pervigilium Veneris.
"It celebrates a Greek feast," Pound wrote, "which had been trans-
planted into Italy, and recently revived by Hadrian: the feast
of Venus Genetrix, which survived as May Day" (SR, 18). His
own poem could easily be celebrating the same feast. Venus is
called "Dione" in the Pervigilium Veneris, and she is the pre-
siding goddess of Pound's feast under the same name: "Dione,
your nights are upon us."*

Pound also used the theme in non-Greek contexts. "After Ch'u

---

* As George Dekker has noted in connection with Canto 47, Aphrodite is
also called Diona in Bion's Lament for Adonis: "Diona was wife to Zeus and,
in fact, his feminine counterpart; therefore Aphrodite, when invoked as Diona,

Yuan," for example, is based on a single passage in Herbert Giles's
longish prose translation of Ch'u Yuan's "The Genius of the Mountain": "Methinks there is a Genius of the Hills, clad in wistaria,
girdled with ivy, with smiling lips, of witching mien, riding on
the red pard, wild cats galloping in the rear, reclining in a chariot,
with banners of cassia, cloaked with the orchid, girt with azalea,
culling the perfume of sweet flowers to leave behind a memory in
the heart."[6] What might have caught Pound's eye in this passage is
its resemblance to a Bacchic procession. He increased the Greek
overtones of the original by adding maidens and grapes:

> I will get me to the wood
> Where the gods walk garlanded in wistaria,
> By the silver blue flood
>   move others with ivory cars.
> There come forth many maidens
>   to gather grapes for the leopards, my friend,
> For there are leopards drawing the cars.
>
> I will walk in the glade,
> I will come out from the new thicket
>   and accost the procession of maidens.
>
>   (P, 108)

It seems probable that Pound had read Frazer's *Golden Bough*
when he wrote of this Chinese sacred wood.* If so, he might have
been struck by the similarities of two legends so widely separated
in their places of origin, and seen in them confirmation of Frazer's
thesis. In any case, the cult of beauty includes Chinese rituals as
well as Greek.

---

as she is in the *Pervigilium Veneris*, represents much more powerful forces
than one normally attributes to her" (*Sailing After Knowledge* [London,
1963], p. 38).

   * Pound's earliest reference to Frazer, so far as I know, is in a letter to
Margaret Anderson written, according to D. D. Paige, in April 1918. The
passage implies, however, an earlier familiarity with the work: "Frazer has
of course done the whole job monumentally, BUT good god how slowly, in
how many volumes. No reader of the *Golden Bough* is likely to relapse into
bigotry, but it takes such a constitution to read it" (LETT, 134). *The Golden
Bough* was in its third edition by 1911. "After Ch'u Yuan" was first published in *Des Imagistes* (1914).

Bacchic rites are also connoted in "April" (P, 92). The stripped olive boughs strike the poet as "Pale carnage beneath bright mist," and they are compared in the epigraph to torn limbs of nymphs. This Imagist haiku seems almost to present the aftermath of a frenzied Bacchic feast, the dismembered parts of the Bacchantes' sacrificial victims.

Another god, Pan, figures indirectly in "The Faun" (P, 109). Here the race of Pan reappears after its hibernal death in Pound's earlier poem, "Pan Is Dead" (P, 72). The speaker comes upon a timid satyr "sniffing and snoozling" among the flowers in his garden. He summons his friends, Auster and Apeliota (Greek for "south wind" and "east wind") to see it, but warns them not to alarm the capriped (goat foot).

The cult of beauty in *Lustra* also involves new reincarnations of Aphrodite/Beatrice. "Gentildonna," as the title suggests, descends from the ladies of *Canzoni*. Though she radiates no light, her *virtù* remains "clinging / in the air she severed" (P, 92). In "Dance Figure," the lady is the bride at the "Marriage in Cana of Galilee," a ceremony implicitly related to the other rites of *Lustra*. The speaker is the groom, and his language is reminiscent of the *Song of Songs*. The bride's beauties are adumbrated by metaphorical comparison to natural objects (P, 91).

Indirectly, the *Song of Songs* also provided one of the most common dramatic movements in Pound's early poetry. It is the "approach"—a figure entering the speaker's field of contemplation from afar. In "Surgit Fama," "The Spring," and "Apparuit" this figure is the goddess herself, and in "The Return" and "The Coming of War: Actaeon" it is a sad and mysterious group of mythical dimensions. These "approaches" in Pound's work probably derive from Cavalcanti's sonnet, "Chi è questa che vien." But that sonnet derives in turn from the *Song of Songs*: "Who is she that cometh forth as the morning rising?" (VI, 9). As Pound asked Harriet Monroe a month before "Dance Figure" was published: "Has our good nation read the Song of Songs?" (LETT, 17).

Pound also invoked the rites of his cult in satiric contexts in *Lustra*, making pagan vitality serve as a contrast to modern sterility and stodginess. In "Salutation the Second," for example, he instructs his songs to

> Dance and make people blush,
> Dance the dance of the phallus
>   and tell anecdotes of Cybele!
> Speak of the indecorous conduct of the gods!
>   (Tell it to Mr. Strachey)
>   (P, 86)

A typical anecdote of the indecorous conduct of Cybele—a fertility goddess—might be found in Catullus (LXIII). But not even a Catullus could make poetry of such stories, Pound implies, in the prudish society of pre-war London.* In "Tenzone" (P, 81), Pound pictures the public fleeing from his vigorous songs "as a timorous wench from a centaur. . . . Their virgin stupidity is untemptable."† In a *BLAST* poem entitled "Our Respectful Homages to M. Laurent Tailhade," Pound called for the erection of a phallic column and for a fertility dance to celebrate the contemporary French satirist whose work was an inspiration to his own satire:

> It is not fitting that we should praise him
> In the modest forms of the Madrigale or the Aubade.
> Let us stamp with our feet and clap hands
> In praise of Monsieur Laurent Tailhade,
> Whose "Poemes Aristophaniques" are
> So-very-odd.
> Let us erect a column and stamp with our feet
> And dance a Zarabondilla and a Kordax. . . .[7]

Pound associated both dances with "such fragments of the worship of Flora and Venus as survived in the spring merrymakings" in

---

* In a letter to his father, written two months after the poem appeared, Pound explained what John St. Loe Strachey typified for him: " 'Strachey' is actually the edtr. of *The Spectator*, but I use him as the type of male prude, somewhere between Tony Comstock and Hen. Van Dyke. Even in America we've nothing that conveys his exact shade of meaning. I've adopted the classic Latin manner in mentioning people by name" (LETT, 21).

† Here the image of poem-as-centaur has a precise significance. In "The Serious Artist" (1913), Pound said: "Poetry is a centaur. The thinking word-arranging, clarifying faculty must move and leap with the energizing, sentient, musical faculties" (LE, 52). The image resembles one later used by Yeats: "I thought that all art should be a centaur finding in the popular lore its back and strong legs" (*Autobiographies*, p. 191).

Provence (SR, 39). Finally, in "Tempora," he contrasted the
primitive worship of Tamuz (Adonis) and Pan to the modern
worship of literary success:

> Io! Io! Tamuz!
> The Dryad stands in my court-yard
> With plaintive, querulous crying.
> (Tamuz. Io! Tamuz!)
> Oh, no, she is not crying: "Tamuz."
> She says, "May my poems be printed this week?
> The god Pan is afraid to ask you,
> May my poems be printed this week?"
>
> (P, 110)

The lady poet of our time is a far cry from the dryads who sum-
moned Pan and Tamuz. In these "ritual" satires, then, the themes
of the *Lustra* lyrics are used as the poet's norm. As in *Hugh Selwyn
Mauberley*, Pound finds the age neither phallic nor ambrosial.

We can see from such poems why "the cult of beauty and the
delineation of ugliness are not in mutual opposition." We can see
that they are in fact complementary, two sides of a coin. Ugliness
in the *Lustra* satires is the negation of beauty, just as satire itself
is an assertion of positive desire "inversely, i.e. as of an opposite
hatred" (LE, 324). Instead of celebrating the life force through
fertility themes, the cult of ugliness reveals death in contemporary
life and letters. This death is both psychic (a spiritual or cultural
desiccation) and physical (an emotional and sexual impotence).
The characters satirized are incomplete, lacking the vital unity or
virtù of the Poundian goddess. The contrast is best seen in the
portraits of women in the two cults. Over against the "Gentildonna" and the "Dance Figure" stand the fragmented women whose
archetype is "Portrait d'une femme" in *Ripostes*. A typical example
is the woman in "Ortus":

> How have I laboured?
> How have I not laboured
> To bring her soul to birth,
> To give these elements a name and a centre!
> She is beautiful as the sunlight, and as fluid.

She has no name, and no place.
How have I laboured to bring her soul into separation;
To give her a name and her being!

Surely you are bound and entwined,
You are mingled with the elements unborn;
I have loved a stream and a shadow.

I beseech you enter your life.
I beseech you learn to say "I,"
When I question you;
For you are no part, but a whole,
No portion, but a being.

(P, 84)

The title of the poem, Pound explained, means " 'birth' or 'spring-ing out' same root in 'orient' " (LETT, 21). Here he attempts to give ontological birth to a woman who lives but does not exist. We recall an earlier definition: "The soul of each man is compounded of all the elements of the cosmos of souls, but in each soul there is some one element which predominates, which is in some peculiar and intense way the quality or *virtù* of the individual."[8] In "Ortus," he seeks that quality amid the chaos. The poem is the clearest and most philosophical statement of the problem which besets all the figures satirized in *Lustra*—they are portions and parts, rather than whole beings with spiritual and physical vitality.

The woman in "The Garden" is another case in point. She too lacks an organizing center: "Like a skein of loose silk blown against a wall / She walks by the railing of a path in Kensington Gardens" (P, 83). Spiritually she is fragmented and diseased: she "is dying piece-meal / of a sort of emotional anaemia." And sexually she is sterile: she is contrasted to the "filthy, sturdy, unkillable infants of the very poor" who will "inherit the earth." Pound's comment has a double meaning: "In her is the end of breeding." The pun on "breeding" epitomizes the inseparability of the psychic and the sexual in *Lustra*; they are aspects of the same thing, and the absence of one kind of vitality usually signifies the absence of the other.

Many of the *Lustra* epigrams, like many Latin epigrams, mock

sexual deficiency. In "Epitaph," Leucis intended a "Grand Passion"
but ended with a "willingness-to-oblige" (P, 99). The graying
"Agathas" has refused love until it is too late (P, 102); the original
title of the epigram was "Agathas intacta."[9] Arides (the arid) is
"bored . . . indifferent and discouraged," and goes to his doom with
an ugly wife (P, 100). The scrawny "Phyllidula" receives much
pleasure in love but gives little (P, 103). The gay Aurelia is married off to preserve the family position, and must suffer the "pal-
sied contact" of Phidippus—the legendary Phidippus having been,
ironically, a grandson of Hercules and a suitor of Helen (P, 111).
In "Simulacra" (meaning both "character sketches" and "appear-
ances, ghosts") two frustrated society ladies appear: a "horse-
faced lady of just the unmentionable age" who walks down a street
reciting Swinburne's erotic poems to herself, and a "really hand-
some young woman" who accosts the poet in the middle of Sack-
ville Street (P, 114). In "The Social Order," a government official
with a wife older than himself adopts "such a caressing air / When
he shakes hands with young ladies" (P, 115). Bastidides, in "The
Temperaments," talks of nothing but sex, but has to be "four times
cuckold" before his wife conceives twins. Yet the frenetic sexual
activity of the apparently "bloodless and sexless" Florialis is also
a sign of disorganization: "Nine adulteries, 12 liaisons, 64 fornica-
tions / and something approaching a rape" simply constitute a
different kind of chaos (P, 100).

In other epigrams, the focus is on emotional and spiritual sterility. "Les Millwin" share the emotional anemia of the woman in
"The Garden": they have "large and anemic eyes." Their psychic
fragmentation is symbolized by the image of their sickly "mauve
and greenish souls," completely detached from them and "lying
along the upper seats / Like so many unused boas" (P, 93). Likewise, the art students from the Slade are split apart, as they hold
up crossed arms in "great futuristic X's" which seem detached
from their bodies. In "Amities" the deficiencies of four "friends" are
presented: the first is "quite correct" and takes "no pleasure" in
anything at all; the second is "wholly parasitic"; the third has com-
pensated for his "obvious flaws" by discovering a moderate chop-
house; and the fourth is commemorated in a Latin epitaph as an

uncultivated man (*vir incultus*) whose dead face is now eaten by worms while the poet profanely rejoices in the company of a merry lady (P, 101).*

This personal confusion is reflected on the social level in "The Bellaires." This good family leads a totally chaotic life amid lawyers, counsels, judges, proctors, "wives, husbands, sisters and heterogeneous connections . . . Replevin, estoppel, espavin and what not" (P, 97–98). They move about from town to town in southern France, presumably to keep one step ahead of their many creditors. Their social fragmentation corresponds to the personal and ontological incoherence of the woman in "Ortus."

The cult of ugliness reaches its extreme in Pound's *BLAST* Satires. Here, as in the last part of "Amities," the poet dwells on images of death and decay to symbolize the spiritual blight of his enemies. In "Salutation the Third" the reviewers of the London *Times* are unfavorably commemorated:

> Let us deride the smugness of "The Times":
> GUFFAW!
> So much for the gagged reviewers,
> It will pay them when the worms are wriggling in their
> vitals;
> These are they who objected to newness,
> Here are their tombstones.
> They supported the gag and the ring:
> A little BLACK BOX contains them.
> So shall you be also,
> You slut-bellied obstructionist,
> You sworn foe to free speech and good letters,
> You fungus, you continuous gangrene.
>
> (P, 145)

And in "Momentum Aere" the moribund critics are presented even more drastically:

* "Amities" is, like "Au Jardin," an ironic treatment of a romantic theme from Yeats's *The Wind Among the Reeds*. Its epigraph is a half-line from Yeats's "The Lover Pleads with His Friend for Old Friends": "Be not unkind or proud, / But think about old friends the most." Pound thinks about them, but not kindly.

As for you, you will rot in the earth,
And it is doubtful if even your manure will be rich enough

To keep grass
Over your grave.

(P, 146)

The critics have *no* life—in mind or in body. The cult of ugliness
in *Lustra* is aptly summarized by the little envoi entitled "Coda,"
for it is essentially a cult of death-in-life:

O my songs,
Why do you look so eagerly and so curiously into people's
    faces,
Will you find your lost dead among them?

(P, 103)

Just as the cult of beauty looks forward to the fertility ritual in
Cantos 39 and 47, so the cult of ugliness looks forward to the
Hell Cantos and to Canto 7:

Thin husks I had known as men,
Dry casques of departed locusts
        speaking a shell of speech . . .
Propped between chairs and table . . .
Words like the locust-shells, moved by no inner being;
    A dryness calling for death;

II. DIMENSIONS OF TRADITION

Our passing references to Chinese sources, Shakespearean allusions, and Yeatsian epigraphs in the foregoing discussion suggest
that we must remain alert for Pound's manipulations of literary
tradition in *Lustra* as in all his poetry. We need especially to be
aware of the influence of Whitman, the use of allusions and epigraphs to provide contexts of satiric judgment, and the handling
of sources in ripostes and translations.

Pound's new style in *Lustra* was due in part to his reconciliation
with Whitman—or more accurately, to his giving freer rein to the
Whitman in himself. He had recognized (and suppressed) this
aspect of his poetic personality since 1909, the date of his essay on

"What I Feel About Walt Whitman." There he admitted: "The vital part of my message, taken from the sap and fibre of America, is the same as his. Mentaly, I am a Walt Whitman who has learned to wear a colar and a dress shirt (although at times inimical to both)."[10] The image was apt, for he distrusted Whitman's nakedness and considered him something of an artistic barbarian. "Now Whitman was not an artist," he declared in another mood, "you cannot call a man an artist, until he shows himself capable of reticence and restraint. . . ."[11] Pound's attitude toward Whitman was highly ambivalent.

The ambivalence is reflected in "A Pact," which registers Pound's reconciliation with Whitman in 1913, but adds an important qualification:

> I make a pact with you, Walt Whitman—
> I have detested you long enough.
> I come to you as a grown child
> Who has had a pig-headed father;
> I am old enough now to make friends.
> It was you that broke the new wood,
> Now is a time for carving.
> We have one sap and one root—
> Let there be commerce between us.
>
> (P, 89)

The qualification is the demand for greater conscious technique implied by "carving." Whitman broke the "new wood" of free verse, and Pound seeks to carve a finer product (with the chisel of absolute rhythm). Whitmanism is thus tempered with the ideal of "poetry-as-sculpture" which Pound took over from Gautier.

The result of this mixed acceptance was a curious hybrid form— the Whitmanian envoi. This form combined the democratic stance of Whitman with the artistic sophistication of the troubadours, the vagabondism of the American open road with the vagabondism of the Provençal byways, Whitman's democracy of the spirit with Daniel's aristocracy of craftsmanship. Pound raised the medieval envoi to a satiric form by infusing it with Whitman's scope and inclusiveness. In this form, the poet addresses his songs and books instead of speaking directly to his readers. He commiserates them

on the abuse they have received, or sends them forth to stir up
prudes and liberate the spiritually oppressed. The songs so addressed are delicate, light-footed, and impudent—a race of fauns
and cupids. *They* are naked rather than the poet.

In "Further Instructions" the songs are "insolent little beasts,
shameless, devoid of clothing" (P, 94). They are distinctively
urban; whereas Whitman could lean and loaf at his ease, observing
a blade of summer grass, Pound's songs "stand about in the streets"
and "loiter at the corners and bus-stops." Amusingly, Pound prom-
ises to conceal the nakedness of his latest song in a green Chinese
coat and "the scarlet silk trousers / From the statue of the infant
Christ in Santa Maria Novella" so that this newest of American
Adams may move in polite company. The metaphor reflects one attitude toward his own literary borrowings, and parallels his picture
of himself as a Whitman in collar and dress shirt.

"The Condolence" emphasizes the qualifications of Pound's
Whitmanism. Here the poet rejects the "asses" who praise his
songs, as they might praise Whitman's, simply for being "virile."
He distinguishes the delicate thoughts of his phantastikon from
this male stupidity, commiserating his song as follows:

> O my fellow sufferers, we went out under the trees,
> We were in especial bored with male stupidity.
> We went forth gathering delicate thoughts,
> Our *"fantastikon"* delighted to serve us.
> We were not exasperated with women,
>   for the female is ductile.
>
>   (P, 82)

The "ductile" female is the radiant woman whom Pound shaped
in *Canzoni*, and he by no means rejects the delicate thoughts of
that phantastikon. (In fact, "delicate" is used so often and so
loosely in *Lustra* that it becomes almost a catchword, as Richard
Aldington demonstrated in his excellent parodies.) *

When Pound addresses other people, rather than his "little
naked and impudent songs" (P, 85), it is often to declare a Whitmanian spiritual kinship with them. But it is an aristocratic kinship

---

* See the Appendix, pp. 197–199.

rather than Whitman's universal embrace, because Pound is nearly always addressing fellow artists. In "Dum Capitolium Scandet" he addresses his posterity in the manner of Whitman, but he means his literary descendants rather than Everyman:

> How many will come after me
>   singing as well as I sing, none better;
> Telling the heart of their truth
>   as I have taught them to tell it;
> Fruit of my seed,
>   O my unnameable children.
> Know then that I loved you from afore-time,
> Clear speakers, naked in the sun, untrammelled.
>
> (P, 96)

And in "The Rest," he addresses the same small audience of kindred souls (oppressed artists and lovers of beauty in America) whom he had addressed in "In Durance" (P, 92–93).

"Pax Saturni" and "Commission" are the envois bearing the greatest formal resemblance to Whitman's poetry. In the first, the poet sends his songs to flatter American vices; the flatteries are arranged in long Whitmanian catalogues, and punctuated by an ironic refrain.[12] In the second, the poet "commissions" his songs to liberate the spiritually oppressed. As C. B. Willard says: "In this poem Pound attempts to recapture not only Whitman's peculiar metric—initial repetition, balanced lines, the catalogue, loose cadence—but his very spirit and tone, his sympathy for the oppressed and suffering."[13] But there is a significant difference; Pound's catalogue involves not physical bondage and pain, but the subtler forms of spiritual tyranny. His songs are sent to speak against "unconscious oppression" and the "tyranny of the unimaginative," and to liberate "the women in suburbs," the "bought wife," and the "adolescent who are smothered in family" (P, 88–89). Again, it is Whitman refined.

The end of "Commission" relates the envoi to the "cults" of *Lustra*:

> Go out and defy opinion,
> Go against this vegetable bondage of the blood.
> Be against all sorts of mortmain.

Here the songs are instructed to bring life to all who suffer under
the "dead hand" of convention and conformity. In other words, the
naked and impudent songs of the Whitmanian envoi are personifi-
cations and emissaries of the vital forces celebrated in the lyrics
of the cult of beauty. This vitality drew Pound to Whitman, and
governed the metaphors he used in speaking of Whitman: "The
vital part of my message, taken from the sap and fibre of America,
is the same as his."

Pound adapted other sources to his own poetic program in
Lustra with equal skill. Many of his satires "place" their subjects
by means of literary allusions and epigraphs. They invoke a network of literary contexts and values against which their subjects
can be judged. The epigraph for "The Garden" is from the opening
line of Albert Samain's "L'Infante": "Mon âme est une infante en
robe de parade." Pound brings his anemic lady into sharper focus
by this reference to the elegant and narcissistic soul of Samain's
poem. In "Albatre" (P, 87) Pound's allusion to Gautier's "Sym-
phonie en blanc majeur" invokes a description of female beauty
which helps to reveal the inadequacies of the affected mistress. In
"Lesbia Illa" (P, 102–103) Pound ironically mourns the marriage
of the modern Lesbia in the same words Catullus used to mourn
the death of a sparrow: "Lugete, Veneres! Lugete, Cupidinesque!"
(See Catullus, III.) The "Shop Girl" (P, 112) is compared to
"Swinburne's women," "the harlots of Baudelaire," and the "shep-
herdess meeting with Guido" Cavalcanti in "In un boschetto trovai
pastorella," a delightful *pastourelle* which ends with the shepherd-
ess fairly flinging herself upon the knight. The epigraph to "The
Bellaires" (P, 97) consists of the opening lines of the thirty-ninth
song in Heine's *Lyrisches Intermezzo*: "Aus meinem grossen
Schmerzen / Mach' ich die kleinen Lieder." But Pound's sorrow is
feigned, and his poem is an implied criticism of both the stupidity
of the Bellaires and the excessive self-pity of Heine's lover. The
epigraph to "The Condolence" (P, 82) is from Lope de Vega;
Pound had translated it in *The Spirit of Romance* as the work of a
"true poet":

> To my solitudes I go,
> From my solitudes return I,

Sith for companions on the journey,
Mine own thoughts (do well) suffice me.

(SR, 208)

It reinforces Pound's contention in "The Condolence" that his songs are misunderstood. This way of "placing" the subject obviously results in various kinds of "criticism in new compositon."

Moreover, two of the *Lustra* poems—"The Lake Isle" and "To a Friend Writing on Cabaret Dancers"—are humorous ripostes to other poems. The former is an answer to Yeats's "The Lake Isle of Innisfree." Whereas Yeats longed for the idyllic isolation of a Thoreauvian cabin, Pound prays for a little tobacco shop in a low neighborhood, with "the whores dropping in for a word or two in passing, / For a flip word, and to tidy their hair a bit." And in stating his own motives, Pound implicitly criticizes the motives of "Innisfree" as escapist:

O God, O Venus, O Mercury, patron of thieves,
Lend me a little tobacco-shop,
             or install me in any profession
Save this damn'd profession of writing,
             Where one needs one's brains all the time.

(P, 117)

But the most elaborate riposte in *Lustra* is "Cabaret Dancers," which answers a sonnet called "The Cabaret Dancer" by Hermann Hagedorn (the anglicized "Hedgethorn" of Pound's first line). Hagedorn's poem appeared in *Poetry* for December 1915; Pound's refutation in *Lustra* (September 1916). The first line of Hagedorn's poem furnished Pound with a epigraph, and the rest of it inspired him with scorn:

Breathe not the word Tomorrow in her ears.
       Tomorrow is for men who send their ships
       Over the sea to moor at alien slips;
For dreamers, dawdlers, martyrs, pioneers,
Not for this golden mote. To her appears
       No hovering dark that prophesies eclipse.
       Grace of the swallow in the swaying hips,
Heart of the swallow, knowing not the years!

Breathe not a word of beauty that shall fade,
Of lagging steps, of bare and lonely sorrow
On roads that other dancing feet have found
Beyond the grove where life with laughter played.
Breathe not a word of that grim land Tomorrow,
Lest she should quake to ashes at the sound.

Pound apparently thought this poem not only ill-made, but positively obnoxious (and rightly so). His answer attempts to break down the pseudotragic and condescending sentimentality of Hagedorn's miserable effusion.

Pound points out that all the cabaret types—Pepita, Euhenia, the pianist, Old Popkoff (the proprietor?)—can look forward to comfortable and prosperous lives: "Good Hedgethorn, they all have futures, / All these people." The shrewd and avaricious Pepita will achieve in her middle age precisely the same bourgeois respectability that "Hedgethorn" himself now enjoys: "The prudent whore is not without her future, / Her bourgeois dulness is deferred" (P, 161–164). Pound summarized his rebuttal in a letter to Harriet Monroe:

What you object to in the "Cabaret" is merely that it isn't bundled up into slop, sugar and sentimentality, the underlying statement is very humane and most moral. It simply says there is a certain form of life, rather sordid, not gilded with tragedy any more than another, just as dull as another, and possibly quite as innocent and innocuous, vide, my singers in Venice. The thing the bourgeois will always hate is the fact that I make the people *real*. I treat the dancers as human beings, not as "symbols of sin." That is the crime and the "obscenity." (LETT, 82)

Pound criticizes not only Hagedorn's grasp of reality, but also his poetic originality. His allusion to Gautier's "Carmen" immediately sets Hagedorn's sonnet in perspective as a derivative and degenerate performance in a mode which Gautier perfected in the mid-nineteenth century:

"CARMEN EST MAIGRE, UN TRAIT DE BISTRE
CERNE SON OEIL DE GITANA"
And "rend la flamme",
    you know the deathless verses.

These lines were for Pound a prime example of the "presentative method" in poetry,[14] and in a letter to Iris Barry only two months before "To a Friend" appeared he placed Gautier in relation to English poetry:

Théophile Gautier is, I suppose, the next man [after Heine] who can write. Perfectly plain statements like his "Carmen est maigre" should teach one a number of things. His early poems are many of them no further advanced than the Nineties. Or to put it more fairly the English Nineties got about as far as Gautier had got in 1830, and before he wrote "L'Hippopotame." (LETT, 89)

All of which makes Hagedorn, writing in 1915 and still incapable of Gautier's objectivity, incredibly out of date.

But Pound's most dramatic use of traditional sources in *Lustra* is in his "translations." The editorial note which originally accompanied "Homage to Quintus Septimius Florentis Christianus" contained a significant declaration of independence: "Mr. Ezra Pound writes of his *Homage to Q.S.F. Christianus*, 'I am quite well aware that certain lines have no particular relation to the words or meaning of the original.' "* Pound was no longer justifying on textual grounds, as he did in his *Seafarer* note, the kind of translation he instinctively practiced. The Greek "Homage" provided a name and a statement of principle for the later, more significant Latin *Homage to Sextus Propertius*, but "Q.S.F. Christianus" was not the only *Lustra* poem to foreshadow the methods of *Propertius*.

"Papyrus," for instance, represents a significant transformation of its source:

> Spring. . . .
> Too long. . . .
> Gongula. . . .
>   (P, 112)

---

* "Notes," *Poetry*, VIII (September 1916), 329. The six epigrams and lyrics of "Christianus" (P, 164–165) are ostensibly translations from *The Greek Anthology*. But a glance at the originals reveals the liberties Pound took. His fifth epigram, for instance, is inspired by two epigrams of Palladas, yet does not actually translate their words. (See *The Greek Anthology*, ed. W. R. Paton, III, Book IX, Nos. 165 and 167.) Pound's second lyric comes from a longer poem by Anyte (III, Book IX, No. 144), and his fourth from Agathas Scholasticus (III, Book IX, No. 153).

As Achilles Fang has pointed out, "the poem itself may be technically considered as an attempted translation of three out of the extant sixteen lines of a seventh-century fragment of Sappho."[15] In
glancing over the text of this song to Gongyla of Colophon, Pound
was no doubt struck by the first three lines, in each of which only
one word survives. By making his poem out of these three lines
alone, Pound achieved an effect similar to that of a compressed
Imagist haiku. The little equation is part of the cult of beauty in
Lustra; as in "The Spring," the new season stirs unsatisfied desire.

In "Liu Ch'e," Pound worked from an earlier English translation
of the Chinese original. To contrast his translation with that of
Herbert Giles is to see what the Imagists were opposing in contemporary poetry, and how they attacked it:

Giles

The sound of rustling silk is stilled,
With dust the marble courtyard filled;
No footfalls echo on the floor,
Fallen leaves in heaps block up the door. . . .
For she, my pride, my lovely one, is lost,
And I am left, in hopeless anguish tossed.[16]

Pound

The rustling of the silk is discontinued,
Dust drifts over the court-yard.
There is no sound of foot-fall, and the leaves
Scurry into heaps and lie still,
And she the rejoicer of the heart is beneath them:

A wet leaf that clings to the threshold.

(P, 108)

With his unrhymed *vers libre*, Pound avoids the metrical monotony
of Giles's couplets; and with his concrete image of the wet leaf, he
gives a far more powerful equation for sorrow than Giles's rhetor-
ical inversion, "In hopeless anguish tossed." "Ibycus and Liu Ch'e
presented the Image," wrote Pound, and his translation highlights
it.[17]

In "Fan-Piece, for Her Imperial Lord," Pound again worked

from one of Giles's translations, and the result was even more
dramatic:

Giles

O fair white silk, fresh from the weaver's loom,
Clear as the frost, bright as the winter's snow—
See! friendship fashions out of thee a fan,
Round as the round moon shines in heaven above,
At home, abroad, a close companion thou,
Stirring at every move the grateful gale.
And yet I fear, ah me! that autumn chills,
Cooling the dying summer's torrid rage,
Will see thee laid neglected on the shelf,
All thoughts of bygone days, like them bygone.[18]

Pound

O fan of white silk,
    clear as frost on the grass-blade,
You also are laid aside.

(P, 108)

The principles of Imagist economy enable Pound to achieve this
astonishing condensation, in which nothing essential is omitted
from the original.

Pound took similar liberties to achieve greater economy and
more vivid imagistic presentation in his "Impressions of François-
Marie Arouet (De Voltaire)." His second "Impression," for instance, is a substantial rewriting of Voltaire's "Stances VIII. À Madame du Chatelet" (1741), as we may see from a brief comparison
of their respective openings:

Voltaire

Si vous voulez que j'aime encore,
Rendez-moi l'age des amours;
Au crepescule de mes jours
Rejoignez, s'il se peut, l'aurore.

Des beaux lieux ou le dieu du vin
Avec l'Amour tient son empire,

Le Temps, qui me prend par la main,
M'avertit que je me retire.[19]

>   Pound

If you'd have me go on loving you
Give me back the time of the thing.

Will you give me dawn light at evening?
Time has driven me out from the fine plaisaunces,
The parks with the swards all over dew,
And grass going glassy with the light on it,
The green stretches where love is and the grapes
Hang in yellow-white and dark clusters ready for pressing.

>   (P, 167)

Pound reduces Voltaire's first quatrain to three lines, expands the
second to five, and adds a great deal of imagery not in the original.
He visualizes the "beaux lieux" in concrete images of dew, grass,
and light; and the "dieu du vin" in images of colorful clusters of
grapes. Instead of Voltaire's measured quatrains, he employs free
verse in irregular strophes.

Even more drastic alterations lie behind the third of Pound's
"Impressions." "To Madame Lullin" exemplifies the Poundian principle that "Dichten=condensare." He has condensed Voltaire's
"Stances XLI, À Madame Lullin, De Genève," thirty-six lines in all,
into a new poem of eight lines:

Voltaire	Pound
Hé quoi! vous etes étonnée	You'll wonder that an old
Qu'au bout de quatre-vingts hivers	man of eighty
Ma muse faible et surannée	Can go on writing you
Puisse encore fredonner des vers?	verses. . . .
Quelquefois un peu de verdure	Grass showing under the
Rit sous les glacons de nos champs;	snow,
Elle console la nature,	
Mais elle seche un peu de temps.	
Un oiseau peut se faire entendre	Birds singing late in
Apres la saison des beaux jours;	the year!

Mais sa voix n'a plus rien de tendre,
Il ne chante plus ses amours.

Ainsi je touche encor ma lyre,
Qui n'obéit plus a mes doigts;
Ainsi j'essaie encor ma voix
Au moment meme qu'elle expire.

"Je veux, dans mes derniers adieux,"   And Tibullus could say of
Disait Tibulle à son amante,   his death, in his Latin:
"Attacher mes yeux sur tes yeux,   "Delia, I would look on
Te presser de ma main mourante."   you, dying."

Mais quand on sent qu'on va passer,
Quand l'ame fuit avec la vie,
A-t-on des yeux pour voir Délie,
Et des mains pour la caresser?

Dans ce moment chacun oublie
Tout ce qu'il a fait en santé.
Quel mortel s'est jamais flatté
D'un rendez-vous à l'agonie?

Délie elle-meme à son tour   And Delia herself fading
S'en va dans la nuit éternelle,   out,
En oubliant qu'elle fut belle,   Forgetting even her beauty.
Et qu'elle a vécu pour l'amour.   (P, 168)

Nous naissons, nous vivons, bergere,
Nous mourons, sans savoir comment;
Chacun est parti du neant:
Ou va-t-il? . . . Dieu le sait, ma chere.[20]

Clearly the title, "Impressions of . . . Voltaire," means Pound's impressions of the original French poems, the Imagist works he was
left with after long pondering and distilling. This kind of "translation" in *Lustra* was preparatory exercise for the masterful *Homage
to Sextus Propertius* (1917).

III. CONTINUITIES IN *Cathay*

The most important translations in *Lustra* are of course in *Cathay*.
A. C. Graham, in the introduction to his own volume of Chinese

translations, indicates the historical significance of *Cathay*: "The art of translating Chinese poetry is a by-product of the Imagist movement, first exhibited in Ezra Pound's *Cathay* (1915), Arthur Waley's *One Hundred and Seventy Chinese Poems* (1918), and Amy Lowell's *Fir Flower Tablets* (1921)."[21] *Cathay* initiated a vogue of Chinese translations which did not diminish until the 1930s. When T. S. Eliot called Pound "the inventor of Chinese poetry for our time," he meant more than simply the earliest in a series, but his statement was also chronologically accurate.[22]

In *Cathay* Pound worked from the posthumous papers of Ernest Fenollosa. Two recent articles by Hugh Kenner provide the most reliable information available at the time of this writing as to Pound's acquisition of the Fenollosa papers, the details of their contents, and the working principles of Pound's translations.* The facts may be briefly summarized as follows: sometime between April and December of 1913, Pound received from Mrs. Mary Fenollosa, in several installments, some sixteen notebooks containing the fruits of Fenollosa's study of the Japanese Noh drama and Chinese poetry. He went to work initially on the plays, publishing his first translation (*Nishikigi*) in *Poetry* for May 1914. Late in 1914 he turned his attention to the poems, and in the following year published all but four of the translations now included under the title, *Cathay*. (The others were added in *Lustra*, 1916.) Kenner describes the notebook containing the poems in this way: "The Fenollosa notes consisted of brushed ideograms, Japanese sounds for these, one- or two-word literal equivalents, and a running crib, hastily scribbled by Fenollosa as a mnemonic of syntax. Any of these components might be lacking; thus 'The Beautiful Toilet' has no running crib, and 'To-Em-Mei's The Unmoving Cloud' no ideo-

---

* Hugh Kenner, "Ezra Pound and the Chinese," *Agenda*, IV (October–November 1965), 38–41, and "The Invention of China," *Spectrum*, IX (Spring, 1967), 21–52. A fair number of the Fenollosa-notebook originals have now been published, here and there, in whole or in part. In the second of the articles just mentioned, Kenner gives extensive versions of the notes for "The Beautiful Toilet," "South-Folk in Cold Country," and "To-Em-Mei's 'The Unmoving Cloud,'" as well as selections from the notes for many others. A fuller version of the notes for "The Beautiful Toilet" appears in *Ezra Pound: Perspectives*, ed. Noel Stock, pp. 178–179, and Lawrence W. Chisholm, in *Fenollosa: The Far East and American Culture* (New Haven, 1963), pp. 251–252, gives the notes for "Song of the Bowmen of Shu."

grams." In the longer of his two articles, "The Invention of China," Kenner discusses in some detail the local problems of translation posed by these sketchy notes, and persuasively defends the solutions Pound adopted. Not knowing Chinese at all, dependent on imperfect English versions, Pound still managed to bring the original poems to life in vigorous and radically original English verse.

Of the finished translations we can speak more confidently, especially if we view them in the context of Pound's other work. In many ways, *Cathay* fits into the pattern of his poetic development and critical preferences. Donald Davie argues persuasively, for instance, that the translations represent a natural stage in Pound's evolution toward the radical metrical innovation of *The Cantos*: "To break the pentameter."[23] But this is not the only kind of continuity in *Cathay*; Pound himself has pointed out others in a little-known essay called "Chinese Poetry" (1918).[24]

The opening lines of this essay show that Pound saw a harmony between Chinese poetry and the principles of Imagism: "It is because Chinese poetry has certain qualities of vivid presentation; and because certain Chinese poets have been content to set forth their matter without moralizing and without comment that one labours to make a translation. . . ." Pound's account of Rihaku (or Li Po, the Chinese poet whose works form a majority of Pound's translations) sees his achievement in terms of Poundian excernment and "criticism in new composition":

He was the head of the court office of poetry, and a great "compiler." But this last title must not mislead you. In China a "compiler" is a very different person from a commentator. A compiler does not merely gather together, his chief honour consists in weeding out, and even in revising.

Thus, a part of Rihaku's work consists of old themes rewritten, of a sort of summary of the poetry which had been before him. . . .

Again Pound is drawing upon the poetry of the past to put across his own program and standards for the present. He tends always to regard the principles and practice of the best poets as similar and universal.

Pound goes on in his article to point out five qualities of Chinese poetry. Not surprisingly, all five are continuous with his own previous poetic interests. First, he illustrates the obscurity of which Chinese poetry is capable, using his *Cathay* translation of "The Jewel

Stairs' Grievance" and a prose gloss similar to his *Cathay* note (P, 132). He relates "these short, obscure poems" in Chinese to the trobar clus tradition of Provençal and Tuscan poetry: "The first great distinction between Chinese taste and our own is that the Chinese *like* poetry that they have to think about, and even poetry that they have to puzzle over. This latter taste has occasionally broken out in Europe, notably in twelfth-century Provence and thirteenth-century Tuscany, but it has never held its own for very long."

By way of contrast, Pound then illustrates the extreme clarity and simplicity of which Chinese poetry is also capable. His examples are "South-Folk in Cold Country" (P, 139), "Song of the Bowmen of Shu" (P, 127), and "Lament of the Frontier Guard" (P, 133). In these war poems, "we find a directness and realism such as we find only in early Saxon verse and in the Poema del Cid, and in Homer, or rather in what Homer would be if he wrote without epithet. . . . There you have no mellifluous circumlocution, no sentimentalizing of men who have never seen a battle-field and who wouldn't fight if they had to. You have war, campaigning as it has always been, tragedy, hardship, no illusions." If Chinese obscurity is related to the trobar clus tradition of *Canzoni*, Chinese simplicity is related to the straightforward realism of *The Seafarer* and *The Odyssey*.

Mysticism is the third quality of Chinese poetry singled out by Pound. The poems and Japanese Noh plays studied by Fenollosa contained spirits which Pound related to the Celtic twilight of Yeats and Fiona MacLeod:

. . . Chinese poetry is full of fairies and fairy lore. Their lore is "quite Celtic." I found one tale in a Japanese play; two ghosts come to a priest to be married, or rather he makes a pilgrimage to their tomb and they meet him there. [Clearly Pound is referring to *Nishikigi*.] The tale was new to me, but I found that Mr. Yeats had come upon a similar story among the people of Aran. The desire to be taken away by the fairies, the idea of souls flying with the sea-birds, and many other things recently made familiar to us by the Celtic school, crop up in one's Chinese reading. . . .

Pound does not illustrate this "lore" in his essay, but one of his *Cathay* translations—"Sennin Poem by Kakuhaku"—provides an example (P, 139–140). Pound called a "sennin" an "air spirit," and related it to the Celtic "Sidhe" (as they appear, for example, in Yeats's "The Hosting of the Sidhe"): "Sennin are the Chinese spirits of nature or of the air. I don't see that they are any worse than Celtic Sidhe" (LETT, 180). Yeats explained the Sidhe as follows: "The gods of ancient Ireland . . . or the Sidhe . . . the people of the Faery Hills, still ride the country as of old. Sidhe is also Gaelic for wind, and certainly the Sidhe have much to do with the wind. They journey in whirling wind. . . ."[25] These Chinese air spirits and "souls flying with the sea-birds" were no doubt related in Pound's mind to the Celtic imagery of disembodied souls and magical winds upon which he had drawn so heavily in A Lume Spento.

The fourth quality of Chinese poetry is the "human." Pound's example is "The River-Merchant's Wife: A Letter," which he relates to the European tradition of heroic epistle and dramatic monologue:

If the reader detests fairies and prefers human poetry, then that also can be found in Chinese. Perhaps the most interesting form of modern poetry is to be found in Browning's "Men and Women." This kind of poem, which reaches its climax in his unreadable "Sordello," and is most popular in such poems as "Pictor Ignotus," or the "Epistle of Karshish," or "Cleon," has had a curious history in the west. You may say it begins in Ovid's "Heroides," which purport to be letters written between Helen and Paris or by Œnone and other distinguished persons of classical pseudo-history; or you may find an earlier example of Theocritus' Idyl of the woman spinning at her sombre and magic wheel. From Ovid to Browning this sort of poem was very much neglected. It is interesting to find, in eighth-century China, a poem which might have been slipped into Browning's work without causing any surprise save by its simplicity and its naive beauty. [Pound then quotes "The River-Merchant's Wife."]

Pound must have experienced the shock of recognition when he found among Fenollosa's papers a poem so similar to his own "western" personae.

The last quality to which Pound calls attention is the use of nature in Chinese poetry: "Especially in their poems of nature and of scenery they seem to excel western writers, both when they speak of their sympathy with the emotions of nature and when they describe natural things." The Chinese convention of associating human emotions with a natural setting happens to resemble a similar convention of Provençal poetry which Pound had earlier praised: "in most Provencal poetry one finds nature in its proper place, i.e. as a background to the action, an interpretation of the mood; an equation, in other terms, or a 'metaphor by sympathy' for the mood of the poem" (SR, 31). In the poems he translated for *Cathay*, Pound found an abundance of "metaphor by sympathy":

> By the North Gate, the wind blows full of sand,
> Lonely from the beginning of time until now!
> $\qquad\qquad$ (P, 133)

> The leaves fall early this autumn, in wind.
> The paired butterflies are already yellow with August
> Over the grass in the west garden;
> They hurt me. I grow older.
> $\qquad\qquad$ (P, 131)

> The clouds have gathered, and gathered,
> $\qquad$ and the rain falls and falls,
> The eight ply of the heavens
> $\qquad$ are all folded into one darkness,
> And the wide, flat road stretches out.
> I stop in my room toward the East, quiet, quiet.
> $\qquad\qquad$ (P, 142)

> And if you ask how I regret that parting:
> It is like the flowers falling at Spring's end
> $\qquad$ Confused, whirled in a tangle.
> $\qquad\qquad$ (P, 136)

> Here we must make separation
> And go out through a thousand miles of dead grass.
> $\qquad\qquad$ (P, 137)

The Chinese use of nature coincided with Pound's own theory of the Image as an equation for moods.

The aspects of Chinese poetry treated in Pound's essay, then, all represent extensions of his earlier poetic interests. All are related, in his mind, to specific European traditions which he had previously discussed and used in his own poetry. Rihaku is like Browning (or Pound), sennin are like Sidhe, Chinese love poetry is like the trobar clus, Chinese war poetry is like *The Seafarer* or like Homer. Pound is determined always to deal with world literature as a single body of material with certain artistic and spiritual unities which transcend differences in time or place of origin.

IV. NOTES TOWARD *The Cantos:* VERSIONS OF PROVENCE

Pound's preoccupation with Imagism and Vorticism did not mean that he had abandoned his earlier interest in Provence and the poetic recreation of history. He carried on the experiments in reconciling Truth and Calliope which had begun with poems like "Marvoil," "Piere Vidal Old," and "Sestina: Altaforte." On the third of June 1913, in the midst of his Imagist activities, he wrote to his father that he was "doing a tale of Bertrans de Born" (LETT, 21). This is the earliest mention of "Near Perigord," which finally appeared in *Poetry* for December 1915. Between these dates, he published a translation of De Born's "Dompna pois de me no'us cal" (March 1914), and "Provincia Deserta" (March 1915). This continued concern with Provence and its history is also seen in the early versions of Cantos 1–3, which Pound probably began in 1915.[26] If "an epic is a poem including history" (LE, 86), these versions of Provence should be regarded as notes toward *The Cantos*.

"Provincia Deserta" attempts to recreate history through a traditional technique of English meditative poetry.* Its structure closely corresponds to the structure of what M. H. Abrams has called the "Greater Romantic Lyric." Abrams applies the term to Romantic descriptive-meditative poems such as "Tintern Abbey" and Coleridge's "conversation poems." But his account of their format can be used to analyze "Provincia Deserta" as well:

---

* The title has several meanings. *Provincia* is the Latin for "province," but was used especially for Provence, the first Roman province in Gaul. *Deserta* may mean either "deserts" or "deserted." The second meaning is more relevant to the poem, but the first recalls Charles Doughty's *Travels in Arabia Deserta* (1888). Pound praised Doughty's book in "Section XI–48. Arabia Deserta" of *Guide to Kulchur*, and may have intended his title to echo Doughty's.

They present a determinate speaker in a particularized, and usually a localized, outdoor setting. . . . The speaker begins with a description of the landscape; an aspect or change of aspect in the scene evokes a varied but integral process of memory, thought, anticipation and feeling which remains closely intervolved with the outer scene. In the course of this meditation, the lyric speaker achieves an insight, faces up to a tragic loss, comes to a moral decision, or resolves an emotional problem. Often the poem rounds upon itself to end where it began, at the outer scene, but with altered mood and deeper understanding which is the result of the intervening meditation.[27]

The main difference is that in Pound's poem the heart of the meditation is not personal insight or resolution but the imaginative penetration and recreation of history. At the center of "Provincia Deserta" stands the living legend of Piere de Maensac, the historical revelation rather than the psychological.

The five-part structure of the poem may be examined in these terms. The first section (from "At Rochecoart" to "Glad to lend one dry clothing") presents a "determinate speaker in a particularized . . . outdoor setting"—Pound himself in modern Provence on a walking tour. He "begins with a description of the landscape"—the scenery of Rochecoart and Chalais. He describes the geography and inhabitants of the region: the various hills, roads, rivers, and arbors; and the charity of the people toward their aged and toward a rain-soaked American traveler. The setting is quotidien, and the language is literal.

The second section (from "I have walked / into Perigord" to "Excideuil, carefully fashioned") begins the dissolution of the present into the past. Bright daylight gives way to "the dark" and "torch-flames." Literal language gives way to metaphor, myth, and art in the torch flames "high-leaping, / Painting the front of that church," and the anthropomorphic "whirling laughter" of the stream. Sonorous place names are used as incantation to summon the past, and the diction itself regresses from the slangy ("old layout") to the formulaic ("carefully fashioned"):

> I have walked
> > into Perigord,
> I have seen the torch-flames, high-leaping,
> Painting the front of that church;

> Heard, under the dark, whirling laughter.
> I have looked back over the stream
>   and seen the high building,
> Seen the long minarets, the white shafts.
> I have gone in Ribeyrac
>   and in Sarlat,
> I have climbed rickety stairs, heard talk of Croy,
> Walked over En Bertran's old layout,
> Have seen Narbonne, and Cahors and Chalus,
> Have seen Excideuil, carefully fashioned.
>   (P, 121–22)

The third section (from "I have said" to "I have said: / 'Riquier! Guido'") marks the resurrection of the first ghosts: "Here Coeur-de-Lion was slain. / Here was good singing." It also marks that "change of aspect in the scene" which accompanies the deepening of meditation in the Greater Romantic Lyric. The sunset drops a magical atmosphere over the landscape, causing images to become extraordinarily clear and precise, and tinging the mountains with Wordsworthian colors of the imagination:

> I have lain in Rocafixada,
>   level with sunset,
> Have seen the copper come down
>   tingeing the mountains,
> I have seen the fields, pale, clear as an emerald,
> Sharp peaks, high spurs, distant castles.

This section ends with a powerful cry, a final incantation which successfully evokes the past.

The fourth part of the poem (from "I have thought of the second Troy" to "So ends that story") is the heart of the meditation. The present disappears entirely, and so does the narrator (the word "I" does not occur in this section after the first line). The past occupies the stage, and the amazing tale of Piere de Maensac lives again:

> I have thought of the second Troy,
> Some little prized place in Auvergnat:
> Two men tossing a coin, one keeping a castle,

One set on the highway to sing.
        He sang a woman.
Auvergne rose to the song;
        The Dauphin backed him.
"The castle to Austors!"
        "Pieire kept the singing—
"A fair man and a pleasant."
        He won the lady,
Stole her away for himself, kept her against armed force:
So ends that story.

Pound gives an elliptical summary of the *vida* of the troubadour,
presenting (as in "Marvoil") a few highly selective details and
tableaux.*

In the last section Pound's poem "rounds upon itself," in Abrams'
terms, "to end where it began, at the outer scene, but with altered
mood and deeper understanding." We have returned to the opening scene; the setting is again the roads of modern Provence, and
the poet again speaks in the first person:

That age is gone;
Pieire de Maensac is gone.
I have walked over these roads;
I have thought of them living.

The intervening drama has enriched and validated the claim of the

---

* In "Troubadours—Their Sorts and Conditions" (1913), Pound gave a
prose summary. He called the *vida* "an epic" in the chronicler's "straightforward prose," and related it to the legend of Helen and Paris (a connection glanced at in "Provincia Deserta" and exploited more fully in Cantos 5
and 23): " 'Piere de Maensac was of Alverne (Auvergne) a poor knight, and
he had a brother named Austors de Maensac, and they both were troubadours
and they both were in concord that one should take the castle and the other
the *trobar*.' And presumably they tossed up a *marabotin* or some such obso-
lete coin, for we read, 'And the castle went to Austors and the poetry to
Piere, and he sang of the wife of Bernart de Tierci. So much he sang of her
and so much he honoured her that it befell that the lady let herself go gay
(*furar a del*). And he took her to the castle of the Dalfin of Auvergne, and
the husband, in the manner of the golden Menelaus, demanded her much,
with the church to back him and with the great war that they made. But
the Dalfin maintained him (Piere) so that he never gave her up. He (Piere)
was a straight man (*dreitz om*) and good company, and he made charming
songs, tunes and words, and good coblas of pleasure' " (LE, 96–97).

last line. "Provincia Deserta" is the creative meditation of a passionate historian.

Having tried this method, however, Pound apparently decided
it was not suited for his epic. There he tends to dispense with the
elaborate autobiographical guidelines which lead to the vision of
the historical moment, and to present only the essential synopsis.
His versions of the De Maensac legend in Cantos 5 and 23, for example, are similar to the central passage of "Provincia Deserta,"
but lack the meditative framework:

> And Pieire won the singing, Pieire de Maensac,
> Song or land on the throw, and was *dreitz hom*
> And had De Tierci's wife and with the war they made:
> > Troy in Auvergnat
> While Menelaus piled up the church at port
> He kept Tyndarida. Dauphin stood with de Maensac.
>
> > > > (Canto 5)

> And my brother De Maensac
> Bet with me for the castle,
> And we put it on the toss of a coin,
> And I, Austors, won the coin-toss and kept it,
> And he went out to Tierci, a jongleur
> And on the road for his living,
> And twice he went down to Tierci,
> And took off the girl there that was just married to Bernart.
>
> And went to Auvergne, to the Dauphin,
> And Tierci came with a posse to Auvergnat,
> And went back for an army
> And came to Auvergne with the army
> But never got Pierre nor the woman.
>
> > > > (Canto 23)

In the context of *The Cantos*, these passages are integrated principally by the parallels between Auvergne and Troy (the De
Maensac legend in Canto 23 is immediately followed by a passage
on Anchises and the fall of Troy). In other words, Pound relies
more on the implied parallelism of his tales than on their medi-

tative gestation in his own mind. *The Cantos* are gists and piths of many poems like "Provincia Deserta."

The next step in Pound's search for a poetic form that could include history is "Near Perigord." Here the search leads him to the question Browning asked in *The Ring and the Book*: can we ever ascertain the "historical truth" about past events? Pound's particular riddle is whether Bertran de Born's poem, "Dompna pois de me no'us cal," was a love song or an instrument of policy dictated by the strategic necessities of De Born's political position. The question arose in Pound's mind from his personal experience of the region:

The historical data for this poem are, first, Uc de St. Circ's statement [in De Born's *vida*] that Bertran de Born was in love with the Lady Maent, wife of Sir Tairiran of Montaignac, and that when she turned him out he wrote a canzon, *Domna pois de me no'us cal.* . . . Second, as to the possibility of a political intrigue behind the apparent love poem, we have no evidence save that offered by my own observation of the geography of Perigord and Limoges. I must leave the philologists and professional tacticians to decide whether Bertrans's proclivities for stirring up the barons were due to his liver or to "military necessity."[28]

The poem may have been conceived at the moment—recorded in "Provincia Deserta"—when Pound "looked south from Hautefort, / thinking of Montaignac, southward."*

Pound borrowed the poetic form that Browning had used to explore Pompilia's murder—the use of multiple viewpoints. Thomas Connolly summarizes the structure of "Near Perigord" as follows:

Pound divides his poem into three parts and, using a technique reminiscent of Browning's *The Ring and the Book*, examines first the historical facts of the case. Then, discarding history, he lets his imagination play about the character of Bertran and tries to recreate the personality of the man in a fictional passage that ends

---

* Pound recommended walking tours like the one commemorated in "Provincia Deserta" to anyone who wishes "emotional, as well as intellectual, acquaintance" with the twelfth century: "Or, again, a man may walk the hill roads and river roads from Limoges and Charente to Dordogne and Narbonne and learn a little, or more than a little, of what the country meant to the wandering singers, he may learn, or think he learns, why so many canzos open with speech of the weather; or why such a man made war on such and such castles" (LE, 95).

with a debate between two of his contemporaries. Finally, he abandons both unsuccessful methods and attempts a dramatic presentation from the point of view not of Bertran, nor of his male companions, nor of the poet, but of the lady to whom Bertran addressed his poem.[29]

None of these approaches is able to reveal with certainty whether De Born's motive was love, intrigue, or a mixture of both; the historical inquiry is baffled.

But the poet is not therefore silenced. According to Hugh Kenner's persuasive interpretation, he is able to fall back on the irreducible verities of the artistic imagination by paraphrasing Dante's description of De Born in the *Inferno* (XXVIII). "This, not anything recoverable from documents or from the testimony of any acquaintance however intimate, is the image of Bertrans de Born that has persisted for six hundred years. It does not directly assist our present enquiries, but it is unchallengeably real. The one reality that no discussion shakes is evinced by art." The image from Dante "catalyzes" the poem, which moves immediately to a comparable "image of Maent herself" in the third section:

> She who could never live save through one person,
> She who could never speak save to one person,
> And all the rest of her a shifting change,
> A broken bundle of mirrors. . . !
>
> (P, 157)

This forces us, Kenner argues, to look at Bertran's canzone primarily as a work of art rather than a document: "Maent herself, like the lady in the canzone, *was* a collection of fragments. Perhaps it was a love-poem. Perhaps it sang of war. . . . But preeminently, it was imitation in the Aristotelian sense: an arrangement of words and images corresponding to the mode of being possessed by the subject."[30]

Except for the emphasis on Aristotelian imitation, this reading is compelling. But the canzone is imitation only if Maent "*was*" what Pound has made her in this third section. In fact we do not know what she *was*, any more than we know what De Born *was*. Our conception of her is governed by the De Born/Pound image of her, just as as our conception of De Born is governed by the

Dante/Pound image of him. The poet's or the historian's image does not "correspond" to her mode of being; it *is* her mode of being as far as we are concerned. The past lives in images held in the living minds of the present. As Pound puts it in Canto 74:

> and that certain images be formed in the mind
> > to remain there
> > > > > > *formato locho*
> > Arachne mi porta fortuna
> to remain there, resurgent ΕΙΚΟΝΕΣ

In the third section of "Near Perigord," Pound realizes that he already possesses, in his own art and in that of De Born and Dante, the phantom he has been pursuing.

In his first version of Canto 1 (1917), Pound wrestled with the same problem and came to the same conclusions. Still searching for an epic form, he experiments here with yet another model—Browning's *Sordello*. *Sordello* was a good form because "the modern world / Needs such a rag-bag to stuff all its thought in." But Browning had already used it ("Hang it all, there can be but one *Sordello*"), so it was incumbent upon Pound to find a new one:

> So you worked out new form, the meditative,
> Semi-dramatic, semi-epic story,
> And we will say: What's left for me to do?
> Whom shall I conjure up; who's my Sordello,
> My pre-Daun Chaucer, pre-Boccaccio,
> > > As you have done pre-Dante?
> Whom shall I hang my shimmering garment on;
> Who wear my feathery mantle, *hagoromo*;
> Whom set to dazzle the serious future ages?
> Not Arnaut, not DeBorn, not Uc St. Circ who has writ out
> > the stories.[31]

As John L. Foster notes, "these cantos are a colloquy with Browning in which Pound seeks illumination concerning two problems: the form his own work is to take, coming as it does after Browning's *Sordello*, and the possibility of recovering the living essence of the past—of reviving it, truly making it new, and using it as a valid standard by which to judge the present."[32]

Pound had confronted both problems in "Near Perigord," and the result of that experiment (as well as his troubadour personae) convinced him that his epic hero could not be "Arnaut, not De Born, not Uc St. Circ who has writ out the stories." In other words, no new version of Provence could provide a satisfactory *mythos* for *The Cantos*. Pound had discovered that he could not really penetrate the life even of a figure (such as Cavalcanti) whom he knows well:

> What have I of this life,
> > Or even of Guido?
> > Sweet lie!—Was I there truly?
> Did I knew [sic] Or San Michele?
> > Let's believe it.
> Believe the tomb he leapt in was Julia Laeta's?
> Friend, I do not even—when he led that street charge—
> I do not even know which sword he'd with him.
> Sweet lie, "I lived!" Sweet lie, "I lived beside him."
> And now it's all but truth and memory,
> Dimmed only by the attritions of long time.

Rather he must fall back on his imaginative conceptions, the images of his own phantastikon.

The closing passage of Canto 1 asserts the power of the phantastikon to create "new form" and out of that form to create "new worlds" which transcend the actual worlds of history:

> "But we forget not."
> > No, take it all for lies.
> I have but smelt this life, a whiff of it.
> The box of scented wood
> Recalls cathedrals. And shall I claim;
> Confuse my own phantastikon,
> Or say the filmy shell that circumscribes me
> Contains the actual sun;
> > confuse the thing I see
> With actual gods behind me?
> > Are they gods behind me?
> How many worlds we have! If Botticelli

Brings her ashore on that great cockle-shell—
His Venus (Simonetta?),
And Spring and Aufidus fill all the air
With their clear-outlined blossoms?
World enough. Behold, I say, she comes
"Apparelled like the spring, Graces her subjects,"
(That's from *Pericles*).
Oh, we have worlds enough and brave *décors*,
And from these like we guess a soul for man
And build him full of aery populations.
Mantegna a sterner line, and the new world about us:
Barred lights, great flares, new form, Picasso or Lewis.
If for a year man write to paint, and not to music—
O Casella!

The artist should not confuse his own phantastikon with actuality, but he can trust it to create new worlds of another order. Three new worlds from painting illustrate the argument—Botticelli's Venus possesses the imagination so strongly that she seems to reappear in a passage of Shakespeare's *Pericles*; the historical question of whether she was modeled on Simonetta is irrelevant to her compelling power as an image.

It was as a result of this argument that Pound settled on Odysseus for his epic hero. In the first version of Cantos 1–3, Odysseus' voyage comes in the last part of Canto 3. But it had to be relocated at the beginning, because Pound could not "hang his shimmering garment on" any of the historical figures who were to be his minor heroes. The historical figures must remain subject to the imaginative metamorphoses of the poet's phantastikon. They must merge with and emerge from the protean archetype of a mythical hero, in the treatment of whom Pound is not bound down to impossible problems of historical reconstruction. The "new world" of *The Cantos* must be flexible enough to include "many worlds and brave *décors*." Pound now faced the task of carrying into practice the lessons he had learned from his versions of Provence. He had to find a way of structuring a complex and substantial modern poem around the myth of Odysseus. He found it when he read Joyce's *Ulysses* and wrote *Hugh Selwyn Mauberley*.

CHAPTER 8

Hugh Selwyn Mauberley as Bhlooming Ulysses

*Ils n'existent pas, leur ambience leur confert
une existence*
(ABC OF READING AND CANTO 77)

Hugh Selwyn Mauberley is Pound's summary farewell to London. It recapitulates many aspects of his earlier poetry, and establishes some basic techniques for *The Cantos*. Its publication in 1920 marked not only the end of Pound's London career, but also a major turning point in his poetic development.

In *Mauberley*, Pound examines the pernicious effects of modern civilization by focusing on the careers of a series of minor artists. As in many of his earlier poems, he takes the *vida* of the secondary artist to be a valid index of the general culture of his society. Nearly all of the modern artists in *Mauberley* fall short of greatness for two reasons: their "age" and their own inherent weaknesses and limitations. In a society that cared for good art, the *scriptor* or *pictor ignotus* might survive his shortcomings to contribute something of value, might become a Waller or a Luini. But in a society hostile to good art, the Mauberleys are doomed to struggle against their own incapacities *and* against public scorn. For such artists, Pound had an apt quotation: *"Ils n'existent pas, leur ambience leur confert une existence."*

The *ambience*, however, is not wholly to blame if its minor artists fail to exist. Pound is also concerned to diagnose the spiritual collapse of the artists themselves. He does not let his sympathy for their cause prevent him from making an objective and unsentimental analysis of the flaws in their will and their aesthetic views.

Satire is "the art of diagnosis" in literature—"surgery, insertions and amputations" (LE, 45)—and Pound's individual sketches involve both satire and dispassionate clinical observation. But the diagnosis is made for the sake of ultimate cure. *Hugh Selwyn Mauberley* is an elaborate autopsy which points the dangers of being an impressionist and aesthete in this "age," and reveals the need for a conception of tradition and artistic creation more vigorous than Mauberley's.

The structure of the poem corresponds to the complexity of its report. Part I prepares us for the account of Mauberley in Part II by presenting a critique of the "age" and brief portraits of other minor artists. In Sections II–V, the taste of the age in art, religion, politics, and war is evaluated; and in Sections XI–XII, the quality of the modern audience. The portraits of other artists in the "Ode" and Sections VI–X provide an aesthetic heritage for Mauberley, and a glance at some contemporary careers with which his may be compared. Excepting the "Ode," these sketches proceed in a roughly chronological order: from the Pre-Raphaelites to the Rhymers and Max Beerbohm to Arnold Bennett and Ford Madox Ford. Mauberley is descended from the British "aesthetic movement," and his own strengths and weaknesses are later shown to be inherited from his forebears (just as his philistine age is essentially continuous with theirs). But his contemporaries have responded to the "age's demands" in different ways: Mr. Nixon has sold out to them, the stylist has fled from them, and the fictional "E.P." of the opening "Ode"—an aesthete like Mauberley—has been buried by them. Pound provides a medical history and background of the disease before turning to the case in hand. By the time we meet Mauberley in Part II, we know his environment, his heredity, and some of the standards by which his responses should be judged.

The voice that knits the sequence is the flexible voice of Pound himself, speaking in various tones of irony, rage, detachment, and impersonal sympathy. His own career provides part of his subject matter, but he treats it with the same objectivity as the careers of others. Thus in the opening "E.P. Ode pour l'election de son sepulchre," Pound writes the literary epitaph that would have been appropriate for himself had he stopped writing about 1911. He calls this early London version of himself "E.P.," as he does frequently in his later correspondence.* The voice in the "Ode" is the same uncompromising voice that judges Mauberley in Part II (especially in "The Age Demanded"); it is the voice that Pound often adopts to dismiss most of his pre-Imagist work.† Later "E.P." appears as a young man about town: visiting M. Verog, taking the advice of Mr. Nixon, waiting in Lady Valentine's drawing room. Here, too, he is strictly functional—a pilgrim, an observer, a recorder, a buffoon, who is used to present the *periplum* of literary London. Behind the voice of this persona is the deeper awareness of the mature poet. Only in "Envoi" and "Medallion" does the controlling viewpoint shift significantly. "Envoi" interrupts the ironic observation of *moeurs contemporaines* to present Pound's positive values; but it does so in a voice that is collective (not just impersonal). The voice of "Envoi" is rich with the overtones of the English lyric tradition of Chaucer, Shakespeare, and Waller; and it represents precisely that vital grasp of "the better tradition" which "E.P." and Mauberley so unfortunately lack. "Medallion," on the other hand, presents Mauberley's values in Mauberley's voice; it should be taken, as John J. Espey suggests, for a poem written by Mauberley himself.[1] It dramatizes his art, and shows a kind of beauty more tenuous but not less real than that of the "Envoi." In this wasteland of life and contacts, "Envoi" and "Medallion" represent the cult of beauty which is "the art of cure."

To unify his sequence, Pound employed the same device that he was to use in *The Cantos*: the assimilation of a number of historical and pseudohistorical figures to the archetypal patterns of quest and heroic struggle found in Homer's *Odyssey*. There can be little doubt that he learned the technique from Joyce's *Ulysses*, which he began to read in late 1917.‡ In reviewing this "super-novel" for

---

* See Patricia Hutchins' account of her correspondence with Pound in connection with the writing of *Ezra Pound's Kensington* (London, 1965): "As this material grew, so we came to write of 'E.P.,' as if he were someone Pound had known intimately" (p. 23).

† See, for instance, Pound's "Foreword" to the 1965 reprint of *A Lume Spento and Other Early Poems*: "As to why a reprint? No lessons to be learned save the depth of ignorance, or rather the superficiality of non-perception— neither eye nor ear. Ignorance that didn't know the meaning of 'Wardour Street.'"

‡ Pound saw much of the manuscript of *Ulysses* before it was published. Joyce would send him the chapters as they were finished, and Pound would

The Dial in 1922, Pound noted that its author had "poached on
the epic . . . Telemachus, Circe, the rest of the Odyssean company,
the noisy cave of Aeolus gradually place themselves in the mind
of the reader. . . . These correspondences are part of Joyce's medievalism and are chiefly his own affair, a scaffold, a means of
construction, justified by the result, and justifiable by it only. The
result is a triumph in form, in balance, a main schema, with continuous inweaving and arabesque" (LE, 406).

Pound employs a similar "scaffold" and "main schema" in *Hugh
Selwyn Mauberley*. Though he does not imitate Joyce's particular
technique of correlating every part of his work in some detail to a
part of the *Odyssey*, he nevertheless uses a looser version of what
T. S. Eliot called "the mythical method."[2] The opening "Ode" sets
up the fundamental equation of the poet-as-Odysseus, engaged in
an arduous quest for his true ideal (Penelope), but mortally
tempted by a false ideal (Circe and the Sirens). The hostile element through which he must fight his way (Poseidon) is the society described in Sections II–V of Part I. The failed minor artists
of the poem, from "E.P." to Mauberley himself, are, like the crewmen of Odysseus, diverted from their quest and destroyed along
the way. Only the "stylist" in Section X reaches a sort of Ithaca.
Mauberley and the others lose their bearings, get marooned, sink
into oblivion. At best, these Elpenors may leave their oars, as Mauberley leaves his "Medallion," to commemorate their struggles.
Such, in general terms, are the principal "correspondences" of the
Mauberley sequence.

II

Having stated some general assumptions, we may undertake a
more detailed examination of the poem by way of the epic correlations. The opening "Ode" is the epitaph that would have been

---

edit and forward them to the *Little Review*. Pound declared Telemachus to
be "echt Joice" in December 1917; see *Letters of James Joyce*, ed. Richard
Ellmann (London, 1966), II, 413. *Telemachus* appeared in the *Little Review*
in March 1918. By the end of 1919, twelve chapters in all had appeared; see
A. Walton Litz, *The Art of James Joyce* (London, 1961), pp. 143–144. Pound
therefore had ample opportunity and time, before he finished *Hugh Selwyn
Mauberley*, to grasp Joyce's structural design.

appropriate for Pound if his career had ended before *Ripostes* and the Imagist movement. The "three years" of the first line are probably 1908–1911, when "E.P." was gathering limbs of Osiris and trying to "resuscitate" the art of poetry through his medieval translations and imitations. *Canzoni*, for instance, with its radiant ladies, its stilted diction, and its Provençal forms, was indeed an attempt "to maintain 'the sublime' / In the old sense." The good intentions of such work were hardly "wrong," but "E.P." was nevertheless going about it in the wrong way. Capaneus and the trout have admirable energy, even a noble integrity, but both are sadly misguided. Born and educated "out of date" in a "half savage country," the young "E.P." does not realize that poetry cannot be resuscitated in its old forms; it must be born anew. The age of lilies, a flower that Pound associated with "the decayed-lily verbiage which the Wilde school scattered over the decadence," had passed.* But "E.P." is still vainly "wringing lilies from the acorn," instead of letting his talent "grow good oak."† He is deceived by the "factitious bait" of a derivative diction and an artificial medievalism. Just as the Sirens tempted Odysseus with knowledge *that he already had* (of "all the things that are in Troy"), so familiar poetic conventions tempt "E.P." from his quest. In observing "the elegance of Circe's hair / Rather than the mottoes on sun-

---

* Writing one of his "Imaginary Letters" in 1918 under the pseudonym of "Walter Villerant," Pound made this comment: "The metal finish alarms people. They will no more endure Joyce's hardness than they will Pound's sterilized surgery. The decayed-lily verbiage which the Wilde school scattered over the decadence is much more to the popular taste. . . ." He went on to add: "Bad Beaudelaire [sic] in English has come from trying to do him in a lilies and clematis vocabulary, fitter for Alfred de Musset." ("Mr. Villerant's Morning Outburst (Four Letters)," *Little Review*, V [November 1918], 11–12.) My reading of "lilies" follows that of Sister Bernetta Quinn, "A Poem Too Interesting for Burial," *Pound Newsletter*, 7 (July 1955), 1–3. Of course the "E.P." of the "Ode" has not achieved the "sterilized surgery" of the later Pound's *Lustra* satires.

† In 1913, Pound supported the idea of "art for art's sake" with the analogy of the entelechy of an oak: "As for touching 'art for art's sake': the oak does not grow for the purpose or with the intention of being built into ships and tables, yet a wise nation will take care to preserve its forests. It is the oak's business to grow good oak." ("America: Chances and Remedies," *New Age*, XIII [1 May 1913], 10.) Clearly "E.P." does not know how to foster the "acorn" within him.

dials," he escapes the age's emphasis on the "march of events" and
its demand that he produce a debased art "made with no loss of
time." But he escapes to the worn conventions of a Pre-Raphaelite
sensualism. (We may recall the imagery of "dim hair," "the soft,
dim cloud of her hair," and "pale hair that the moon has shaken"
in Pound's *Exultations*.) The true Odysseus is not mastered by
Circe and detained by the elegance of her hair; in *The Cantos* he
dominates her, and she becomes "the trim-coifed goddess." "E.P."
loses a year, however, while fishing in the still waters surrounding
the "obstinate isles" of dead convention. He fails to catch the tide
that might bear him onward to his "true Penelope." He is not only
out of key with his "time," but also out of key with himself and
with the rhythm or entelechy of his own artistic development. He
is abandoned, and "passes from men's memory" without leaving
any artistic testament equivalent to the one Villon began to set
down in *"l'an trentiesme / De son eage."* And his work takes no
place among tradition's timeless order of monuments, presents "No
adjunct to the Muses' diadem."

   "E.P." fails in his artistic quest because he does not clearly perceive its goal. Modern poetry can be revived only by a strong in-
fusion of the spirit of Flaubert's prose; in this sense Flaubert is
his "true Penelope." But "E.P." fishes on, either unaware of Flaubert or unable critically to see that Flaubert can give him what all
the elegant Circes of the nineteenth century cannot provide. In
short, "E.P." does not realize (or does not act on the realization
of) what Ford Madox Ford began to teach Pound in 1911. Ford
ridiculed Pound's *Canzoni* by rolling on the floor in gales of
laughter because, as Pound later put it, the book "displayed me
trapped, fly-papered, gummed and strapped down in a jejune
provincial effort to learn, *mehercule*, the stilted language that then
passed for 'good English' in the arthritic milieu that held control
of the respected English critical circles, Newbolt, the backwash of
Lionel Johnson, Fred Manning, the Quarterlies and the rest of
'em. And that roll saved me two years, perhaps more."[3] This imagery of entrapment and "backwash" corresponds to the imagery in
the "Ode": "The chopped seas held him, therefore, that year."
Ford showed Pound his true Penelope and a way to revolutionize

modern poetry by emphasizing the Flaubertian "prose tradition" of exact presentation, which in turn led Pound to Imagisme. "Mr. Hueffer believes in an exact rendering of things. . . . You would find his origins in Gautier or in Flaubert," declared Pound in the same article which announced to readers of *Poetry* the appearance of creatures called Imagistes.[4] "I think this sort of clear presentation is one of the noblest traditions of our craft. . . . It is what may be called the 'prose tradition' of poetry. . . . It is to modern verse what the method of Flaubert is to modern prose."[5] But in the "Ode" young "E.P." does not move on toward Flaubert's prose tradition. After his three active years he remains trapped and arrested in the contemplation of a false ideal, the first of *Mauberley's* gallery of failed artists.

The "Ode" establishes the basic perspective of Pound's subsequent portraits. "E.P." is not Mauberley—there is nothing, for instance, in Mauberley's portrait to correspond to "E.P." 's half-savage origin or his Capanean intensity. But he has much in common with Mauberley and with the aesthetes of the Nineties from whom they both derive. They are all plagued by an inner disharmony, an inability to distinguish the true Penelope clearly enough, and a lack of the tenacity needed to pursue the quest toward Ithaca. The "Ode" also establishes a basic technique of *Mauberley* in presenting a fairly coherent critical analysis of its subject in a few images. Throughout the sequence, images imply whole critical arguments. Fortunately, we can often find the key to their significance in Pound's prose, which served as a testing ground for much of this "criticism in new composition."

Sections II–V of Part I establish the "age" as Poseidon, the hostile element through which the artist's quest must be pursued. Though "all things are a flowing" in history seen *sub specie aeternitatis*, the modern artist from Flaubert to Mauberley finds himself in a particularly uncongenial phase. He is immersed in "a tawdry cheapness" that "shall outlast our days." This is dramatized by Pound's implicit comparison of the war of 1914 to the Trojan War. Neither Odysseus nor Agamemnon found his house in order upon returning from Troy, but the soldiers of the twentieth century come home to a totally diseased society:

came home, home to a lie,
home to many deceits,
home to old lies and new infamy;
usury age-old and age-thick
and liars in public places.

If the Greek army became disillusioned as the Trojan war dragged
on, the armies of 1914 suffer "disillusions as never told in the old
days." The Greeks at least fought for a Helen, but the modern
soldiers die for "an old bitch gone in the teeth, / For a botched
civilization." Throughout the war sections of *Mauberley*, the Greek
analogy provides an implicit contrast to war in the modern "age."
Similarly, Greek ideals function in every stanza of Section III to
reveal modern degeneracy, culminating in the ironic echo of
Pindar's heroic salute.

The Homeric quest also underlies Pound's treatment of the
Nineties in "Siena Mi Fe; Disfecemi Maremma." M. Verog himself
is like the sole survivor of an Odyssean postwar voyage in which
he "lost all companions." His noble lineage is emphasized and he is
not only "perfecting the catalogue" of the Royal College of Sur-
geons, but also giving Pound a Homeric catalogue of his companions in battle. He talks of war (General Galliffet), and the
Grecian title of his book reflects the martial strain in the man's own
spirit. (*In the Dorian Mood* recalls not only Greek music and
Victor Plarr's book, but also the "strong loneliness" and "eternal
moods" of Pound's earlier poem, "Δώρια.") *

London is the Maremma which "undid" the Rhymers, and in
Verog's report it bears a striking resemblance to Circe's isle. Lionel
Johnson dies by "falling from a high stool in a pub," just as Elpenor
died by falling from Circe's loft. Dowson succumbs to the tempta-
tions of harlots, who are for him the most alluring embodiment of
Circe or the Sirens. The men Verog knew suffer from a Circean
befuddlement of mind, an inability to distinguish truly. Thus Johnson mixes his Catholicism with his alcoholism, Dowson thinks extensive whoring will cost him less than a bourgeois existence in

---

* The pseudonym which Pound chose to give to Victor Plarr reminds one
strongly of "Virag," the name of Leopold Bloom's father and the Hungarian
word for "flower."

hotels, and Selwyn Image is a bundle of indiscriminate and contradictory enthusiasms—"impartially imbued / With raptures for Bacchus, Terpsichore and the Church." Pound treats these splendid follies with affectionate humor and something like elegiac tenderness. But he leaves no doubt as to where "E.P." and Mauberley have inherited their confusions.

"Brennbaum" involves a Hebraic version of the Hellenic quest. Pound may have been mistaken in assuming that Max Beerbohm was Jewish, but thematically it was a happy mistake. For "the heavy memories of Horeb, Sinai and the forty years" recall the Hebrew exile and the quest for Canaan. The implication of the epigram (which could so easily have appeared in *Lustra*) is that "Brennbaum" has relinquished his inherited quest for the sake of impeccability. This is reinforced by the irony of his name, for no burning bush will be revealed to this modern Moses. Brennbaum has lost the spiritual intensity of ancient Judaism, just as the "franchise" has replaced the ritual of "circumcision" in his society. Like Mauberley in his desert exile, Brennbaum's "manna" is "insubstantial," and his "hosannah" is merely "subjective." These images from the Old Testament harmonize with the quest motif from the *Odyssey*.

Mr. Nixon, of course, undertakes *his* Odyssean quest "in the cream gilded cabin of his steam yacht," an appropriately luxurious setting for his materialistic voyagings. He has triumphed over all hazards—the "reviewer" and even the Polyphemic "Dr. Dundas." He advises the aspiring writer to do the same—"to advance with fewer / Dangers of delay." He has indeed achieved his Penelope—cash—but of all the artists in the sequence he is most truly "wrong, wrong from the start."

Nixon is likened to "a friend of Bloughram's," and the allusion at once establishes an analogy between Nixon's advice to the young Pound and Blougram's advice to the young Gigadibs in Browning's "Bishop Blougram's Apology." The "cream gilded cabin" in Nixon's steam yacht is a literal version of the metaphoric "cabin" that Blougram uses to contrast his lot in life to that of Gigadibs: "We mortals cross the ocean of this world / Each in his average cabin of a life." Blougram's "cabin" is prudently and comfortably furnished, but Gigadibs' is bare because it could not contain the stock

of art treasures that Gigadibs had brought aboard as his sole
equipment. Thus Blougram chides:

> You peep up from your utterly naked boards
> Into some snug and well-appointed berth,
> Like mine for instance (try the cooler jug—
> Put back the other, but don't jog the ice)
> And mortified you mutter "Well and good;
> He sits enjoying his sea-furniture;
> 'Tis stout and proper, and there's store of it:
> Though I've the better notion, all agree,
> Of fitting rooms up. Hang the carpenter,
> Neat ship-shape fixings and contrivances—
> I would have brought up my Jerome, frame and all!"
> And meantime you bring nothing: never mind—
> You've proved your artist-nature:

Now Mr. Nixon lives in Blougram's cabin. His scorn for the Nineties and his advice to "give up verse" parallels Blougram's scorn
for the "artist-nature" that will suffer hardships on the voyage because of a devotion to Correggio paintings and Balzac novels. For
both Blougram and Nixon, the most important thing about the
Odyssean quest is that it be made in comfort. Neither takes his
bearings from a traditional ideal, and neither respects those who
do. For, as Nixon makes clear, the penalty of failure in the true
quest is tragic: "The Nineties tried your game / And died."

The implied analogy between Pound and Gigadibs is also important in this connection. For Gigadibs' reaction to his interview
with Blougram is to set out on a voyage to Australia within a
week. Far from being persuaded to play the game of the Establishment, he quits journalism and "having bought, not cabin-furni-
ture / But settler's-implements," he goes to seek a personal fulfill-
ment in tilling the soil of his Ithaca. This voyage, too, is recalled by
Pound's allusion to Browning's poem, and it furnishes a significant
contrast to the Blougram–Nixon luxury excursion.

A more important contrast is provided in Section X by "the
stylist." In some respects the stylist is the nearest thing to a successful Odysseus in the whole poem. He has reached his Ithaca, has
anchored in a "haven from sophistications and contentions." He

has put himself and his Penelope into a fruitful harmony with nature which enables him to carry on his art independently of the "world's welter" that engulfs the other artists:

> Nature receives him;
> With a placid and uneducated mistress
> He exercises his talents
> And the soil meets his distress.

He demonstrates that failure in the modern Odyssean quest is not inevitable. Nevertheless, the stylist pays a price for his success, and certain ironic touches in the portrait question the adequacy of this Ithaca. The stylist's arrangements savor of escapism and wilful primitivism. In his quaint and rustic cottage, with its thatched and sagging roof and its creaking latch (few visitors), he runs the danger of becoming a permanent provincial. A "haven from sophistications and contentions" might soon prove to be not Ithaca, but a lotos land providing a tempting escape from the turbulent complications of serious aesthetic debate. And "a placid and uneducated mistress" is not, perhaps, all that a true Penelope might be. Pound has reservations about the wisdom of turning the quest into this kind of Rousseauvian retreat.

Still, the stylist is a serious artist, unlike the young time-server who waits in Lady Valentine's drawing room in Section XII. This ironic persona (an "E.P." who has taken Mr. Nixon's advice) is comparable to an Odysseus languishing in the charming establishment of Calypso. But whereas Calypso gave Odysseus beautiful raiment and detained him for love, our modern suitor knows that his "coat has never been / Of precisely the fashion / To stimulate, in her, / A durable passion." As a poet, he sometimes has the kind of delightful psychic experience which enables him to understand the myths of metamorphosis. But he is not able to find the appropriate objective equations for it (equations such as Pound's earlier poems, "The Tree" and "A Girl"). His visions remain subjective only:

> "Daphne with her thighs in bark
> Stretches toward me her leafy hands"—
> Subjectively.

Like Mauberley in Part II, he is capable only of "lifting the faint susurrus / Of his subjective hosannah."* He waits, timorous and thwarted.

If this figure is no Odysseus, Lady Valentine is by the same token no Calypso or Daphne. Daphne's yearning and fertile garb have no counterpart in the "well-gowned approbation" of the ironically named Lady Valentine. Her relationship to her poet is a far cry from the medieval relationship of the noble lady to her troubadour. Unlike the Countess of Beziers, she is capable neither of loving her Marvoil nor of understanding his songs. Her ideas of poetry are indistinct; for her, the art is a means to an end, a social passport which enables her to mix with classes above and below her own. Her vocation is:

> Poetry, her border of ideas,
> The edge, uncertain, but a means of blending
> With other strata
> Where the higher and lower have ending;
>
> A hook to catch the Lady Jane's attention,
> A modulation toward the theatre,
> Also, in the case of revolution,
> A possible friend and comforter.

In Lady Valentine, Pound presents an ironic evaluation of aristocratic patronage in the modern age.

Lady Valentine's portrait is complemented by an analysis of the bourgeois and the popular segments of the modern audience. The modern middle-class reader is mocked in the *Lustra*-style epigram which constitutes Section XI of *Mauberley*. Far from fitting De Gourmont's definition of "les femmes" as the conservators of the classical tradition of the erotic Milesian Tales, she leads a completely bourgeois existence in suburban Ealing, and is conscious of nothing beyond the social distinctions so important to her new station. Like the Lady Valentine, she has neither culture nor passion.

Pound turns in the latter part of Section XII to the popular

---

* On the Caedmon recording, Pound places strong ironic emphasis on "subjectively" and "subjective" in these two passages.

audience. If Dr. Johnson could survive on Grub Street after having rejected the patronage of a degenerate aristocracy, perhaps the twentieth-century poet can survive on Fleet Street. Pound therefore conducts what Laforgue called "l'âme que les Lettres ont bien nourrie" on another Odyssean voyage to Fleet Street, and provides another glimpse of the *periplum* of literary London. But this glimpse shows only that modern journalism has prostituted itself to the money values of a usurious capitalism; it foreshadows the more extensive denunciation of the modern press in *The Cantos*.

> Beside this thoroughfare
> The sale of half-hose has
> Long since superseded the cultivation
> Of Pierian roses.

In a press controlled by advertisers ("the sale of half-hose"), there is no room for the cultivation of classical beauty which Sappho associated with the roses of Pieria. Pound evaluates the modern audience by the Greek standards of passion and beauty implied in his allusions to the Milesian Tales, Daphne, and Sappho; he finds it neither "phallic" nor "ambrosial."

These various Homeric correlations prepare us for the voyage of Hugh Selwyn Mauberley himself in Part II of the sequence. We first meet Mauberley taking his bearings, as it were, from Jacquemart's engraving of the head of Gautier and from the head of the empress Messalina engraved on a Roman coin. His ambition is to incorporate into poetry the values of clear presentation and sculptural form which Pound associated with Gautier's work: "to present the series / Of curious heads in medallion." His "true Penelope" is Flaubert, whose prose method of exact presentation Pound habitually associated with the poetic method of Gautier.[6]

But though Mauberley seems to recognize his Penelope at the outset more clearly than does the "E.P." of the opening "Ode," he too proves unable to pursue the quest to Ithaca. His art is not vigorous, and he lacks the skill to "forge Achaia." Like "E.P.," he has only three creative years. He suffers from the same malady as his ancestors of the Nineties—confusion and an inability to discriminate:

Drifted . . . drifted precipitate,
Asking time to be rid of . . .
Of his bewilderment; to designate
His new found orchid. . . .

To be certain . . . certain . . .
(Amid aerial flowers) . . . time for arrangements—
Drifted on
To the final estrangement;

Unable in the supervening blankness
To sift TO AGATHON from the chaff

Here psychic confusion is dramatized in the broken speech-pat-
tern, just as it was in "La Fraisne," "Cino," and "Piere Vidal Old."
Mauberley (unlike the stylist) can find no firm standing ground:
no principle of discrimination for his art, and no viable arrangement for his life. He simply drifts.

Mauberley resembles Jenny, the Pre-Raphaelite faun of "Yeux
Glauques," in that he is "questing and passive"—pursuing a true
ideal but pursuing too weakly. He floats into a state of refined and
passive subjectivity, broken only by occasional exquisite impressions. But since he has found no way to designate and arrange
them in art, he stops writing altogether:

A pale gold, in the aforesaid pattern,
The unexpected palms
Destroying, certainly, the artist's urge,
Left him delighted with the imaginary
Audition of the phantasmal sea-surge.

The Homeric allusion in these lines emphasizes his abandonment
of the Odyssean quest.* The voyage ends when he becomes marooned on the "scattered Moluccas," the lotos land of his sub-

* As Pound told W. H. D. Rouse in 1935, the "imaginary / Audition of the
phantasmal sea-surge" is an attempt to translate Homer's "para thina po-
luphloisboio thalasses" (*Iliad*, I, 34). See LETT, 274–275. Mauberley is like
"Stele," the subject of an epigram in Pound's "Moeurs contemporaines"
(1918): "Now, quenched as the brand of Meleagar, / he lies by the poluphois-
boious sea-coast" (P, 181).

jective impressions. Odysseus' black ship has become a "coracle of Pacific voyages," washed up on an "unforecasted beach."

Thus Mauberley joins the ranks of the fallen crewmen of Odysseus. The shade of Elpenor in Hades asks Odysseus to set up his oar and inscribe on his tomb the epitaph which Pound translated as: "A man of no fortune, and with a name to come." Similarly, Mauberley is commemorated by oar and epitaph:

> Then on an oar
> Read this:
>
> "I was
> And I no more exist;
> Here drifted
> An hedonist."

He shares the fate of Conrad's Decoud, the sceptical hedonist of *Nostromo*.

Pound, then, employed the Joycean "mythical method" to good advantage in *Hugh Selwyn Mauberley*. And the writing of *Mauberley* helped to break the impasse in which his "versions of Provence" had left him. Pound had not been making much progress on *The Cantos* while *Mauberley* was under weigh. He had drafted seven by the end of 1919, but he had not really solved the formal problems mused over in the "Three Cantos" of 1917. (Eventually six of the seven had to be drastically rewritten and rearranged.) He seemed stymied, and put the poem aside for a time: "no further reference to the composition of the Cantos seems to have been made until 1922, some three years later."[7] Early in 1922 something happened to unblock Pound's way. In May *The Dial* published "Canto VIII," the poem we now know as Canto 2. This marked the beginning of "another period of intensive work on the long poem . . . stretching from the spring of 1922 to the early part of 1925," a period in which "the poem—or at least the first part of it—took what is now its final shape."[8] In July 1923, the Malatesta cantos were published in *Criterion*, and "within a month or perhaps two months of the publication of these Cantos, Pound had entirely revised the beginning of the poem. . . ."[9] What probably accounted for this burst of activity was the publication of *Ulysses* in book

form in February 1922. Pound had to formulate his thoughts about
Ulysses for his *Dial* review, dated "May 1922," and it is no coincidence that "Canto VIII" appeared in the same month. By the next
summer, when he had finished the Malatesta sequence and sat
down to revise the earlier cantos, he perhaps saw that by moving
the Nekuia episode from the end of Canto 3 to Canto 1 he could
make Malatesta the first of a potentially innumerable series of historical heroes all patterned on Odysseus. He would have been the
abler to see this for having done something similar in *Mauberley*,
and for having recently reconsidered the "scaffold" of the finished
Ulysses.

Whether his own "main schema" came to him in the summer of
1923 or later, it had certainly taken shape by the publication of
A Draft of XVI. Cantos in January 1925. Three months earlier
Pound wrote: "Am . . . ready for another long chunk; and trying to
find some bhlooming historic character who can be used as illustration of intelligent constructivity."[10] His plan was now clear to
him; he could ransack history for embodiments of the Odysseus
principle. He could include figures from past and present, from
history and pseudohistory, without having to "hang his shimmering garment on" any particular one. The way was open for the
"many worlds and brave *décors*" of El Cid, Confucius, Hanno,
Adams, Jefferson, Mussolini, and other factive heroes.

Joyce would no doubt have been delighted to know that Pound
was hunting for yet another "bhlooming" Ulysses. Pound had done
him fine service, in getting his works published and helping out
financially. Now Joyce had repaid the debt handsomely by writing
the book that helped make possible two of Pound's greatest poems.
After all, Joyce might have said to himself, it is no coincidence that
Ulysses was finished on Pound's birthday.[11]

III

The fall of Hugh Selwyn Mauberley, the modern Elpenor, is
partly a drama of aesthetic theory. Mauberley is not modeled on
any particular historical person, and to search for his "original" is
to misunderstand Pound's intention. He is *the type of the impressionist*, and his failure is inseparable from his aesthetic. Pound's

critique of Mauberley is closely related, in its images and principles, to his Vorticist critique of impressionism as outlined in the
polemical prose of the *BLAST* period. Part II of the sequence is
the anatomy of an impressionist.

In distinguishing impressionism from Vorticism, Pound followed
the basic strategy of Vorticist polemic, which was to identify rival
aesthetic theories as fundamentally mimetic, and to contrast them
with the more "creative" and formalist principles of Vorticism. The
first issue of *BLAST* lumped naturalism, impressionism, and futurism together in this way: "Intrinsic beauty is in the Interpreter
and Seer, not in the object or content. We do not want to change
the appearance of the world, because we are not Naturalists, Impressionists or Futurists (the latest form of Impressionism), and
do not depend on the appearance of the world for our art."[12] Vorticism reaffirmed the creative imagination and asserted the value of
nonrepresentational form: "Our respect is not for the subject-
matter, but for the creative power of the artist; for that which he is
capable of adding to his subject from himself; or, in fact, his capability to dispense with external subjects altogether, to create from
himself or from elements. . . ."[13]

The essence of Pound's criticism was that impressionism is simply a passive recording of external impressions, without any active
or creative transformation on the part of the artist. He argued that
"the *conception* of poetry is a process more intense than the *reception* of an impression,"[14] and he elaborated this idea in his essay
on "Vorticism": "There are two opposed ways of thinking of a
man: firstly, you may think of him as that toward which perception
moves, as the toy of circumstance, as the plastic substance *receiv-
ing* impressions; secondly, you may think of him as directing a
certain fluid force against circumstance, as *conceiving* instead of
merely reflecting and observing".[15] The impressionist is a "toy of
circumstance" in that he is played upon by sensory impressions,
and does not rearrange or alter them. Pound traced the impressionist theory of perception back to Bishop Berkeley and the
eighteenth-century associationist tradition of the tabula rasa: "Impressionism sought its theoretic defence in, if it did not arise from,
Berkeley's theory of the minimum visible, i.e. of the effect of points
of light and colour on the retina." Pound asserted that the im-

pressionist derives his pleasure "from the stroking and pushing of
the retina by light waves of various colours."*

He went on to argue that the impressionist, as a mechanical
recorder, is comparable to the motion-picture camera; both share
the aesthetic of simple mimesis. "The logical end of impressionism
is the cinematograph. The state of mind of the impressionist tends
to become cinematographical. Or, to put it another way, the cinematograph does away with the need of a lot of impressionist art."[16]
Elsewhere he compared the impressionist to a seismograph. In
describing an artist's technique as machinery that can conduct a
high voltage of electricity, Pound adds this qualification: "These
are bad expressions if they lead you to think of the artist as wholly
passive, as a mere receiver of impressions. The good artist is perhaps a good seismograph, but the difference between man and a
machine is that man can in some degree 'start his machinery
going.' He can, within limits, not only record but create."[17] The
creative Vorticist is more than a mere cinematograph or seismograph.

The relevance of this analysis to *Mauberley* should be clear, for
Mauberley in Part II becomes increasingly passive, increasingly a
"toy of circumstance" and a prisoner of his own impressions. "Invitation, mere invitation to perceptivity" leads him into not only a
social isolation from the world of letters, but also a psychological
isolation. As he drifts into passivity, he is sustained only by "selected perceptions," an occasional "Minoan undulation," or the
glimpse of "pale gold" and "unexpected palms." Gradually he becomes a type of the passive and superficial impressionist sensibility:

---

* "Vortographs," *Pavannes and Divisions*, p. 255. According to Berkeley,
the *minimum visibile* is the smallest point that can be perceived. A field of
vision is made up of a finite number of these points, and this number remains
the same no matter what the eye beholds: "Of these visible points we see at
all times an equal number. It is every whit as great when our view is con-
tracted and bounded by near objects, as when it is extended to larger and re-
moter. . . . The visive faculty . . . can take in at a view but a certain determinate number of *minima visibilia*, beyond which it cannot extend its prospect."
(*An Essay Towards a New Theory of Vision*, LXXXII–LXXXIII.) Pound
seems to mean that impressionist technique aims primarily at affecting this
finite number of points.

> A consciousness disjunct,
> Being but this overblotted
> Series
> Of intermittences;

The term "overblotted" expresses with precision Pound's view of the impressionist mind as a tabula rasa. Mauberley's perception is passive ("Thus, if her colour / Came against his gaze"). He becomes a retina, stroked and pushed by the light waves emanating from "tawn" foreshores, "cobalt" water, the "grey and rose" flamingoes. Perhaps this is what Pound meant when he told Felix Schelling that "Mauberley is a mere surface" (LETT, 180). Mauberley illustrates Pound's dictum that "the state of mind of the impressionist tends to become cinematographical." And after three years of seeking some principle of selection for his art, he comes to rest upon the principle of the seismograph:

> Unable in the supervening blankness
> To sift TO AGATHON from the chaff
> Until he found his sieve . . .
> Ultimately, his seismograph:

Once we view Mauberley's fate in connection with the aesthetics of Vorticism, certain other aspects of his portrait fall into place. Mauberley begins as a proto-Imagist, an imitator of Gautier, a lesser poet of *emaux et camées*. He moves, during his three creative years, amid "phantasmagoria," a word that Pound had explicitly associated with Imagisme and *phanopoeia*.* Thus far he pursues a worthy goal. But he becomes confused, and proves unable to designate or arrange the "aerial flowers" of his phantasmagoric Arcadia. In other words he lacks the Vorticist *virtù*, the ability to "produce

---

* In reviewing the *Others* anthology in 1917, Pound set up his familiar distinction between *melopoeia, phanopoeia*, and *logopoeia*. He associated "phantasmagoria" with the second of these, which he calls "imagism, or poetry wherein the feelings of painting or sculpture are predominant (certain men move in phantasmagoria; the images of their gods, whole countrysides, stretches of hill land and forest, travel with them)." See *Instigations* (London, 1920), p. 234. This passage makes it unnecessary to seek the source of the word far afield in a passage of James's *The Ambassadors*, as Kenner and Espey have done.

'order-giving vibrations'" which can "departmentalize such part
of the life-force as flows through him."[18]

He is particularly unable to establish a fruitful relationship between his own work and a living poetic tradition. Pound had
argued that "all the past that is vital, all the past that is capable
of living into the future is pregnant in the vortex, NOW."[19] But
Mauberley is

> Incapable of the least utterance or composition,
> Emendation, conservation of the "better tradition,"
> Refinement of medium, elimination of superfluities,
> August attraction or concentration.

Pound had long ago noted this incapacity in the school of impressionism that derived from Flaubert and came to him through Ford.
"Impressionism has, however, two meanings. . . . There is a school
of prose writers, and of verse writers for that matter, whose fore-
runner was Stendhal and whose founder was Flaubert. The followers of Flaubert deal in exact presentation. They are often so
intent on exact presentation that they neglect intensity, selection,
and concentration" (LE, 399). There are some dangers in having
Flaubert for true Penelope, especially for the poet. For, as Pound
argued in "The Serious Artist," the best poetry has a "passionate
simplicity" which is "in some way different from the clear statements of the observer," a "poignancy" which goes beyond "the
formal phrasing of Flaubert" (LE, 53). Mauberley is a hard impressionist rather than a soft, but he lacks *maestria*.

He is ultimately reduced to the single impression as his unit of
selection. He attempts to found his life on the beautiful impression, and to wall out everything else in the "manifest universe":

> By constant elimination
> The manifest universe
> Yielded an armour
> Against utter consternation.

His relationship to the "manifest universe" is just the opposite of
Remy de Gourmont's, as Pound described it. De Gourmont's
"thoughts had the property of life. They, the thoughts, were all
related to life, they were immersed in the manifest universe while
he thought them, they were not cut out, put on shelves and in

bottles."[20] But Mauberley's "selected perceptions" *are* "cut out" and isolated one from another. Yet only in the presence of these perceptions does his faint "desire for survival" become an "Olympian *apathein*"; only through them does he retain his fitful grasp on life. His temperament becomes more and more like that which Pound once ascribed to John Gould Fletcher: "Fletcher is sputter, bright flash, sputter. Impressionist temperament, made intense at half-seconds" (LETT, 49).

Mauberley's decline is also manifested in his failure to love, as John J. Espey shows in his excellent analysis of the second poem in Part II.[21] For Pound, there had always been an intimate connection between what he called, in an essay on Remy de Gourmont, "amour and aesthetics."[22] Phallic and ambrosial are but two sides of the same coin for Pound, and it is significant that in Part II Mauberley is twice explicitly associated with ambrosia but never (except indirectly and ironically) with the phallus. This idea carried over into Pound's Vorticism; as he bluntly stated in a discussion of "the caressable" in art, "the ideal vorticist is not the man of delicate incapabilities, who, being unable to get anything from life, finds himself reduced to taking a substitute in art."[23]

Gradually Mauberley's creative energy, his "artist's urge," dwindles as he moves farther and farther from all these sources of life. He moves out of the vortex into the "placid water" of his imaginary Moluccas, and he dies "an hedonist." Pound's Vorticist estimate of hedonism was stated in *BLAST*: "Hedonism is the vacant place of a vortex, without force, deprived of past and future."[24] In Odyssean terms, Pound might say that the Vorticist confronts Charybdis, while the hedonist becomes a lotos-eater.

It was while blasting and bombardiering in his Vorticist polemics, then, that Pound first plotted the downfall of Hugh Selwyn Mauberley. The character of Mauberley is the dramatic embodiment of certain radical defects which the Vorticists saw in impressionism, and Vorticist aesthetics constitute the implicit value system by which he is judged in the poem. But Vorticism also furnishes the critique of modern taste in Part I of the sequence, and provides the link between the age's demands and Mauberley's response.

We must first realize that the age has *a definite aesthetic* of its own in *Hugh Selwyn Mauberley*. It demands a representational or

mimetic art, a photographic reproduction of observable reality.
Like a latter-day Narcissus, it wants an unaltered picture of its own
"accelerated grimace." It requires a "mould in plaster" and a "prose
kinema."

Indeed, this demand for mimetic art seemed to Pound the greatest barrier to the acceptance of Imagist poetry and Vorticist sculpture, which are fundamentally formalist and abstractionist. Early
in 1912, he had said: "in every art I can think of we are clogged
and dammed by the mimetic."[25] He was constantly trying to edu-
cate the public in the new conventions of nonrepresentational art.
In defending Gaudier-Brzeska's statues to a St. Louis audience, he
explained: "If sculpture were judged by the closeness with which
it copies pre-existing material objects, the plaster cast or mould of
the object would be the apex of the achievement. . . . Brzeska's
statues have form. . . . It is for the spectator to decide whether the
forms of this sculpture are *in themselves* delightful."[26] Many reit-
erations of this argument no doubt lie behind the statement in
Mauberley that "The 'age demanded' chiefly a mould in plaster."

Pound opposed the new cinema on similar grounds. The cinema
simply provides the mimesis of kinesis, and gives the age "an
image / Of its accelerated grimace." In "Kinema, Kinesis, Hepworth, etc." (1918) he refused to call the cinema an Art: "We hear
a good deal about the 'art' of the cinema, but the cinema is not Art.
Art with a large A consists in painting, sculpture, possibly architecture. . . . Art is a stasis."[27] He is probably echoing the argument
of Stephen Dedalus in Chapter V of *Portrait of the Artist as a
Young Man*. (Nevertheless, it is surprising that Pound, usually so
quick to perceive the possibilities of new art forms, should casually
have dismissed what has become perhaps the most creative medium of our day.)

The phrase "prose kinema" refers to the naturalistic novel, the
second-rate fiction on which the age feasts its eyes. Like the cinema, it provides Narcissus with a mirror image of himself, unre-
fracted by the lens of artistic form. It operates according to the
aesthetic Pound once called "the 'slice of life,' or crude realism."[28]
Pound showed great acumen in linking these two forms of popular
entertainment, for he saw that the cinema grew out of the naturalistic novel and would eventually capture the reading audience.

When Marshall McLuhan says "the realistic novel . . . was a complete anticipation of film form," he is explicating *Hugh Selwyn Mauberley*.[29] By 1934, Pound could declare: "The cinema supersedes a great deal of second-rate narrative, and a great deal of theatre" (ABC, 76).

In sum, the popular aesthetic of simple mimesis seemed to Pound the antithesis of Vorticism. It says, in effect, "our respect *is* for the subject-matter, and *not* for the creative power of the artist; *not* for that which he is capable of adding to his subject from himself." Now the link between this aesthetic and Mauberley's impressionism is that both are (in Vorticist eyes, at least) mimetic theories. Impressionism is different in degree but not in kind from naturalism. Both depend on the "appearance of the world" rather than the creative power of the artist. Both are passive and mechanical, and so the cinema affects them equally. (It "does away with the need of a lot of impressionist art," and it "supersedes a great deal of second-rate narrative.") This relationship greatly heightens the irony of Hugh Selwyn Mauberley's decline from imagism to impressionism. For Mauberley drifts into what is simply a more sophisticated version of the crude mimetic realism which the "age demands." The only difference is that his seismograph is a more delicate instrument than the kinema; his consciousness records certain exquisite impressions rather than continuous images of the accelerated contemporary world. (This latter was the task of Marinetti's Futurism, which Pound dismissed as "accelerated Impressionism.")[30] The important fact, however, is that he ceases to be "capable of adding to his subject from himself." He has, in a sense, succumbed to the age's demand for mimesis at the precise moment when he thinks he has escaped far away to his imaginary "Moluccas." Or, to put it another way, his earlier sculptural ambitions have been infected and perverted, without his realizing it, by the degenerate popular aesthetic of his time.

IV

Pound's analysis of vision and failure in modern art is borne out by a careful logic of eye imagery in the poem. He uses images of eyes, gazes, and reveries to suggest the exact quality of various vi-

sions of beauty, and to gauge degrees of commitment to the artist's Odyssean quest.[31] The image is established in the second
poem of the sequence, where the age's demands are contrasted to
"the obscure reveries / Of the inward gaze." Here the reveries
seem to have a value comparable to the unseeing gaze of Yeats's
dancers, symbolizing the rapt contemplation of a subjective revelation. They are in complete harmony with the Vorticist doctrine that
"intrinsic beauty is in the Interpreter and Seer, not in the object or
content." This kind of insight reappears in the third section of
Mauberley, when the poet notes that the "saint's vision" is lost to
the modern age. In Sections IV and V, the eyes become those of the
fair young soldiers killed in the war, and we are reminded of the
line from Remy de Gourmont which Pound quoted with approval:
"J'ai plus aimé les yeux que toutes les autres manifestations corpo-
relles de la beauté."[32] Ironically, however, the soldiers' vision is one
of hell and death. They "walked eye-deep in hell," and they are
"quick eyes gone under earth's lid."

In "Yeux Glauques," the eyes of the Pre-Raphaelite muse symbolize both the strength and the limitation of Pre-Raphaelite vision. They are beautiful and immortal; preserved in Burne–Jones's
picture of "King Cophetua and the Beggar Maid" at the Tate Gallery, they can still teach Pound to rhapsodize. "Foetid Buchanan"
mutters in vain against this beauty, just as the Trojan elders mut-
tered against Helen's. But though this muse embodies the "faun's
flesh," she lacks something of the "saint's vision." Her gaze is
"clear," but it is "thin" and "vacant"; in Odyssean terms her gaze
is "questing" but "passive." Jenny—confused, enervated, and exploited by her society—becomes typical of the entire English tradition from which Mauberley descends. Her bewilderment is shared
by the Rhymers, and her "yeux glauques" resemble the "sky-like
limpid eyes" of "Brennbaum," whose childlike gaze symbolizes the
weakness of his commitment to his inherited Hebraic quest. Nevertheless, this kind of vision, however "thin" or "limpid," signifies a
true insight far superior to the blindness of that Tiresian oracle of
modern letters, Mr. Nixon, who is certain that "no one knows, *at
sight*, a masterpiece." Rather than be a success on Nixon's terms,
it is better to be like M. Verog, sole survivor of his tragic generation,

Detached from his contemporaries,
Neglected by the young,
Because of these reveries.

In Part II, Hugh Selwyn Mauberley's tenuous commitment to
the quest for beauty is related to that of his ancestors through the
pattern of eye imagery. His is a delicate visual art, devoted to cap-
turing the exquisite nuances of visual impressions. But it lacks the
capacity for a complete and direct apprehension of beauty. It is not
an art of the full face, but an "art in profile"; it focuses not on the
eye but on "the relation / Of eye-lid and cheek-bone." Thus Mauberley misses the invitation to love contained in the eyes of his
Venus—"the wide-banded irides / And botticellian sprays implied
/ In their diastasis." (If he were with Pound in the Pisan tent in
Canto 81, he could not perceive the "new subtlety of eyes" that
Pound suddenly apprehends: "Saw but the eyes and stance between the eyes, / colour, diastasis.") For Mauberley's own vision is
faulty, even when his eyes are open widest. He passes his Venus
"inconscient, full gaze." He is a passive and partial observer, who
perceives reality in refracted form:

Thus, if her colour
Came against his gaze,
Tempered as if
It were through a perfect glaze

His is a "*porcelain* revery," and his Minoan undulations are always
"seen . . . amid ambrosial circumstances."

Mauberley's limited vision ultimately destroys his art, for it
tends naturally to the "constant elimination" of the "manifest universe." It tends, in other words, to a point where only single impressions will be passively received in isolation. Indeed, he seems
to have a premonition of the "scattered Moluccas" toward which
he is drifting when

The coral isle, the lion-coloured sand
Burst in upon the porcelain revery:
Impetuous troubling
Of his imagery.

When the porcelain revery is finally shattered, he is left with only

an "overblotted / Series / Of intermittences." Ultimately his pleasure is derived, as Pound put it, only "from the stroking and pushing of the retina by light waves of various colours"—such as the
"coral" isle, the pale "gold," the "tawn" foreshores, the "grey and
rose" flamingoes. The glaze over Mauberley's vision has condi-
tioned it to be partial and passive.

But since this glaze has been the only source of unity and coherence in the world Mauberley perceives, it is also the sole basis
of his art during his three creative years. So much is clear from
"Medallion," the perfectly characteristic product of Mauberley's
"porcelain revery." Mauberley's portrait of a lady is a "Luini in
porcelain," a picture of a "sleek head" made by a man whose sole
poetic aim is "to present the series / Of curious heads in medallion." The poem's whole raison d'être is visual; it illustrates a certain way of apprehending reality-as-porcelain. Though limited
and partial, it presents a thoroughly integrated apprehension of
its subject.

And its conclusion has a powerful and complex logic by virtue
of the eye images which have preceded it:

> The face-oval beneath the glaze,
> Bright in its suave bounding-line, as,
> Beneath half-watt rays,
> The eyes turn topaz.

The "half-watt rays" may be taken two ways, both of which represent a qualified triumph and justification of Mauberley's brief
quest. They may symbolize (1) the feeble enlightenment of the
modern electric age, or (2) the feeble creative energies of Mauberley himself. In either case, Mauberley has succeeded in transforming the lady's eyes into beautiful gems despite the inadequate
artistic forces at his command. In celebrating "topaz" eyes he is
carrying on the work of his ancestors who celebrated "yeux glauques." This kind of beauty may not promise a fertile future, for to
achieve it Mauberley has had to petrify the living eyes of Venus
Anadyomene. Nevertheless it is perfect in its kind; the "half-watt
rays" do illuminate the lady with their own particular yellow gleam
of porcelain, gold, honey, amber, and topaz. He may have missed
those "botticellian sprays" in life, but he can still commemorate
Venus with the botticellian "suave bounding-line" of his art, and

it will never be said that for him poetry was a "border of ideas, /
The edge, uncertain." Mauberley is keeping alive the only tradition
he really understands—the finely chiseled art of Gautier's *Emaux et
camées*. Like Elpenor, he will not be entirely forgotten; before
sinking into the "cobalt of oblivions," he leaves one perfect in-
scription.

V

If visual and sculptural values are important to *Hugh Selwyn
Mauberley*, auditory and musical values are scarcely less so.
Pound's poem includes a critique of music and song in Mauberley's
"age." To understand the "Envoi," we must examine another dimension of Pound's "criticism in new composition."

Early in the poem, Pound presents a synoptic comment on modern taste in music, a comment which parallels his analysis of impressionism in literature. In Section III, he notes that in our time
"the pianola 'replaces' / Sappho's barbitos." Here, as in the case of
"mould in plaster" and "prose kinema," he is using two symbols
which have already-established meanings in his earlier writings.
He habitually used the pianola (player piano) to signify the mechanization and dehumanization of modern music, a trend for which
he blamed nineteenth-century impressionist and program music.
And he used the barbitos to signify the traditional kinship between
music and poetry.

Pound had a hierarchy of musical instruments, classed by their
mechanization. The pianola was the *non plus ultra* of dehumanized
music. "I think the organ has given way to the piano largely because the organ is too mechanical," he said in 1918. "The pianola
is worse, and should be relegated to sea-side dance halls. . . . There
is more aesthetic satisfaction in a few simple notes played by a
person who intends something than in a procession of notes shot
through a punched sheet of paper, but unintelligible to the execu-
tant."[33] Earlier he had praised Arnold Dolmetsch's reconstructions
of eighteenth-century instruments, because they could express "the
players' exact mood and personality" far more than the piano or
pianola, their modern replacements: "The clavichord has the
beauty of three or four lutes played together. . . . You have your
fingers always en rapport with the strings; it is not one dab and

then either another dab or else nothing, as with the piano; the music is always lying on your own finger-tips . . . [and now] we have come to the pianola. And one or two people are going in for sheer pianola" (LE, 433). The pianola, in other words, alienates the performing artist from the medium. (A similar critique lies behind the contrast between the "Bechstein" electric piano and the "lark squawk" of Janequin's "Canzone degli Uccelli" in Canto 79.)

Pianolas were "replacing" human artists because nineteenth-century impressionist and program music had softened and enervated the seventeenth- and eighteenth-century tradition of concentration and participation. "This old music was not theatrical. You played it yourself as you read a book of precision. A few people played it together. It was not an interruption but a concentration. . . . Impressionism has reduced us to such a dough-like state of receptivity that we have ceased to like concentration. Or if it has not done this, it has at least set a fashion of passivity that has held since the romantic movement" (LE, 433–434). The passivity induced by impressionist music leads to the passivity involved in playing the pianola: "Our ears are passive before the onslaught of gramophones and pianolas."[34]

The argument parallels Pound's analysis of impressionism in painting and poetry. The pianola is to music what the kinema and "seismograph" are to painting and poetry; once more this mimetic aesthetic culminates in mechanism and passivity. Impressionism leads inevitably to alienation because it seeks to imitate what is separate from the self; its basis is "this impression which works from the outside, in from the nerves and sensorium upon the self." Impressionist music "starts with being emotion or impression and then becomes only approximately music" (LE, 434). It has little respect for sound as such; its pleasures do not derive from the formal arrangements of notes, but from the recognition of the thing being imitated by the music. A new Vorticist music, Pound said, might come "from a new computation of the mathematics of harmony," but it would never attempt to please its audience with "a mimetic representation of dead cats in a fog-horn. . . ."[35]

Now, Hugh Selwyn Mauberley reveals his characteristically impressionistic conception of music in the first stanza of his "Medallion." He celebrates the "grand piano," the instrument in Pound's hierarchy most appropriate for him. (Mauberley occupies a middle ground between the vulgarity of the pianola and the formal mastery of the clavichord or lute.) The piano is an instrument which, in Pound's view, prevents a vital relationship between the musician and the music ("one dab and then either another dab or else nothing, as with the piano"). This reflects the impending disjunction between Mauberley and his own art. Then, too, Mauberley thinks of music not as a formal arrangement of sounds, but as a mimetic reproduction of some impression. He immediately translates the piano's high note into a "profane protest." His conception of music "starts with being emotion and impression and then becomes only approximately music."

At the opposite end of the hierarchy from pianos and pianolas is Sappho's barbitos. For Pound, this instrument symbolized not only the ideal relationship between the musician and his music, but also the ideal relationship between music and poetry. He argued that in the greatest lyric epochs, poetry was conceived as song and written in conjunction with music, and that "poetry atrophies when it gets too far from music" (ABC, 61). Sappho's barbitos, the original lyre of lyric poetry, images the happy union of the two arts: "It is not intelligent to ignore the fact that both in Greece and in Provence the poetry attained its highest rhythmic and metrical brilliance at times when the arts of verse and music were most closely knit together, when each thing done by the poet had some definite musical urge or necessity bound up within it. The Romans writing upon tablets did not match the cadences of those earlier makers who had composed to and for the Cythera and Barbitos" (LE, 91). When poetry is written primarily to be read, its inner melody is in danger of disappearing: "It is open to doubt whether the Aeolic singing was ever fully comprehended even in Rome. When men began to write on tablets and ceased singing to the *barbitos*, a loss of some sort was unavoidable" (LE, 101). There is an analogy between Imperial Rome and modern Britain here, as in *Homage to Sextus Propertius*. If anything, we are worse off than the Romans. We not only write our poetry on "tablets," but now we also write our music on "a punched sheet of paper" for our pianolas:

> The pianola "replaces"
> Sappho's barbitos.

This critique of music and poetry helps to explain the "Envoi"
of *Mauberley*. So far we have said only that the "Envoi" presents
Pound's positive values in the poem, and symbolizes that grasp of
"the better tradition" which Mauberley lacks. But to make these
claims good, we must consider some more specific questions. What
"tradition" is involved in the "Envoi"? Why did Pound choose
Waller's "Go Lovely Rose" as his source? What does the "Envoi"
have to do with Mauberley himself and with the criticism of contemporary culture presented in the rest of the poem? The answers
are closely related to each other, and are to be found in Pound's
music criticism and his *ABC of Reading*.

"Envoi" is based on a lyric written by Edmund Waller and set
to music by Henry Lawes toward the end of the seventeenth century. (In fact, it is addressed to a woman who "sang me once that
song of Lawes"—that is, who sang "Go Lovely Rose" itself to the
poet.) Pound's choice of this source was not casual. During the
three years before he published *Mauberley* and left England, he
had been writing regular music reviews for *The New Age* under
the name of "William Atheling." In these reviews, he found himself
invoking Lawes's settings of Waller's poems more and more frequently, as a model of the correct relationship between poetry and
music. Eventually these songs became synonymous in his mind
with the great period of the English lyric "from Henry the Eighth's
time down to fat Anne's . . ." (ABC, 156).

Pound described his "noble" alter ego as follows: " 'William
Atheling' wrote fortnightly in the *New Age* from 1917–1920; he
was more a secondary personality than a nom de plume, that is to
say he had a definite appearance (bald-headed) and a definite
script (crabbed and with an old-fashioned slant); he sympathized
with Arnold Dolmetsch's opinions, even when not wholly in agreement therewith. He shared my own interest in the fitting of *motz
el son*; the fitting of words and tunes. . . . He regretted the lost culture of Henry Lawes."[36] As persona in charge of music, Atheling
was much concerned with this lost culture.

"I would point out Lawes," wrote Atheling, "as an example of
how the words of a poem may be set and enhanced by music."[37]
He often did so, as in this review written in September 1918:

It is only too easy to ruin fine words with a poor setting, but it is quite possible to preserve their beauty, and if possible to enhance them; to emphasise their speech-beauty by a very slight exaggeration of each sound-quality *keeping* in each case the quality of the word-sound, but, as it were, dwelling on it, holding it to the ear, as a good poet might conceivably do in composing it. . . . Lawes has done this in setting some poems by Waller. (One of the rare cases where a poet has commended his setter.)[38]

In 1919, the unavailability of Lawes's *First Book of Ayres* called down Atheling's "anathema" upon the heads of the English publishers.[39] And if he chanced to review a concert that included a certain song in which "the words do not fit the notes," Atheling was apt to remark: "Even the deified Purcell is not up to Lawes (First Book of Ayres, especially) in these matters."[40] In the course of his brief career as judge of music, Atheling managed to condemn quite a few people by the standard of Lawes.

Lawes's settings had clearly become for Pound one of those "luminous details" which give insight into a whole phase of literary history. They were symptoms of a lost culture, and could be used to define the age itself: "The great lyric age lasted while Campion made his own music, while Lawes set Waller's verses, while verses, if not actually sung or set to music, were at least made with the intention of going to music" (ABC, 60–61). This was an age in which "poetry AND music . . . were very generally an accomplishment," an age in which "each thing done by the poet had some definite musical urge or necessity bound up within it." In other words, this was the time when Sappho's barbitos sounded in England.

The result was a cultural climate extremely conducive to the production of good lyric poetry, *even by poets with very little innate talent*. Pound's primary example of a poet who benefited in this way is Edmund Waller. "Waller," he declared, "was a tiresome fellow," but much of his work is good because it participated in a "style of the period." In poems like "Go Lovely Rose," he profited immensely from the fact that "the musical criteria of the times were of prime order" (ABC, 154). Inherently, his "natural talent is fathoms below My Lord Rochester's. BUT when he writes for music he is 'lifted'; he was very probably HOISTED either by the composer or by the general musical perceptivity of the time and of his acquaintances. His inborn lack of melody, if you compare it with Rochester's, is emended" (ABC, 154–55). This Pound calls one of the "ADVANTAGES ACCRUING FROM THERE BEING A 'STYLE OF THE PERIOD.' " And since no one, in Pound's opinion, did more to establish the style of Waller's period than Lawes did through his music, Pound felt justified in speaking of "the lost culture of Henry Lawes."

The "Envoi" in *Mauberley* is Pound's attempt to revive this lyric art, which he declared "well worth an effort to recover."[41] It reaches out beyond its source in "Go Lovely Rose" to summarize, by a masterful combination of themes and images, the entire lost culture of the English lyric tradition. As Espey says, "the echoes of the long line of English poets from Chaucer down are so varied and interwoven as to make a complete unraveling almost impossible."[42] Pound also sets the "Envoi" in the context of a wider European tradition by his skillful transition from Sappho's "Pierian roses" to Waller's "Go Lovely Rose." This serves to recall the cluster of values surrounding "Sappho's barbitos" in Section III. The "Envoi" is earnest that the tradition invoked by such allusions really exists; it proves the allusions to be more than mere empty gestures. To say, as A. L. French does, that Pound's positive ideal is insufficiently realized in *Mauberley*, that he "evidently thought that a bare *mention* of Sappho was enough to bring in, by implication, the whole Greek ethos," is to miss the point of "Envoi."[43] Pound obviously cannot bring in "the whole Greek ethos," if only because he is writing in English. But he can and does bring in the English tradition most closely associated with the *melopoeia* of Sappho's barbitos—namely, the "lost culture of Henry Lawes."

The music of "Envoi" demonstrates how modern poetry may draw fresh life from the poetry of the past. Pound has lengthened the tetrameter line of Waller's "Go Lovely Rose" to a pentameter; he has changed Waller's five-line stanzas to irregular strophes of seven, nine, and ten lines; and he has loosened the rhymes and caesuras. Where Waller had written:

> Tell her that's young,
> And shuns to have her graces spied,
> That hadst thou sprung

> In deserts, where no men abide,
> Thou must have uncommended died

Pound wrote:

> Tell her that sheds
> Such treasures in the air,
> Recking naught else but that her graces give
> Life to the moment,
> I would bid them live
> As roses might, in magic amber laid,
> Red overwrought with orange and all made
> One substance and one colour
> Braving time.

Nearly all the short lines in Pound's poem can be combined into the regular pentameter of the longer lines ("Life to the moment, / I would bid them live"; "One substance and one colour / Braving time"). But Pound avoids monotony by splitting them with heavy caesuras, by inverting initial feet, and by using enjambement on either end of the short lines. The "Envoi" thus seems to follow "the sequence of the musical phrase" rather than the "sequence of a metronome" (LE, 3). Clearly the poet of the "Envoi" must be contrasted to Mauberley, who becomes "Incapable of the least utterance or composition, / Emendation, conservation of the 'better tradition.' "*

The "Envoi" provides the key to the music/time images that recur throughout *Mauberley* in such phrases as "out of key with his time" and "diabolus in the scale." For three years Mauberley and "E.P." are out of key with the age but in tune with themselves. After this brief period of inner harmony, however, they both fall

---

* The reference to Reinach's *Apollo* in Mauberley's "Medallion" may symbolize Mauberley's inadequate critical sense. In his Vorticist writings, Pound contrasted Reinach's scope to Gaudier–Brzeska's wider view of world sculpture: "Here is a man as well-furnished with catalogued facts as a German professor of the old type, before the war school; a man who knows the cities of Europe and who knows not merely the sculpture out of Reinach's Apollo but who can talk and think in terms of world-sculpture. . . ." (See "Affirmations–V. Gaudier–Brzeska," *New Age*, XVI [4 February 1915], 380–382.) This description of Gaudier–Brzeska ("a man who knows the cities of Europe") echoes Homer's description of Odysseus ("pollon d'anthropon iden").

out of key with themselves, losing contact with the rhythms of their art and becoming diabolus in another scale. At this point time itself (not just the "times") becomes their greatest enemy. Mauberley drifts aside, asking "time to be rid of . . . / Of his bewilderments" and "time for arrangements." He notes the missed invitation to love "a year late," just as "E.P." was held in chopped seas "that year." Time is passing them by (all things *are* "a flowing" in this poem), and they are strangely out of harmony with it. Mauberley's ultimate response is to deny the existence of what he cannot master; on his scattered Moluccas he loses all sense of time, "not knowing, day to day, / The first day's end, in the next noon." Time is also denied by "E.P." when he contemplates the elegance of Circe's hair "rather than the mottoes on sun-dials." They have been driven to this extreme by an age which conceives of history as a "march of events" and demands an art "made with no loss of time"—in other words, an age which thinks of time primarily as a factor in a production schedule geared to the quantitative satisfaction of immediate needs.

But the "Envoi" presents a different response. It suggests that the artist transcends time not by ignoring it, but by confronting it and wresting beauty from its fluid destructive power. The poet immortalizes those graces which give "life to the moment," and bids them live "braving time" until "change hath broken down / All things save Beauty alone." Heracleitus can be given the lie only by an active and vital art. The poet himself must brave time, as he does in "Envoi" by recreating the music of the past.

The "Envoi," then, stands as a commentary on Mauberley and his age. It reminds us what the age has lost by valuing the pianola above the barbitos and the culture of Henry Lawes. And it shows us that the age's loss is Mauberley's loss. For Mauberley is a poet of Waller's order of talent who cannot be "HOISTED" by the "general musical perceptivity of the time and of his acquaintances." His age has no perceptivity, musical or otherwise, and his "acquaintances" are people like Mr. Nixon and Lady Valentine. He badly needs the "ADVANTAGES ACCRUING FROM THERE BEING A 'STYLE OF THE PERIOD,'" but he has the misfortune to be born in a period that has no style. At the same time, he lacks the grasp of vital traditions that enables the poet of the "Envoi" to forge a style from the past.

Having neither external support nor inner strength, he must inevitably pass from men's memories into the cobalt of oblivions. For, as Pound said of such artists, *"ils n'existent pas, leur ambience leur confert une existence."*

Richard Aldington's Parodies of *Lustra*

Although Richard Aldington signed the Vorticist Manifesto in the first issue of *BLAST*, he was not in complete harmony with the aims of the group as expressed by Pound, Lewis, and Gaudier–Brzeska. In particular he opposed the general Vorticist detraction of Greek art in favor of Egyptian. His parodies of Pound's *Lustra* satires appeared in *The Egoist* immediately following his article on "Anti-Hellenism. A Note on Some Modern Art."[1] There Aldington reaffirmed the values of Greek art: "And the upshot of all this somewhat incoherent writing is that, though I admit as I have admitted before the great value of, say, the sculpture of Mr. Epstein and the painting of M. Picasso and the latest poems of Mr. Pound and even the works of Signior Severini, Mr. Barzun and so on, I find that there is still a strange allure about these ordinary uninteresting things which the Greeks loved—health and beauty and youth in the midst of friends."

In addition to this dissent, Aldington also disliked the satires Pound was writing during his Vorticist period. In reviewing the first issue of *BLAST*, he declared them unnatural and tedious: "It is not that one wants Mr. Pound to repeat his Provencal feats, to echo the 'nineties—he has done that too much already—it is simply the fact that Mr. Pound cannot write satire. Mr. Pound is one of the gentlest, most modest, bashful, kind creatures who ever walked this earth; so I cannot help thinking that all this enormous arrogance and petulance and fierceness are a pose. And it is a wearisome pose."[2]

Aldington was not the only one to parody Pound's Imagist work, but Pound thought he was the best. When Leroy Titus Weeks published his parodies in *Poetry* (April 1915), Pound replied: "I could,

in general, advise him and the rest of the American parodists of my
work to leave off until they have studied the very excellent parodies made by Mr. Richard Aldington."³ Here, then, are those "very
excellent parodies."

PENULTIMATE POETRY
Xenophilometropolitania.

I.
TENZONE ALLA GENTILDONNA.

Come, my songs.

II.
CANTATA.
"Men pols lois puelh voys."
—Arnaut of Marvoil.

Come my songs,
Let us observe this person
Who munches chicken-bones like a Chinese consul
Mandilibating a delicate succulent Pekinese spaniel.

III.
ELEVATORS.

Come my songs,
Let us whizz up to the eighteenth floor,
Let us present our most undignified exterior
To this mass of indolent superstition.
To this perverted somnambulistic age;
Let us soar up higher than the eighteenth floor
And consider the delicate delectable monocles
Of the musical virgins of Parnassus:
Pale slaughter beneath purple skies.

IV.
ANCORA.
Rest me with mushrooms,
For I think the steak is evil.

V.
CONVICTED.

Like an armful of greasy engineer's-cotton
Flung by a typhoon against a broken crate of ducks' eggs
She stands by the rail of the Old Bailey dock,
Her intoxication is exquisite and excessive,

And delicate her delicate sterility.
Her delicacy is so delicate that she would feel affronted
If I remarked nonchalantly, "Saay, stranger, ain't
    you dandy."

VI.
GITANJALI.

Come my songs,
(For we have not "come" during three of these our
    delectable canzoni)
Come, my songs, let us go to America.
Let us move the thumbs on our left hands
And the middle fingers on our right hands
With the delicate impressive gestures
Of Rabindranath Tagore. (Salaam, o water-cress of
    the desert.)
O my songs, of all things let us
Be delicate and impressive.
I implore you my songs to remain so;
I charge you in the name of these states.

VII.
ALTRUISM.

Come my songs,
Let us praise ourselves;
I doubt if the smug will do it for us,
The smug who possess all the rest of the universe.

VIII.
SONG OF INNOCENCE.

The wind moves over the wheat
With a silver crashing,
A thin war of delicate kettles.

IX.

| The apparition | of these poems | in a crowd: |
| White faces | in a black | dead faint. |

Notes

Notes

CHAPTER 1

1. T. S. Eliot, *Selected Essays* (New York, 1960), pp. 4–5.
2. "Praefatio aut tumulus cimicium," *Active Anthology* (London, 1933), p. 9.
3. For the printed announcements of Pound's lecture courses, see Charles Norman, *Ezra Pound* (New York, 1960), pp. 30–34.
4. "I Gather the Limbs of Osiris, Part II," *New Age*, X (7 December 1911), 130. Hereafter called simply "Osiris."
5. "Osiris, Part IV," *New Age*, X (21 December 1911), 179.
6. *New Age*, X (4 January 1912), 224.
7. "Osiris, Part II," *New Age*, X (7 December 1911), 131.
8. "Osiris, Part IV," *New Age*, X (21 December 1911), 179.
9. "Osiris, Part III," *New Age*, X (14 December 1911), 155.
10. *Studies in the History of the Renaissance* (London, 1873), pp. viii–ix.
11. *Sonnets and Ballate of Guido Cavalcanti* (London, 1912). This introduction is dated November 15, 1910), and is reprinted in *The Translations of Ezra Pound* (New Directions, 1953). Pater's passage is mentioned on p. 18 of the modern edition.
12. "The Critic as Artist," *Intentions*, 4th ed. (London, 1909), p. 188.
13. "A Visiting Card" (1942), in *Impact: Essays on Ignorance and the Decline of American Civilization*, ed. Noel Stock (Chicago, 1960), p. 56.
14. See Donald Davie, *Articulate Energy* (London, 1955), especially the chapters on Hulme and Fenollosa; Graham Hough, *Image and Experience* (London, 1960); and Frank Kermode, *Romantic Image* (New York, 1957).
15. *Opere di Dante Alighieri*, ed. Moore and Toynbee, 4th ed. (Oxford, 1924), p. 222.
16. Dante Gabriel Rossetti, *Poem and Translations, 1850–1870* (London, 1959), p. 48.
17. *La Vita Nuova* (XLIII), in *Opere di Dante Aligheri*, p. 233.
18. By N. Christoph de Nagy, in *The Poetry of Ezra Pound: The Pre-Imagist Stage* (Berne, Switzerland, 1960), pp. 126–31 and 171.

CHAPTER 2

1. "Religio, or the Child's Guide to Knowledge," *Pavannes and Divisions* (New York, 1918), p. 23.

2. "Axiomata," *New Age*, XXVIII (13 January 1921), 125–126.

3. *The Poetry of Experience* (New York, 1963), pp. 46–47.

4. SR, 87, and "Osiris, Part IX," *New Age*, X (25 January 1912), 298.

5. "Osiris, Part VI," *New Age*, X (4 January 1912), 224.

6. "Introduction" to *Sonnets and Ballate of Guido Cavalcanti*. See *The Translations of Ezra Pound*, p. 23.

7. Coffman, *Imagism: A Chapter in the History of Modern Poetry* (Norman, Oklahoma, 1951), p. 137.

8. "How I Began," *T.P.'s Weekly*, XXI (6 June 1913), 707. Reproduced in *Ezra Pound: Perspectives*, ed. Noel Stock (Chicago, 1965), p. 1.

9. See Earl Miner's excellent discussion of haiku and the "super-pository" technique in *The Japanese Tradition in British and American Literature* (Princeton, 1958). See also his "Pound, *Haiku*, and the Image," in *Ezra Pound: A Collection of Critical Essays*, ed. Walter Sutton (Englewood Cliffs, N.J., 1963), pp 115–128.

10. "Vorticism," *Fortnightly Review*, XCVI (1 September 1914), 461–471. Reprinted in *Gaudier–Brzeska: A Memoir* (London, 1916), pp. 94–109. Subsequent references to this important essay will be to the latter. Richard Ellmann and Charles Feidelson, Jr. have also reprinted the essay in *The Modern Tradition* (New York, 1965).

11. *Imagism*, p. 207.

12. "The Book of the Month," *Poetry Review*, I (March 1912), 133.

13. Langer, *Philosophy in a New Key* (Cambridge, Mass., 1942). See especially Chapter IV, "Discursive and Presentational Forms."

14. Fletcher, *Life Is My Song* (New York and Toronto, 1937), p. 137.

15. "Vortex. Pound," *BLAST*, I (June 1914), 154.

16. "Vorticism," *Gaudier–Brzeska*, pp. 100–101.

17. "Affirmations—IV. As For Imagisme," *New Age*, XVI (28 January 1915), 349–350.

18. "Affirmations—II. Vorticism," *New Age*, XVI (14 January 1915), 277–278.

19. "Vorticism," *Gaudier–Brzeska*, p. 106.

20. See "Fields of Force," Chapter 25 of Kenner's *The Poetry of Ezra Pound* (London, 1951), pp. 233–241.

21. Pound also used a lengthy passage from Pater's translation early in *The Spirit of Romance* (p. 17).

22. Pater, *Marius the Epicurean* (New York, 1901), p. 49.

CHAPTER 3

1. See Charles Norman, *Ezra Pound*, pp. 27–29.

2. See *Music and Moonlight* (London, 1874), p. 1. I am indebted for this identification to Nemi d'Agostino, "La fin de siecle inglese e il giovane Ezra Pound," *English Miscellany*, VI (1955), 135–162.

3. N. Christoph de Nagy has studied the matter in some detail in *The Poetry of Ezra Pound: The Pre-Imagist Stage*.

4. *The Translations of Ezra Pound*, p. 20. For an account of Pound's allusions to Rossetti, see T. W. West, "D. G. Rossetti and Ezra Pound," *Review of English Studies*, IV (1953), 63–67; De Nagy, *The Poetry of Ezra Pound*,

pp. 66–67; and above, pp. 14–15, 17, 18. For a discussion of Pound's translations, see Anne Paolucci, "Ezra Pound and Dante Gabriel Rossetti as Translators of Cavalcanti," *Romantic Review*, LI (1960), 256–267. The best general treatment of Rossetti's influence on Pound is that of Thomas H. Jackson, in *The Early Poetry of Ezra Pound* (Harvard University Press, 1968), pp. 17–28. Mr. Jackson's book appeared so recently that I have been unable to indicate our many points of agreement, or to incorporate the convincing conclusions of his discussion of Pound and Plotinus (pp. 77–89).

5. See De Nagy, *The Poetry of Ezra Pound*, p. 95. Mosher published Fiona MacLeod's *From the Hills of Dream* in 1901.

6. See Charles Norman, *Ezra Pound*, p. 4.

7. *The Symbolist Movement in Literature*, 2nd ed. (London, 1908), pp. 8–9.

8. *Ibid.*, pp. 120–132.

9. *Essays and Introductions* (London, 1961), pp. 193–194. Pound had almost certainly read Yeats's *Ideas of Good and Evil* before May 1909, because he advised William Carlos Williams in a letter of that date to "Read . . . Yeats' essays" (LETT, 8).

10. The phrase is used by Arthur Symons in connection with Villiers de l'Isle–Adam's *Axël*, in *The Symbolist Movement*, p. 44.

11. "Hark to Sturge Moore," *Poetry*, VI (June 1915), 140.

12. For a discussion of the fire imagery, see De Nagy, *The Poetry of Ezra Pound*, Chapter III.

13. For an account, see Herbert N. Schneidau, "Pound and Yeats: The Question of Symbolism," *Journal of English Literary History*, XXXIII (1965), 220–237.

14. See LETT, p. 180, and *The Translations of Ezra Pound*, pp. 222 and 236.

15. *Guide to Kulchur* (London, 1938), p. 295. Italics added.

16. De Nagy, *The Poetry of Ezra Pound*, p. 63, has identified the source of the epigraph of this poem (*La Vita Nuova*, IX).

17. "The Decadent Movement in Literature" (1893), reprinted in *Dramatis Personae* (London, 1925), p. 106.

18. See *Sophist*, 266e: "We must remember that there were to be two parts of the image-making class, the likeness-making and the fantastic [phantastikon], if we should find that falsehood really existed and was in the class of real being" (Loeb Classical Library ed., p. 451).

19. "Preface to the Second Edition of London Nights," in *Studies in Verse and Prose* (London, 1904), p. 284.

20. See M. H. Abrams, "The Correspondent Breeze: A Romantic Metaphor" in *English Romantic Poets: Modern Essays in Criticism*, ed. M. H. Abrams (New York, 1960), pp. 37–54. Wind is associated with death in both of Pound's "Villonauds" (ALS, 24–27) and in "For E. McC" (ALS, 61–62).

21. "M. Antonius Flamininus *and* John Keats," *Book News Monthly*, XXVI (February 1908), 445–447.

22. The title of this poem comes from an Italian paraphrase of it made by Marc Londonio, and reproduced by Pound in the notes to *Personae* (1909), p. 59. Londonio's first line is "Nel biancheggiar di delicata rosa."

23. Cf. "M. Antonius Flamininus *and* John Keats," p. 446: "You livers in cities know not this wind of the dawn."

24. Pound's first line, "Goddess of the murmuring courts," echoes the

first line of Rossetti's poem, "Master of the murmuring courts." See De Nagy, *The Poetry of Ezra Pound*, p. 67.

25. "Vorticism," *Gaudier–Brzeska*, pp. 97–99.

26. *Ibid.*, p. 97.

CHAPTER 4

1. *The Complete Poetic and Dramatic Works of Robert Browning*, Cambridge ed. (Boston and New York, 1895), p. 1009. Hereafter cited as *Works*.

2. *Ibid.*, pp. 1008–1009.

3. *Ibid.*, p. 1008.

4. *The Disappearance of God* (Cambridge, Mass., 1963), p. 107.

5. *Autobiographies*, p. 87.

6. See Robert Langbaum, *The Poetry of Experience*, pp. 188–189.

7. *The Poetry of Ezra Pound*, p. 119.

8. On the difference between Pound's Marvoil and the impression of the man left by his works, see De Nagy, *The Poetry of Ezra Pound*, pp. 120–121.

9. See "Provincia Deserta" (P, 121–123) and *Guide to Kulchur* (New Directions [1952]), p. 111.

10. *The Poems of Algernon Charles Swinburne* (London, 1904), IV, 148.

11. Ida Farnell, trans., *The Lives of the Troubadours*, pp. 85–86.

12. See Arthur W. E. O'Shaughnessy, *An Epic of Women and Other Poems* (London, 1870), pp. 55–64.

13. "How I Began," *T. P.'s Weekly*, XXI (6 June 1913), 707. Note that Pound disclaimed De Born's values *before* World War I. The second "vigorous" poem was "Ballad of the Goodly Fere."

14. *The Poetry of Ezra Pound*, pp. 125–126.

15. P, 106. Pound's translation first appeared in *Poetry and Drama*, II (March 1914), 23–24. It was reprinted in *Lustra* (London, 1916), pp. 39–41. I have added the words with which "Na Audiart" ends ("que be'm vol mal"). For the Provençal original of this and of other poems relevant to Pound, see *Poésies complètes de Bertran de Born*, ed. Antoine Thomas (Toulouse, 1888), pp. 110–113.

16. For this Pound extrapolates one step further from his later free translation of "si be'm vol mal" as "with a full heart" (P, 106).

17. See above, p. 16.

18. *The Poetry of Ezra Pound*, 117–118.

19. Arthur Symons, *Images of Good and Evil* (London, 1899), p. 178.

20. *The Poetry of Ezra Pound*, p. 119.

21. "How I Began," *T. P.'s Weekly*, XXI (6 June 1913), 707.

22. SR, 95. See also LE, 431–432.

23. "Affirmations—IV. As for Imagisme," *New Age*, XVI (28 January 1915), 350.

24. "Osiris, Part VI," *New Age*, X (4 January 1912), 224.

25. Browning, *Works*, p. 163.

26. See Richard Ellmann, *Yeats: The Man and the Masks* (London, 1949).

27. Yeats, *Autobiographies*, 469.

28. See Charles Norman, *Ezra Pound*, pp. 39–40, 51, 53–54.

29. "Vorticism," *Gaudier–Brzeska*, p. 98.

CHAPTER 5

1. "Osiris—Part II," *New Age*, X (7 December 1911), 131.

2. I quote Pound's earlier translation, which first appeared in "Osiris—Part III," *New Age*, X (14 December 1911), 155. A later translation may be seen in *The Translations of Ezra Pound*, p. 39. For a comparison of the two versions, see Donald Davie, *Ezra Pound: Poet as Sculptor* (New York, 1964), pp. 104–106.

3. J. E. Shaw, *Guido Cavalcanti's Theory of Love: The "Canzone d'Amore" and Other Related Problems* (Toronto, 1949), p. 115.

4. See Praz, *The Romantic Agony*, 2nd ed. (Cleveland and New York, 1963), chapters IV and V, and Kermode, *Romantic Image*, Chapter IV. See also "Afterword: The Ladies of Helicon" in Thomas H. Jackson's *The Early Poetry of Ezra Pound* (Harvard University Press, 1968), pp. 229–241.

5. Ellmann, *The Identity of Yeats*, pp. 20–21.

6. "Osiris—Part III," *New Age*, X (14 December 1911), 155. See *The Translations of Ezra Pound*, pp. 106–107.

7. "Introduction" to *Sonnets and Ballate of Guido Cavalcanti* (published 1912, dated November 1910); see *The Translations of Ezra Pound*, p. 18.

8. "The Alchemist" was first published in *Umbra: The Early Poems of Ezra Pound* (London, 1920), but Pound there dated it as "unpublished 1912." See *Umbra*, p. 8.

9. It first appeared in *Quest*, IV (October, 1912), 37–53, and has been reprinted as Chapter V in editions of *The Spirit of Romance* since 1932. *Quest* was a journal edited by G. R. S. Mead, and devoted largely to matters of occultism and supernaturalism. See the excellent discussion by Herbert Newton Schneidau in "Pound and Yeats: The Question of Symbolism," *Journal of English Literary History*, XXXII (1965), 226–228.

10. Pound used this phrase of his recent work in 1918: "The metal finish alarms people. They will no more endure Joyce's hardness than they will Pound's sterilized surgery." See "Mr. Villerant's Morning Outburst (Four Letters)," *Little Review*, V (November 1918), 11.

11. T. Wilson West notes that these lines are probably adapted from Rossetti's poem, "The Bride's Prelude." Rossetti speaks of a recess "That the sun flooded: it o'er spread / Like flame the hair upon her head / And fringed her face with burning red." See "D. G. Rossetti and Ezra Pound," *Review of English Studies*, IV (1953), 66.

12. Rosenthal, *A Primer of Ezra Pound* (New York, 1960), p. 5.

13. See N. Christoph de Nagy, *The Poetry of Ezra Pound*, p. 41.

CHAPTER 6

1. "Ezra Pound: His Metric and Poetry" (1917), in *To Criticize the Critic* (New York, 1965), pp. 172–173.

2. "La fin de siecle inglese e il giovane Ezra Pound," *English Miscellany*, VI (1955), 148.

3. N. Christoph de Nagy, *The Poetry of Ezra Pound*, p. 13.

4. See *The Metamorphic Tradition in Modern Poetry* (New Brunswick,

N. J., 1955), p. 25. The chapter on Pound first appeared as "The Metamorphoses of Ezra Pound" in *Motive and Method in The Cantos of Ezra Pound*, ed. Lewis Leary (New York, 1954), pp. 60–100. This is the best discussion of the metamorphosis theme in Pound's poetry.

5. Robert Langbaum, *The Poetry of Experience*, pp. 95–96.

6. "The Broken Mirrors and the Mirror of Memory," *Motive and Method in The Cantos of Ezra Pound*, ed. Lewis Leary, p. 15.

7. *Ibid.*, pp. 15–17.

8. *Ibid.*, p. 10.

9. For the identification of the Heine originals, see N. Christoph de Nagy, *The Poetry of Ezra Pound*, pp. 174–175.

10. For the original, see *The Greek Anthology*, ed. W. R. Paton (London: Loeb Classical Library, 1916), I, Book V, No. 85.

11. *Pavannes and Divisions*, p. 23.

12. Rossetti's translation. See *Poems and Translations*, p. 402.

13. Davie, *Ezra Pound: Poet as Sculptor*, pp. 25–27.

14. See Kenneth Sisam's letter to the *Times Literary Supplement* (25 June 1954).

15. "Osiris—Part I," *New Age*, X (30 November 1911), 107.

CHAPTER 7

1. "Vorticism," *Gaudier–Brzeska*, p. 109.

2. For Pound's earliest comments on the reviving of myth and the classical sensibility, see "M. Antonius Flamininus *and* John Keats," *Book News Monthly*, XXVI (February 1908), 445–447. He praises these two poets for their "ability to give us the beauty of the old mythology."

3. In Ovid's *Metamorphoses* (IV, 168), Leuconoë tells the story of Leucothoë, who was beloved of the sun and transmuted by him after her death into a source of fertility.

4. For the original, see *Lyra Graeca*, ed. J. R. Edmonds (Loeb Classical Library), II, 85.

5. "Vorticism," *Gaudier–Brzeska*, p. 95.

6. Giles, *A History of Chinese Literature* (New York, 1901), pp. 52–53. I owe this reference to Achilles Fang, "Fenollosa and Pound," *Harvard Journal of Asiatic Studies*, XX (1957), 236.

7. *BLAST*, II (July 1915), 21. For Pound's high estimation of Tailhade, see also "The Approach to Paris—V," *New Age*, XIII (2 October 1913), 662–664.

8. "Osiris—Part VI," *New Age*, X (4 January 1912), 224.

9. *Poetry*, IV (August 1914).

10. Herbert Bergman printed Pound's essay in *American Literature*, XXVII (1955–1956), 56–61. The spelling is Pound's.

11. "Patria Mia," *New Age*, XI (26 September and 24 October 1912), 516 and 611.

12. "Pax Saturni," *Poetry*, II (April 1913), 8–10.

13. C. B. Willard, "Ezra Pound's Debt to Walt Whitman," *Studies in Philology*, LIV (1957), 579.

14. See "The Approach to Paris—V," *New Age*, XIII (2 October 1913),

662. There is one other allusion to "Carmen" in Pound's poem. "We can't preserve the elusive *'mica salis'* " probably refers to Gautier's last stanza:

> Elle a, dans sa laideur piquante,
> Un grain de sel de cette mer
> D'où jaillit, nue et provocante,
> L'acre Vénus du gouffre amer.

15. "A Note on Pound's 'Papyrus,'" *Modern Language Notes,* LXVII (March 1952), 188–190. The fragment was published by J. M. Edmonds in *The New Fragments of Alcaeus, Sappho and Corinna* (London, 1909), p. 14. Fang thinks this was Pound's source.

16. Giles, *A History of Chinese Literature,* p. 100. Achilles Fang first pointed out the source of "Liu Ch'e" and "Fan-Piece, for Her Imperial Lord" in "Fenollosa and Pound," *Harvard Journal of Asiatic Studies,* XX (1957), 236.

17. "Vorticism," *Gaudier–Brzeska,* p. 95.

18. *A History of Chinese Literature,* p. 101.

19. *Oeuvres Completes de Voltaire* (Paris, 1828), XVIII, 144–145.

20. *Ibid.,* pp. 201–202.

21. A. C. Graham, "The Translation of Chinese Poetry," *Poems of the Late T'ang* (Baltimore, 1965), p. 13.

22. T. S. Eliot, "Introduction" to *Ezra Pound: Selected Poems,* 3rd ed. (London, 1934), p. xvi.

23. Davie, *Ezra Pound: Poet as Sculptor,* pp. 41–46.

24. "Chinese Poetry," *To-Day,* III (April–May 1918), 54–57 and 93–95.

25. *The Collected Poems of W. B. Yeats,* pp. 61 and 524.

26. For this date, see Myles Slatin, "A History of Pound's Cantos I–XVI, 1915–1925," *American Literature,* XXXV (1963), 183–195.

27. M. H. Abrams, "Structure and Style in the Greater Romantic Lyric," in *From Sensibility to Romanticism,* ed. Frederick W. Hilles and Harold Bloom (New York, 1965), pp. 527–528.

28. "On 'Near Perigord,'" *Poetry,* VII (December 1915), 143–146.

29. Thomas E. Connolly, "Ezra Pound's 'Near Perigord': The Background of a Poem," *Comparative Literature,* VIII (1956), 110. This article amply explicates the names and allusions to historical events in the poem.

30. Hugh Kenner, "The Broken Mirrors and the Mirror of Memory," in *Motive and Method in The Cantos of Ezra Pound,* ed. Lewis Leary, pp. 8–10.

31. *Poetry,* X (June 1917), 113–121.

32. Foster, "Pound's Revisions of Cantos I–III," *Modern Philology,* LXIII (1966), 238–239.

CHAPTER 8

1. John J. Espey, *Ezra Pound's Mauberley* (Berkeley and Los Angeles, 1955), pp. 15–16. I have accepted Espey's excellent account of the overall structure of the sequence, and my own interpretation starts from there.

2. T. S. Eliot, "Ulysses, Order, and Myth," in *Criticism,* ed. Schorer, Miles, and McKenzie (New York, 1958), p. 270.

3. "Ford Madox (Hueffer) Ford: Obit," *The Nineteenth Century and After*, CXXVI (August 1939), 179.

4. "Status Rerum," *Poetry*, I (January 1913), 125.

5. "The Approach to Paris—V," *New Age*, XIII (2 October 1913), 662.

6. See the essay mentioned above, in note 5 to this chapter.

7. Myles Slatin, "A History of Pound's Cantos I–XVI, 1915–1925," *American Literature*, XXXV (1963), 188.

8. *Ibid.*, p. 189.

9. *Ibid.*, p. 191. In a letter of 24 August 1923, Pound told his father that he had "revised earlier part of the poem." In a July letter he also states that he has "rewritten beginning of poem."

10. *Ibid.*, p. 194. From a letter of 1 November 1924.

11. See Richard Ellmann, *James Joyce* (New York, 1965), p. 538.

12. "Long Live the Vortex," *BLAST*, I (June 1914), 7.

13. "Affirmations—III. Jacob Epstein," *New Age*, XVI (21 January 1915), 311–312.

14. "The Book of the Month: High Germany," *Poetry Review*, I (March 1912), 133.

15. "Vorticism," *Gaudier-Brzeska*, p. 103. See also "Vortex. Pound," *BLAST*, I (June 1914), 153.

16. "Vorticism," *Gaudier–Brzeska*, p. 103. Pound had argued this as early as March 1912; see "The Book of the Month: High Germany," *Poetry Review*, I (March 1912), 133.

17. "Affirmations—IV. As for Imagisme," *New Age*, XVI (28 January 1915), 349–350.

18. *Ibid.*

19. "Vortex. Pound," *BLAST*, I (June 1914), 153.

20. *Pavannes and Divisions*, pp. 119–120.

21. *Ezra Pound's Mauberley*, pp. 71–83.

22. *Instigations*, p. 343. De Gourmont was a main influence on this strain of Pound's thought, as Espey demonstrates. But so also were Propertius and the medieval love poets of Provence and Tuscany. See "Psychology and Troubadours" in *The Spirit of Romance*.

23. "Affirmations—III. Jacob Epstein," *New Age*, XVI (21 January 1915), 311–312.

24. "Vortex. Pound," *BLAST*, I (June 1914), 153.

25. "Osiris—Part XI," *New Age*, X (25 February 1912), 370.

26. "E.P. Files Exceptions," *Pavannes and Divisions*, pp. 248–249.

27. "Art Notes. By B. H. Dias. Kinema, Kinesis, Hepworth, etc.," *New Age*, XXIII (26 September 1918), 352. "B. H. Dias" was Pound's nom de plume for art reviews in *The New Age*.

28. *Patria Mia and the Treatise on Harmony* (London, 1962), p. 64n.

29. *Understanding Media* (New York, 1966), p. 252.

30. "Vorticism," *Gaudier–Brzeska*, p. 94.

31. John J. Espey has noted this image pattern (*Ezra Pound's Mauberley*, p. 76), but has not interpreted it at length.

32. *Pavannes and Divisions*, p. 122. The image appears in Pound's earlier work in such poems as "The Picture," "Of Jacopo del Sellaio," and "Dans un Omnibus."

33. "Music. By William Atheling. Prom.," *New Age*, XXIII (19 September 1918), 335.

34. "Appendix V. Arnold Dolmetsch," *Pavannes and Divisions*, p. 260. Cf. the gramophone in Eliot's *Waste Land*.

35. "Vorticism," *Gaudier–Brzeska*, p. 108.

36. "Notes for Performers by William Atheling, with marginalia emitted by George Antheil," *Transatlantic Review*, I (February 1924), 109.

37. *Ibid.*, p. 114.

38. "Music. By William Atheling. The Avoidable," *New Age*, XIII (5 September 1918), 303.

39. "Music. By William Atheling. Post Mortems," *New Age*, XXV (5 June 1919), 103.

40. "Music. By William Atheling. 'Cellists, etc.," *New Age*, XXIII (30 May 1918), 73.

41. "Notes for Performers by William Atheling," *Transatlantic Review*, I (February 1924), 114.

42. *Ezra Pound's Mauberley*, p. 98.

43. A. L. French, " 'Olympian Apathein': Pound's *Hugh Selwyn Mauberley* and Modern Poetry," *Essays in Criticism*, XV (October 1965), 430.

APPENDIX

1. *The Egoist*, I (15 January, 1914), 35–36.

2. *The Egoist*, I (15 July, 1914), 272–273.

3. *Poetry*, VI (June 1915), 158. See also Horace Holley's "Imagists" in *The Egoist*, I (15 June, 1914), 236.

Index to Poems Discussed

Containing the titles of the poems by Ezra Pound discussed or mentioned in this book. Italicized page numbers refer to the most detailed discussions.

Index